BEYOND THE HUSTLE

BEYOND THE HUSTLE
DISCOVERING YOUR PURPOSE

Roberto Hernandez

© 2025 Roberto Hernandez
BEYOND THE HUSTLE
DISCOVERING YOUR PURPOSE
© 2025 Roberto Hernandez

All rights reserved solely by the author. The author guarantees all contents are original and do not infringe upon the legal rights of any other person or work. No part of this book may be reproduced in any form without the permission of the author. The views expressed in this book are not necessarily those of the publisher.

All Scripture quotations, unless otherwise indicated, are taken from the Holy Bible, New International Version®, NIV®. Copyright ©1973, 1978, 1984, 2011 by Biblica, Inc.™ Used by permission of Zondervan. All rights reserved worldwide. www.zondervan.com. The NIV and "New International Version" are trademarks registered in the United States Patent and Trademark Office by Biblica, Inc.™

Printed in the United States of America.
ISBN-13: 978-17359627-57

Purpose Life Publishing
Miami, Florida

TABLE OF CONTENTS

Acknowledgements vii
Introduction: Learning To Be You Again xi
1   The Discovery Of Your Hidden Self. 1
2   Finding Your Niche, Escaping The Hustle. 13
3   The Unforced Rhythms Of Grace 33
4   Provoking People To Pinpoint And
    Pursue Their Purpose. 55
5   Your Purpose Is Found In Two Places 83
6   Finding Meaning In The Product
    Reviving The Hidden You In You! 133
7   Tapping Into Your Gift 175
8   Discovering Your Work Beyond Your Job 201
9   14 Question - Steps Toward Self-Discovery 241
10 Vision: How You Will Accomplish Your Purpose 249
11 The True Definition Of Leadership:
    What Qualifies You To Lead 289
12 "The Edge Of Purpose". 319

ACKNOWLEDGEMENTS

I'm excited to announce the launch of this book. The beginning of furthering my understanding on this journey toward self-discovery came through an encounter I had in Naples, Florida in 2010. Trust me, I know I have more to learn. From that moment on, though, I became even more aware of how meeting certain people in life helps us connect the dots toward other more important and meaningful relationships that are intended in confirming and getting us closer to our life assignment. As the saying goes, "Iron sharpens iron." People are always a factor in our growth, since we aren't called to do life alone or to fulfill our assignment in isolation.

I'm dedicating this book to Matthew and Trista Sue Kragh. I was introduced to Trista through her husband, Matthew, after a small dialogue in a fast-food restaurant. Trista not only allowed me to work alongside her and the vision she had, but also took a lot of time to train, mentor, and educate me toward one of the hardest tasks in the world... Helping me unlearn what I thought I knew to be right. I must tell you; it was quite the experience. Firstly, because it came from a woman, and one who was a little younger than me. Secondly, she was one who did not fit the script in my mind of what an overseer should look like. People had their opinions of who should've been training and/or mentoring me, and it wasn't a little redheaded woman from a quiet city in Southwest Florida (SWFL). I thought it was fun, especially when I exposed this to my students or the people I'm called to influence (my audience). I respectfully gave her that grace; to be called my mentor and overseer, since 2010.

Unlearning was harder than learning. It's like overcoming any kind of addiction, such as food, drugs, laziness, etc. It takes commitment to build a new habit and time to let that habit take root. However, I knew there was information and wisdom that I was supposed to get from and through her, in order for me to end up where I envisioned myself being. What I wanted to do was tied to this process.

Ultimately, what made it easier for me to submit to this entire process of education through her was finding out that she was being trained by the late Dr. Myles Munroe.

My first question to her was, "Who are you under?" Or "Who overwhelms you with knowledge?" She wasn't hesitant in her answer, and I liked that. I had heard of Dr. Myles Munroe and listened to his teachings in the mid 90's. I remember reading one of his books while pastoring (overseeing a group) as a missionary in Trinidad and Tobago. It was the first book I read in its entirety, Single, Married, Separated, and Life After Divorce. Even though I wasn't married at the time, and still am not, it was a game-changer for me. It helped me change the dynamics in my perception of the purpose of marriage, how couples should view each other, and life as a unit. I was already a huge fan of his philosophy on leadership, potential, vision, purpose, now (at that time) relationships, and learned a lot about the human physique. I even used his principles during that time to help others. It worked. Most of my insight came through his materials that I had studied. I came to understand through that first book that even choosing a mate in one's life should be based more on purpose than on any other factor, even love. If we are to effectively flow, impact and influence our world finding a suitable person or "The One" to compliment oneself is based more on working

ACKNOWLEDGEMENTS

in one's purpose, niche, and area of gifting with as few distractions as possible.

Trista introduced me to Dr. Myles Munroe who immediately embraced me and took me into his circle of training, or under his wing, so to speak. I spent approximately an additional 4 years in Naples, FL to scrub my brain from old ideologies. It was a perfect combination of him and her. Dr. Munroe's Training Seminars, friendship, and smaller late-night huddles of wisdom, and then after that, accompanied by Trista's training, teachings, correction, and often conversations. These provided the repetition I needed to grab hold of these new truths I was being introduced to and studying. Most of these are to be caught, not merely taught. How? By intentionally studying until that light of understanding came on and became my very own. You learn from them, but never become them.

For that reason, I also want to dedicate this book to the late Dr. Myles Munroe, his wife the late Ruth Munroe, and their two great children Charisa and Myles Jr (Chairo), for allowing us to borrow him, their father, for so many hours at a time. May they be fueled and empowered (blessed) in their life assignment and in their unique manner through which they have taken their parent's baton to go into all the world and make more students of divine truth. For me this has been the best education in my life thus far. Some of his mentees use the (hashtag) #TrainedByTheBest. I guess he was our best to help catapult us into our life assignments. For many of us that is. I've also noticed after their passing (Him and his wife) on November 9, 2014, how many of his students evolved. Some started their own businesses, others initiated their personal life visions, other ministries (different acts of service), and some published their own books, etc. It is good to think on and/or consider who overwhelms, helps or contributes toward your growth? True Leadership is the result of what happens in one's absence, not just their presence.

BEYOND THE HUSTLE

There is a principle that I've caught a few years ago that confirms and suits Dr. Myles and Ruth Munroe's leadership role very well. It states in John's view, this first century leader's historic account of the good news, **"unless a kernel of wheat falls to the ground and dies, it remains only a single seed. But if it dies, it produces many seeds."** *(John 12:24)* May Dr. Myles and Ruth Munroe RIP and the seven others who passed in that horrific plane crash as well. May his legacy live on through the "seed" potential in others.

INTRODUCTION

LEARNING TO BE YOU AGAIN

> "He's so beat up, it's hard to tell what he's like. I just can't help feeling they've got him so screwed up running in a circle, he's forgotten what he was born to do. He just needs to learn how to be a horse again." **–Tom Smith, Seabiscuit's trainer** (From the motion picture, Seabiscuit)

I remember hearing these words while watching this movie, on a Saturday afternoon in 2010. I was staying at a friend's guest home, and he suggested I watch the movie after my lengthy flight. It was the day before I was scheduled to speak at a local church in Camden, New Jersey on "Defining One's Purpose." These words resonated with how I was viewing people during this time in my life, especially in religious settings but, really all over the world.

I believe that most people never find their purpose in life and live with a huge regret of never pinpointing or living their dream—what they envision for their lives—because they either get sidetracked by living under others' unauthorized opinions about who they are and what they should be doing, or they never intentionally take the time to seek and figure it out for themselves. Sometimes we need to be still and study ourselves and our Source in order to be introduced to ourselves again, or for the first time. Thus, I call myself a Self- Discovery Coach.

This was when I started getting a clearer revelation on the message of self-discovery and assisting people with their purpose. I believe that many who profess to be close to their Source (God, that is) are amongst those who are the furthest from their purpose. We run in circles and are guilty of not knowing who we truly are. In fact, just like Seabiscuit, we must learn how to become ourselves again.

It was during this time I also felt I was becoming one with my assignment. I wanted to encourage as many people as possible to discover who they truly are and to know their purpose in life. I believe that I was acquiring revelation and receiving some tested principles during this time, which assisted me to help many self-discover, pinpoint, and pursue their purpose. Ultimately, the goal when this happens is to impact, empower, and influence our world, through everyone's own unique calling, gift, and niche.

The Western spiritual settings of our era have primarily been focused on training and teaching people to love and have intimacy with their Deity (God, that is, who is our Source). However, as a society, many of its leaders are running people in circles. We do not encourage individuals to discover who they truly are. Instead, we tell them—compel them—that they need to serve in some capacity within their spiritual communities, such as their church. This often involves participating in church chores, local church housekeeping, being part of a study or home group, and attending services every week while remaining accountable to someone to make sure they are doing everything by that group's standards.

INTRODUCTION

Unfortunately, this cycle continues endlessly, with the emphasis placed more on what happens inside the four walls of those settings and not on impacting the external society. Activities with this goal in mind, where the aim is the world at large, will ultimately contribute to not just our personal and corporate growth, but our maturity. Our purpose should entail a worldwide vision, not an internal ambition to build an organization. In one sense, the church has become a prison, keeping its follower's captive, while their leaders act as wardens. Aren't we reminded by the famous words, 'Go into all the world,' to do just that? Show up on a great platform where, if we show up, perhaps God can show off! The word 'world'—originally the Greek word 'Kosmos,' which means institutions of control and powers of influence—indicates that our focus should ultimately be on becoming world-changers. We are to get into the systems of the earth and start rectifying what is erroneous. Let's go!

Loving God isn't enough. It's in obeying Him that takes us from where we are to where we are supposed to be as **"The steps of a good man are ordered by the LORD, And He delights in his way." (Psalm 37:23 NKJV)** The more revelation we get into our life assignment, the more we move into dominion and taking this thing by force as **"But the path of the righteous is like the light of dawn, which shines brighter and brighter until full day." (Proverbs 4:18 ESV).** In these verses we see movement: path and steps, as a captain cannot steer a ship that is stagnant. There must be movement. I believe that loving God isn't enough. It's in discovering our purpose and executing by taking steps in the path that enables us to experience success in the very thing for which we were born. As the wise king Solomon also stated, **"Many are the plans in a person's heart, but it is the Lord's purpose that prevails" (Proverbs 19:21 NIV).** "Prevail" means that it proves more powerful than opposing forces and even teachings, like what you think to be right, such as our rituals and especially, manmade customs, devices, and/

or traditions. It's a plan that goes beyond the walls of our buildings into carrying an assignment that's greater than us. The aim is for a lost world.

Many believers are **"so screwed up from running in circles that they've forgotten what they were born to do"** or never learned who they are. The challenge in life is to learn to be ourselves again. I believe we have been educated out of ourselves through an unauthorized society that isn't qualified to point the way. Just like in the case of Seabiscuit who **"needed to learn how to be a horse again."**

Seabiscuit has become one of my favorite movies. Why did this film inspire me? Because I could relate to that horse! Seabiscuit did not fit the image of a great racehorse. He was relatively small and knobby-kneed, with a laid-back demeanor that suggested he would much rather sleep than step into the starting gate. It seemed he could not run a lick when he lost the first 17 starts of his career, leaving him the butt of bad jokes in his own barn.

I've been there, and perhaps you have too; down and out, or not off to a great start, even doubting ourselves and our capabilities. Even worse, people often **judge us by our outward appearances**, as if they were **judging a book by its cover**. Yet there is far more to each of us than the human eye can see, and much of this truth will be explored in the chapters that follow.

> **Ultimately, "You, dear children, are from God and have overcome them, because the one who is in you is greater than the one who is in the world." (1 John 4:4 NIV).**

Why does this story of Seabiscuit impact many of its viewers in a profound way? During the Great Depression, a time when Americans were looking for someone — or something — to root for, an underdog came along in the form of a small, lazy thoroughbred… "Out of nowhere, Seabiscuit inspired hope at a time

INTRODUCTION

in our history when people were really struggling. He came out into the open and entertained many.

You are a Celebrity When You Are Celebrated.

I believe that when we finally emerge as offspring (sons) of our Source (God), we too will be celebrated in our unique service to a world around us in need of our inner potential. Your purpose entails you releasing yourself to it through your individuality. But that will only come by not heeding to the world's standards and unauthorized inputs of who we are to become. When we tap into God rather than the world, we will tap into our hidden capabilities needed to fulfill our purpose. This right and privilege is for every single person reading this book.

First Century Writer Paul stated, *"For the creation waits with eager longing for the revealing of the sons of God." (Romans 8:19 ESV)* I believe that there is celebration energy all around when a person manifests or reveals their true selves. This experience is not to be bottled up or capped but released to a desperate world in need of your gift. This is a true celebration: when we become our true selves—made in the image and likeness of God, our very Source—and emerge with our unique gifts, according to the measure of grace given to us by God Himself, to serve our generation, we effectively fulfill our purpose.

This is where the creation is eagerly longing for this experience, for you to fully emerge and for them to benefit from your individuality.

CELEBRITY STATUS FROM A WORLDLY LIGHT

The term "celebrity" refers to a person who is widely recognized and acclaimed, often in the realms of entertainment, sports, or public life. Celebrities typically enjoy significant fame and attention from the public and media, often due to their achievements, talents, or public persona.

1. **Latin Origin**: It comes from the Latin word "celebritas," which means "fame" or "renown." This word is derived from "celeber," meaning "famous" or "celebrated."

2. **Middle English**: The term was absorbed into Middle English as "celebrite," and by the late 14th century, it evolved into the modern form "celebrity."

YOU ARE GOD'S CELEBRITY: CHOSEN, NOT JUST SEEN

> **"I will make you famous, and you will be a blessing to others… and all the people on earth will be blessed through you." (Genesis 12:2)**

Over time, "celebrity" has come to encompass not just the quality of being famous but also the lifestyle and culture surrounding famous individuals, including their influence on society, fashion, and trends. The rise of mass media and social media has further amplified the visibility and reach of celebrities, making the concept even more pervasive in contemporary culture. In the passage above God told his servant Abraham that He would make him known, 'famous' and that the people on earth will be blessed because of him. Famous means, "well known, <u>celebrated</u>, popular, famed, distinguished, or notable."

In today's world, many celebrities are celebrated not just for their fame, but increasingly for their commitment to using their gifts and talents to serve others and uplift their generation. These individuals understand that their influence extends far beyond the silver screen or concert stage—it carries a responsibility to inspire and effect positive change in society. Remember, the aim is the world, where the real problems lie.

INTRODUCTION

Take, for example, An athlete who uses their platform to mentor at-risk youth and builds community sports facilities; or the musician who promotes literacy and fights human trafficking through their work. Through their art, they not only entertain but also educate and mobilize their fans to act. By hosting benefit concerts, donating a portion of their earnings to charitable causes, or participating in advocacy campaigns, they demonstrate that true celebrity status comes from a place of service.

Similarly, actors and actresses often leverage their visibility to support various humanitarian efforts. They might visit underserved communities, engage in charitable projects, or use their voice to bring attention to important causes. By doing so, they embody the idea that their gifts—whether it be acting, singing, or public speaking—are meant to serve a greater purpose: to uplift and empower others.

These celebrities inspire their generation to recognize their potential and encourage them to pursue their passions while making a difference. They remind us that living fully means not only achieving personal success but also contributing to the well-being of others, using their significance. In celebrating these individuals, we acknowledge the power of using one's gifts to create a lasting impact, fostering a culture where service to others is as valued as personal achievement. In this way, they become role models, encouraging future generations to embrace their talents while serving the world around them.

A **platform** is any position of influence to reach an audience, while a **pulpit** is a platform of spiritual authority, carrying the responsibility to teach and inspire according to God's truth.

Today, we are called to be a light for others in a world that is in darkness, in need of the right type of entertainment: restoration, hope, refreshment, and a little revival. So that they can see our good works and ultimately praise, commend, admire, applaud, pay tribute to, speak highly of, and compliment not us, but our

Father in heaven, who has blessed us by allowing us to share in His image and likeness—though a unique borrowed light.

The phrase "made in His image and likeness" refers to the biblical concept, found in **Genesis 1:26-27**, that **humans are created by God to resemble Him, reflecting His character and nature, and given a unique dignity and purpose.**

Check out how simply this verse is worded. Matthew 5:16 states, **'In the same way, let your light shine before others, that they may see your good deeds and glorify your Father in heaven' (Matthew 5:16).** Notice where the attention ultimately goes: to our Source, because of what He allows us to enjoy and serve with.

Tom Smith, (Seabiscuit's trainer) also on hard times, saves a lame horse from being put down by making the statement, **"Every horse is good for something…you don't throw a whole life away just because he's banged up a little."** If you are still breathing your purpose isn't over. Life has a way of hurting us, but it doesn't mean it is the end. Sometimes the deeply bruised are the more mightily used in their lifetime and in their assignment – our purpose. Our wounds can turn into wisdom and our mess into a message. Thats the real beauty of God's purpose prevailing over everything we can think, plan, or imagine.

When Seabiscuit is first introduced, he is described as **"small, hurting, walking with a limp, and having a wheeze in his breathing,"** but Tom Smith did not pay attention to these imperfections. Instead, he looks the horse in the eyes and immediately knows who he is. He saw potential. Potential is that capped capability and unreleased energy. Potential was everything Seabiscuit could be but hadn't yet fully become. All he could do but hadn't yet done.

Seabiscuit was a Thoroughbred racehorse. A Thoroughbred is a purebred stallion bred specifically for racing. Notice that this

INTRODUCTION

is what he was, but wasn't doing, until a trainer came along who believed in what he was—a purebred stallion

He was one of the most famous and beloved racehorses in American history, known for his incredible underdog story and his racing successes during the Great Depression era.

Champion horses are usually large, muscular, sleek, and without imperfections. Seabiscuit did not fit this description at all. He was used to race against "real" racehorses, to help build their confidence. Imagine that! As stated in the movie, when they did race him, **"He did what he was taught to do, lose."** What have the unauthorized feeds of this society been teaching you about yourself? This is the reason I will focus on "unlearning" or renewing our minds, almost like a regress before we can progress. We must be retaught and re-self-discover before advancing to our true, full selves. Society has a way of grooming us into what it sees fit concerning us. Now we must learn how to win. And win while staying in our lane.

This is the reason First Century Writer Paul stated, **"Do not be conformed to this world, but be transformed by the renewing of your minds, so that you may discern what is the will of God – what is good and acceptable and perfect" (Romans 12:2 NRSV).** Will is synonymous with Intent. What were you intended for? What did God purpose for you before the creation of the world. You were born in a troublesome time to be a solution. You were born for greatness, I assure you, and this is what we must rediscover — to lift the spirits of a world burdened by depression.

Renew means to 'resume an activity after an interruption.' It also entails going back, as the prefix 're' means just that—once more, afresh, renewed. It is 'a return to a previous state.' You must go back to yourself, before unauthorized interruptions or opinions come along and settled in.. This renewal will bring us back to the will of God, which also means the intent or purpose for which we were created. Most times, it means getting back to our untainted childhood dreams and sticking with them in our own convictions. You must believe in yourself and the God within you.

Though we may not presently fit the part of greatness in the eyes of society—and may even have doubts about our own unique greatness—there is something that we too are called to do to inspire those around us. Even if we have not yet seen amazing achievements and successes in our own lives before reading this book, these can be brought out of us when we discover our purpose and surround ourselves with the right people and/or a suitable environment. We love stories like Seabiscuit, because deep down we believe we have it in us to live our best lives while making an impact. We were made for more in life, to make an impact, not just to make an income.

YOUR PURPOSE WILL PROPEL YOU TO POWER

When we find our purpose for our lives, we'll stop operating in the mere "hustle and bustle-mode" of strictly giving it the old college try and move into a sweet spot where life doesn't seem like some burdensome experiment. Instead of toiling and struggling through frustration, we'll experience a more fulfilled journey of success.

The part in Seabiscuit that really got a hold of me and added fuel to this idea of self-discovery and defining one's purpose in this story was when the new trainer, Tom Smith, was called in to take on the challenge of training this lost cause of a thoroughbred. Smith said, **"They got him so screwed up running around in circles that he's forgotten what he was born to do."**

Smith was known for his unorthodox methods, but they struck a chord with Seabiscuit. Smith sensed the greatness that was within him. He and the new rider, Red Pollard, made sure to bring it out of the horse. Victories soon followed

INTRODUCTION

I'm fired up right now while writing this portion of the book. I desperately want to be the one that helps draw out of you the very PURPOSE for which you were born. I believe that lying dormant in you there is way more than what we are presently seeing. You know it as well. I want to be the person described in Proverbs 20:5 where it states, **"The purposes of a person's heart are deep waters, but one who has insight draws them out."**

Here are other translations:

> The purpose in a man's heart is like deep water, but a man of <u>understanding</u> will draw it out. (ESV)
>
> Knowing what is right is like deep water in the heart; a <u>wise</u> person draws from the well within. (MSG)
>
> The purposes in the human mind are like deep water, but the <u>intelligent</u> will draw them out. (NRS)
>
> The purpose in the heart of a man is like deep water, but a man of <u>good sense</u> will get it out. (BBE)
>
> The heart's real intentions are like deep water; but a person with <u>discernment</u> draws them out. (CJB)

Tom Smith and Red Pollard were two key figures in the story of Seabiscuit, the famous racehorse. Tom Smith was Seabiscuit's trainer, known for his unconventional methods and deep understanding of horses. Red Pollard was Seabiscuit's jockey, who formed a close bond with the horse and played a crucial role in their success on the racetrack. The partnership between Tom Smith, Red Pollard, and Seabiscuit became legendary in the world of horse racing.

These two broke the curse of having Seabiscuit **so screwed up running in a circle, he's forgotten what he was born to** do. Both together helped Seabiscuit learn how to be the Thoroughbred racehorse it always was born to be and win.

I, together with the words in this book, want to **bring out what lies dormant in you—your true potential**—so that you too can **emerge and serve your purpose as a unique light** to a dark world. You are a **solution** to the Kosmos, to the world as a whole. Let's go!"

I believe that we can work together at drawing out your purpose from way deep in the hidden crevasses and secret chambers of the core of your being. There is a better you hidden and lying dormant in you. Let's take steps to discover your true self. A person needed in your generation ready to be celebrated, cherished, commemorated, crowned, cheered, championed and considered.

Mission: I'm "Passionate about Provoking You to Pinpoint and Pursue Your Purpose."

Vision: Helping Competent Leaders Discover Themselves, Their Value, and Impact Their Sphere in Society with the Right Message, in the Right Method.

CHAPTER 1

THE DISCOVERY OF YOUR HIDDEN SELF

"And in the end, it's not the years in your life that count; it's the life in your years."
- Abraham Lincoln

Many of us are like Seabiscuit; running around in circles, either forgetting what we were born to do or not having the knowledge of our identity and purpose. Forgetting what we were once passionate about is common, since we easily get distracted with lots of competing alternatives. There are many good things that aren't right or best suited for our lives or purpose and we tend to drift about – wasting time, energy, and resources. This is where my focus comes from for this book. We work hard going nowhere. This time not like a racehorse, but more like a rocking horse, moving back and forth, but staying in the same sloppy state. Lots of movement, but no mission accomplished.

Many of us are on this path of hit or miss, trial and error experimentation. We're living haphazardly in the quest of trying to find our sweet spot, whether we realize it or not. The sweetest place for a human to be is right smack in the middle of what he or she was born to do. Their purpose, which is the Original Intent for their lives. This is what makes us all winners and causes us to attain our personal success – discovering who we were created to be.

I call this self-discovery. "Becoming", instead of just "Doing". Doing without becoming will make you a mere "Hustler" and will make you waste a lot of time in your life. Someone who is running around in circles, getting nowhere fast. Nailing it in one's niche, or suitable place, is contrary to hustling, or running in circles. Identifying one's niche propels you into your unique greatness. From this moment on through this book, I'll assist you in looking inwardly, before you can GO anywhere outwardly. Your future isn't ahead of you, it's in you! So, Stop, Read, Ponder, Listen, and Learn.

Seabiscuit's story is truly remarkable and inspiring. Despite his humble beginnings and initial struggles, he rose to become one of the most celebrated and beloved racehorses of his time. The partnership between Seabiscuit, his trainer Tom Smith, and his jockey Red Pollard exemplifies the power of belief, dedication, and perseverance in achieving greatness.

Seabiscuit's success on the racetrack, culminating in being named Horse of the Year in 1938, is a testament to the transformative impact of having the right guidance and support. His record-breaking career and his ability to capture the hearts of thousands of fans reflect the enduring legacy of his underdog story.

Isn't it amazing that this was the same time Napoleon Hill wrote *Outwitting the Devil* — 1938? What a coincidence! I discovered this while writing, and honestly, I do not believe it was mere chance. Hill's writing focuses on how the majority of humanity drifts from their purpose because a dark force intentionally prevents them from fully emerging.

CHAPTER 1

This must mean that when you eagerly seek and discover your true purpose, you become a great threat to his plan — to keep people in darkness — since he is called the prince of darkness.

Prince of Darkness:

- **Ephesians 6:12 (KJV)**:

    "For we wrestle not against flesh and blood, but against principalities, against powers, against the rulers of the darkness of this world, against spiritual wickedness in high places."

This verse refers to the spiritual forces of darkness, often associated with the devil, who is sometimes called the "prince of darkness."

Blinding the Minds:

- **2 Corinthians 4:4 (KJV):**
- *"In whom the god of this world hath blinded the minds of them which believe not, lest the light of the glorious gospel of Christ, who is the image of God, should shine unto them."*

This verse explains how the "god of this world" (a reference to the devil) blinds the minds of unbelievers, preventing them from seeing the light of the gospel and their true selves.

Outwitting the Devil by Napoleon Hill is a thought-provoking book in which Hill explores the concept of fear, doubt, and negativity as tools of control used by the "Devil" to keep people from reaching their true potential. Written in 1938 but not published until decades later, the book takes the form of a fictionalized interview between Hill and the Devil. In this interview, the Devil admits to using subtle methods—such as the manipulation of fear, distractions, and societal conditioning—to prevent individuals from finding their purpose and living fulfilling lives. The core message is that the key to overcoming these forces lies in mastering one's thoughts, taking control of one's mind, and living with a clear sense of purpose and self-discipline. The book encourages readers to break free from these invisible chains in order to live a life of success and spiritual fulfillment.

Interestingly, this revelation coincides with something that happened to me, along with a clear insight I personally received that confirmed this truth. At the time, I was completely unaware of the book Outwitting the Devil. Yet, after speaking in various settings, several people began approaching me and asking if I had ever read it. Eventually, a friend insisted I stop what I was doing and listen to Napoleon Hill's audiobook. I promised him I would, and chose to do so while walking along the beach in Fort Lauderdale. I couldn't believe what I heard. I'll share more about this experience later in the book.

To fully understand your true self and live in your God-given identity, you must be aware of three enemies: the world, which seeks to conform you to its ways (Romans 12:2); the Devil, who deceives and distorts your true identity (John 8:44), as Napoleon Hill mentions in his book; and your own mind, which must be renewed to align with God's purpose for your life (Romans 12:2)

HERE ARE THE REFERENCES:

1. **Romans 12:2 (NIV)** – *"Do not conform to the pattern of this world, but be transformed by the renewing of your mind."*

2. **John 8:44 (NIV)** – *"You belong to your father, the devil, and you want to carry out your father's desires. He was a murderer from the beginning, not holding to the truth,*

CHAPTER 1

for there is no truth in him. When he lies, he speaks his native language, for he is a liar and the father of lies."

3. **Romans 12:2 (repeated)** – Emphasizes the need for renewing the mind to align with God's will.

This passage, used again, grounds the message in biblical principles and reinforces the importance of transformation through the renewal of the mind. This is where this book comes into play. As a man thinks in his heart, so he becomes (Proverbs 23:7). The way you think shapes your identity and determines your destiny.

Even in retirement at Ridgewood Ranch in California, Seabiscuit continued to enchant and uplift spirits, with thousands of visitors coming to pay homage to the legendary horse. His lasting impact on horse racing and popular culture serves as a reminder of the indomitable spirit and resilience that can lead to greatness, even in the face of adversity. Seabiscuit's legacy as a symbol of hope and inspiration continues to resonate with people around the world, reminding us that with determination and belief, anything is possible.

The quality of one's life is not measured by its duration, but by the depth of its impact and the authenticity of one's pursuits. To die finished, having lived a life of purpose and significance, is far more meaningful than simply existing for a long time without true effectiveness.

Your value or gift is God's provision, but what you do with it—like developing it—becomes your skill and prosperity. Your gift will ultimately make room for you and bring you to the right places, where you can influence, impact, and make your mark. You must practice what you were born to do so that you can be fully sharpened and refined to serve your world effectively. Are you ready to do this?

I believe this correlates with that special quote we used with this chapter by Abraham Lincoln, **"And in the end it's not the years in your life that count; it's the life in your years."**

In his book "Rags-to-Riches Story," Tom Pedulla eloquently captures the extraordinary journey of Seabiscuit, It took someone looking at Seabiscuit and seeing what no one else saw in him. He also highlighted that an 89-race career allowed him to finish as the all-time leading earner with $437,730 in purse money. Like I mentioned earlier, he retired to Ridgewood Ranch in California. In a testament to his popularity, Seabiscuit entertained more than 50,000 visitors in the seven years he spent there before he died. **"During hard times when spirits needed raising, 'The Biscuit' surely did his part" (Tom Pedulla, A True Rag-to-Riches Story, April 21st, 2016).**

Everything God created has a purpose. Sometimes, we just need someone— including ourselves— to understand our inner selves. If a horse can get it right and leave its mark, how much more important are you?

> **"For we are God's workmanship, created in Christ Jesus to do good works, which God prepared in advance for us to do." (Ephesians 2:10, NIV)**

We are God's masterpiece and the crown of all He created, as stated here in this book called Ephesians. The word 'workmanship' in Greek means 'masterpiece' and 'poem.'

We were intended for something masterful. Don't underestimate yourself.

> **"The greatest pursuit of mankind is significance, meaning, and purpose." -Dr. Myles Munroe, Pursuit of Purpose**

CHAPTER 1

Everyone wants to be successful, but being able to define one's purpose in life is what will ultimately secure one's full satisfaction in living in peace and achieving true success. There are those who become successful, but not in what they are passionate about. Being successful in the wrong endeavor equates to failure. I have encountered many people who are successful in the traditional sense (measured by material possessions rather than fulfillment) who have approached me asking, 'What else do I lack?'

If this is the case, it is a question that should also be asked by individuals themselves and those around them. This signifies a form of failure and can prevent one from leaving a true impact or legacy—something for others to remember them by. You can only impart what you truly possess. Let's face it, we all want to succeed, be great, or significant at something. Regardless of who we are or where we live – in civilized or uncivilized societies – there appears to be a unique internal desire and longing to achieve success or greatness. Truth be told, we genuinely aspire to excel in something, to be in a place where we are not just toiling or stuck in a constant work-hard mode. We strive to be relevant in a specific area that is uniquely suited for us. Despite the billions of people on earth, each of us has a sense of our own uniqueness. Whether it manifests as a feeling of being the odd one out or a belief that we are destined for more, our inner being yearns for individuality, originality, and greatness.

This feeling exists for a reason. It is not meant to frustrate you but to drive you towards your purpose. There is something that you do better than others, something that brings you ease when you are doing it. That 'something' is your purpose, your passion and your value.

PURPOSE VS PLEASURE

Sigmund Freud stated that our ultimate pursuit is for pleasure at any cost. However, I believe that if a person remains solely fixated on pleasure, they have not fully broken through. An individual may seek pleasure as a means to numb the void of purpose.

The types of successes that we are introduced to in today's society seem to be sidetracking us from our true selves. They consist of grandiose rewards defined by the media – prestige, fame, wealth, luxury, and power.

Our world's relentless pursuit of this type of success has led to our downfall and unglamorous ends. Our focus has shifted towards the pursuit of material possessions and a persona that we can't truly relate to. It's a regrettable situation.

In this book, I will teach you how to achieve true success by embracing your authentic self and tapping into your real-life purpose. Before we can make any significant impact, we must first understand who we are meant to be. Prior to enhancing our career prospects, honing our skills and talents, and pursuing educational endeavors, we must delve deep into our individual sense of purpose. Defining our life's purpose enables us to live authentically rather than being caught in the 'Hustle and Bustle mode' of life, merely going through the motions. Everything else, including education, should follow the process of discovering our purpose.

> "THE GREATEST DISCOVERY IN THE HUMAN EXPERIENCE IS SELF-DISCOVERY, BECAUSE WITH IT COMES AN UNDERSTANDING OF OUR ORIGIN IN THE CREATOR, OUR INHERENT VALUE, AND THE MANNER IN WHICH WE ARE TO FULFILL OUR PERSONAL PURPOSE."

CHAPTER 1

- DR. MYLES MUNROE

In life, from a very early age, we are trained to pursue material achievements. Our parents, peers, and other relatives drill into us the importance of working hard to become "somebody." We are encouraged to go to school, get the best grades, and excel in our endeavors. Today, our bookstores are filled with materials that teach us how to reach the top of our fields so that we can accumulate wealth, power, and influence. Best-selling books and magazines constantly promise shortcuts to success, painting glamorous pictures of the rich and famous.

I am always reminded of the wise words of King Solomon, who admonishes us to **"cast but a glance at riches,"** because they come and go. What we possess or can attain should never define who we truly are. Ultimately, these things **"…will surely sprout wings and fly off to the sky like an eagle"** (Proverbs 23:5 NIV). If we rely on material wealth for our identity, we may find ourselves standing alone, completely lost, in a state of limbo and truly disappointed.

This pursuit of material achievements is no longer limited to living in the "right" neighborhood, attending the "right" college, or landing the "right" job. With the rise of social media, it has a much broader reach. We often find ourselves glancing at other people's pages and comparing ourselves to those who may have a lot of followers, exuberance, confidence, style, fame, and fortune. Looking outwardly instead of discovering our true identity—tapping into and staying true to our intrinsic values and potential—will only contribute to our waywardness. This external comparison confuses us further and causes us to drift away from our true selves.

The first-century writer Paul also warned those around him about such attitudes when he stated: *"We do not dare to classify or compare ourselves with some of those who commend themselves. But when they measure themselves by one another, and compare themselves with one another, they do not show good sense" (2 Corinthians 10:12 NRSV).* Truly, a bold and uncompromising statement from Paul — don't you agree? He is basically saying that you show a lack of judgment when you compare yourself to others as the standard for worth, success, or authority. Knowing who you are, staying true to yourself, and focusing on your own lane will keep you out of the comparison game.

When I started working out at a public gym, I had to wear bigger t-shirts at first and simply go through the motions. I refused to look at others in the mirror who were in better shape than I was, so I wouldn't get discouraged. Instead, I focused on myself—always observing my own progress without taking my eyes off me. There were many great bodies to look at, but I refused to do so. If I had to greet someone or make small talk, I'd just look at their face and keep it moving. I learned the eating habits, followed the workouts, tapped into my internal motivation—and I went to work. Before I knew it, I began receiving compliments from others and was even asked for advice on how I did it. That's when I started wearing less baggy t-shirts.

This lines up with one of Paul's instructions to his mentee: **'Give yourself wholly to these things; that your profiting may appear to all.'** *(1 Timothy 4:15, KJV). The verse prior states,* **'Neglect not the gift that is in thee'** *(verse 14). Do you see how we are called to work from the inside out?*

TRULY, IF YOU FOCUS ON YOUR PRIVATE HABITS, YOUR PUBLIC FRUIT WILL SPEAK LOUDER THAN YOUR WORDS.

In 2006-2010, when the financial crisis hit, I was in Florida. During that time, many people committed suicide. One former

CHAPTER 1

wealthy man shot himself at a nearby cabana, from a hotel that I was staying at in Southwest Florida. This wrong pursuit, which sometimes is combined with greed, has had endless disappointments in our societies. Not just suicide but divorce, violence, environmental destruction, and white-collar crimes have seemed to escalate in every community. Success in a career, though rewarding, does not automatically yield the desired end toward our true personal fulfillment. I have spoken in many settings where people had this type of success and still asked me at the end of my seminars or speaking engagements, "But what else am I lacking?"

I really like when students whom I speak amongst ask me this, "But what else is there?" Or, "What am I lacking?" Why? Because, as you'll find out later in this book, purpose is found in two places. Not limited to one place, or even just your career or job! A genuine pursuit of Purpose also sets the ground for learning. Questions are the true expression of perpetual students (disciples) and those who seek to know will inevitably attract their right directive information. I believe this with ALL MY HEART. Students ask questions and questions denote readiness. **"The hunger of the student determines the topic of the teacher." (Myles Munroe).**

Personal fulfillment through self-discovery is the true measure of success, because it comes from **being who you are meant to be** and **doing what you are meant to do**. I call it **minding your own business**.

There are some internal clues that you already came equipped with that I'll do my very best to help you identify. Truly, your future isn't farfetched, it's inside of you. My first mentor used to say, "God placed it where He knew you wouldn't miss." (Trista Sue).

Proverbs 12:5 says, **'The thoughts of the righteous are right,'** meaning those who are in alignment with God think in harmony with His will. Proverbs 23:7 adds, **'As a man thinks in his heart,**

so is he,' referring to what you already possess deep within your subconscious. And Romans 11:29 reminds us, **'For the gifts and calling of God are without repentance'**—they are already in you. Also, 'without repentance' means that God isn't having second thoughts about how you are designed, wired, and uniquely made. There is no remorse or regret about how you came into this world

You see, I told you, these things aren't far-fetched; they are already within you. So stop running all over the world and investing in countless programs that haven't yet led you to the most important discovery in the human experience.

As Dr. Myles Munroe once said, **'The greatest discovery in life is self-discovery. Until you find yourself, you will always be someone else.** Become yourself. Lets Rock and Roll!

CHAPTER 2

FINDING YOUR NICHE, ESCAPING THE HUSTLE

> "To find out what one is fitted to do, and to secure an opportunity to do it, is the key to happiness." - John Dewey

The word "hustle" has become a trend in today's society. Everyone is using it to define themselves as hard workers and people who are constantly on the move. Many showcase their relentless activity through social media, demonstrating that they are always moving, regardless of the weather, circumstances, or conditions.

While being 'on the move' can be productive—after all, no captain can steer a ship that is stagnant—it's important to recognize that movement alone doesn't always indicate meaningful progress. Hustling often reflects activity more than actual productivity. A person can be in constant motion without making any real advancement. This often happens when people engage in activities that don't align with their true passions or purpose, leading to a lingering sense of aimlessness.

The dictionary defines the word "hustle" as "forcing (someone) to move hurriedly or unceremoniously in a specified direction." In

BEYOND THE HUSTLE

this context, "hustle" is not necessarily a positive term. Back in the 1980s, the word often carried a negative connotation. Athletic coaches would urge their players to "hustle, hustle, hustle," which made sense within the focused environment of sports. However, street thugs and con artists would also "hustle" people out of their money, giving the term a more dubious meaning.

In that era, hustling wasn't a glamorous way of saying you were getting things done; instead, it implied that someone was being played, so to speak. It meant compelling, forcing, manipulating, tricking, or coercing someone. Hustling is akin to convincing someone to buy into something they don't really need. Have you ever felt like you were hustled?

In 2019, the movie "Hustlers," starring Constance Wu and Jennifer Lopez, was released. The film follows a stripper named Destiny (Wu), who is working to make ends meet. Destiny's life changes forever when she becomes friends with Ramona (Lopez), the club's top money earner. Ramona shows Destiny how to navigate the wealthy Wall Street clientele who frequent the club. However, when the 2008 economic collapse cuts into their profits, the women, along with two other dancers, devise a daring scheme to take their lives back.

They develop the art of slipping roofies into men's drinks to make them lose consciousness, allowing the women to run up their credit cards and drain their bank accounts. Forced by recession, they turn to these desperate measures to survive, becoming "hustlers." Economic downturns push us to find new, innovative, and creative ways to solve problems for ourselves and our families—not to create more problems. Unfortunately, these hustlers chose shortcuts that ultimately led to their downfall, as is often the case with actions taken in darkness. In the end, light exposes all hidden agendas. What seems like a shortcut often becomes the longest, most painful route.

CHAPTER 2

I recall having two off-duty police officers, who were also realtors, at one of my speaking events while I discussed the topic of "hustle" versus finding what one is fitted to do—one's niche. In the middle of the session, one of them exclaimed, "That's the truth." The other added, "We often use 'hustle' in a negative way when making arrests and filling out our police reports."

I believe you get it now, right? The term 'hustle' never truly had a positive connotation to begin with.

How did "hustle" become a positive term in today's world? Why does everyone refer to themselves as "hustling" or being a "hustler" when trying to express that they're getting things done or staying on the move?

Perhaps the shift began with the 2006 release of rapper Rick Ross's song *Hustlin'*, which features the now-famous line, "Every day I'm hustlin'." In the song, he describes gangster life in Miami—referred to as "MIA." The music video shows people selling water, fruit, and other goods, exchanging them for cash. Ross is portrayed as a boss figure, receiving large amounts of money for pushing his products. The term "yayo" used in the song is slang for cocaine, derived from Miami's street and Spanish-language culture or street lingo.

It's possible we have Rick Ross—among others—to thank for turning 'hustling' into a widely accepted term associated with ambition, drive, and survival, rather than manipulation or deceit.

TRUE HUSTLERS *CREATE MOMENTUM*

I believe that for "hustle" to have a positive meaning or effect, two things are required.

First, the person must be engaged in something productive and especially suited for them. Why? Because when a person is doing what they are meant to do, they won't have to move forcefully or unceremoniously; it becomes a natural flow. The only opposing forces they would need to overcome are their own fears, doubts, laziness, and procrastination. Additionally, let's not forget the opposition that often comes from "haters" or individuals who rise up to hinder one's progress out of jealousy. When you focus your attention on your niche or unique area of concentration, you create your own strength and momentum—a positive force not to be reckoned with. We grow, gain strength, and excel when we are on paths that are aligned with who we are and suitable to our design.

This doesn't mean you won't face opposition; it means you now have an advantage—because you've found something you are uniquely fitted to do. All that's needed now is the right opportunity to walk in it, even in the face of obstacles.

The reason you must identify your niche is because it naturally attracts both resistance and support—people and circumstances that will either challenge or champion your journey.

A description of this momentum is captured in the words of the wise King Solomon: *"**The path of those who are properly aligned (the righteous) is like the morning sun, shining ever brighter till the full light of day."** (Proverbs 4:18, NIV)*

Just as the morning sun gradually increases in brilliance, so too does a person on the right path gain strength, clarity, and influence over time, building unstoppable momentum as they align with their true purpose. There are distinct traits that define the momentum born from doing what one is truly designed for:

1. Clarity of focus – It is single-minded and undistracted, with a clear sense of direction.

2. Unshakable persistence – It remains steadfast in the pursuit of purpose, regardless of obstacles.

CHAPTER 2

3. Limitless passion – It is fueled by a deep, enduring drive that doesn't fade over time.

4. Laser-like intensity – It demands intentional effort and carries a strong sense of calling and destiny.

5. Expansive vision – It embraces a long-term commitment to excellence, growth, and impact.

Here are some firm and specific **characteristics of momentum** that arise from doing what is truly suited for a person—qualities that deserve an even closer look.

1. Passion: Engaging in activities that align with one's true interests and strengths can ignite passion and enthusiasm, driving momentum forward.

2. Flow: When individuals are immersed in tasks that resonate with their skills and values, they experience a state of flow, where time seems to fly by and productivity is heightened.

3. Motivation: Pursuing tasks that are well-suited to one's abilities and aspirations can fuel intrinsic motivation, leading to sustained effort and progress. When its intrinsic it doesn't need outside demands.

4. Resilience: Being in alignment with one's purpose and strengths can enhance resilience, enabling individuals to navigate challenges and setbacks with determination.

5. Creativity: Working in areas that are a natural fit can stimulate creativity and innovation, fostering new ideas and solutions to almost anything.

6. Confidence: Success and fulfillment in tasks that are suited to one's unique abilities can boost self-confidence and self-belief, further propelling momentum.

In that productive, fitted niche mode, a person must always be available, present, and ready to serve. It starts with discovering one's gift, then developing and refining it, followed by readiness to offer it to others at every opportunity. This aligns with John Dewey's quote, **"To find out what one is fitted to do, and to secure an opportunity to do it, is the key to happiness."**

Therefore, a true hustler shows up consistently for what they are passionate about—always present, prepared, and committed to doing what servant-leaders do best: serve.

Momentum is the force or energy gained by a person, process, or movement as a result of continued progress or activity. In a personal development context, momentum refers to the compounding drive and forward motion that builds when one consistently takes purposeful action aligned with their goals, values, and strengths. It creates a sense of flow, confidence, and acceleration toward meaningful outcomes.

A RIGHT WAY AND A WRONG WAY

The advice given by the first-century leader Paul to his mentee Timothy highlights the true posture of a servant-leader. He writes that a leader must **"not wrangle, but be mild toward all men, apt to teach, patient, with modesty admonishing those who resist the truth; if perhaps God may grant them repentance to know the truth"** (2 Timothy 2:24–25, Douay-Rheims Bible).

This passage underscores that influence—not control—is the aim. A servant-leader does not impose truth but gently guides others toward it, trusting that transformation comes through God's work in the heart and mind.

CHAPTER 2

In the end, if done rightly, this approach can influence how others think—leading them to embrace truth by conviction, not coercion. That was the essence of this successor's mission: to shape thinking, not control behavior. The moment we shift toward controlling people's actions, we cross into manipulation. True transformation begins in the mind, and a servant-leader must honor that.

Our goal should always be to engage the mind, because thinking is a voluntary act—something people must do for themselves. Even when offering correction or guidance, a servant-leader must lead with truth and love, not force. Afterward, it is up to the individual to decide whether or not to act on the truth you've shared. And if they do—you've won them over, just as Proverbs 11:30 says, "He who wins souls is wise."

We win through influencing, not imposing. That's true wisdom. We did our part, and God did His. Together, we collaborated in the process. Bingo!

A wrangler is a person who must work hard or engage in lengthy and complicated quarrels or excuses. No one wants to be oversold. When we try to oversell, we overkill. This is also a form of hustling. Notice many of the words in this translation and passage: mild, apt, patient, modest—even when admonishing. Ultimately, this is how we influence thinking. These qualities are the opposite of "forcing someone to move hurriedly or unceremoniously in a specified direction by imposing your beliefs or way of doing things on them.

A person with the gift of Timothy—the recipient of this counsel, whose role was to teach and shed light on the truth—would be "hustling" only if he resorted to imposing like a wrangler, engaging in lengthy debates or detailed arguments just to get his point across. When someone takes this approach, their focus shifts to influencing behavior rather than inspiring a change in mindset (repentance). This can easily slip into manipulation. True influence happens through inspiration, not imposition. Otherwise, it becomes just another form of hustling.

Even in sales, one of the most powerful principles taught is the importance of listening—truly listening—to identify the client's **X factor**: that underlying need, pain point, or desire that drives their decision-making. When we take the time to understand this fully, we're not just making a sale—we're offering a tailored solution that can genuinely serve and even transform their situation. Listening isn't just a soft skill; it's a strategy. The goal is not to push a product, but to meet a need—and in doing so, you build trust, loyalty, and long-term impact. In business, just like in leadership, saving the sale often starts by saving the person.

Two Ears to LISTEN, One Mouth to TALK:

> **"Wisdom is the reward for a lifetime of listening when you'd have preferred to talk."**
> **- D.J. Kaufman**

Could this be why the book of wisdom states, ***"Transgression is at work where people talk too much, but anyone who holds his tongue is prudent"*** (Proverbs 10:19, NSV)? In modern terms, a transgression is more than just a mistake—it's an offense that violates a principle, standard, or boundary. In our interactions with others—whether in business or purpose-driven leadership—talking too much, overselling, or imposing our views can cross into that territory. It disrupts trust and hinders the very transformation we hope to inspire.

When we impose rather than influence, we trespass—not just on personal space, but on the sacred process of someone else's growth. Just as "trespass" originally referred to entering someone's property without permission, it now extends to violating emotional or moral boundaries. In contrast, when we listen well, discern carefully, and engage respectfully, we create space for genuine influence. We guide others toward their purpose without

CHAPTER 2

force. This is the essence of servant leadership: exercising restraint, honoring boundaries, and building influence through wisdom, not pressure.

Influencing others toward their purpose is a skill—one that requires humility, timing, and emotional intelligence. It's not about rushing results, but about respecting the process.

> **"Let everyone be quick to hear [be a careful, thoughtful listener], slow to speak [a speaker of carefully chosen words and], slow to anger [patient, reflective, forgiving]" (James 1:18 AMP).**

> **"Often, the most powerful form of communication is restraint—saying less to convey more."**
> —Roberto Hernandez

Hustling often involves excessive toiling and the need to constantly convince others to accept your point of view. But as Albert Einstein wisely noted—even when you do have a valid perspective—"If you can't explain it simply, you don't understand it well enough." When someone has true understanding, especially of their purpose, they can communicate naturally and effectively, drawing from what's already within them.

In contrast, someone who lacks understanding yet insists on expressing their opinions—without listening or seeking deeper insight—can easily be seen as unwise. As Proverbs 18:2 says, **"A fool takes no pleasure in understanding, but only in expressing his opinion."**

Often, when we talk too much or feel the need to force our point, hidden motives begin to surface. It's no longer about helping the other person—it's about satisfying our own need to be heard, validated, or to feel important. In business, and especially in sales, this tendency can reveal an even deeper issue: you're more focused on the transaction than the person.

People can sense when the conversation shifts from their needs to your commission. And they pull away. Remember, to make a commission you have to make a sale, but to make a fortune, you must genuinely make a friend. Have you ever been around someone who just loves the sound of their own voice? It becomes clear that true influence—rooted in wisdom—always begins by listening.

As a coach, I learned that asking the right questions and simply listening as the client speaks can produce incredible results. It made me realize how simple—and powerful—my role really is. Why? Because I don't have to impose anything on the client. My job is to draw out what's already within them and, when the time is right, gently guide them toward the changes they're ready to make. Coaching is not about giving answers—it's about creating space for self-discovery, clarity, and alignment with purpose.

HUSTLE AND BUSTLE

We have also heard of "being in the grind" or in the "hustle and bustle." To "bustle," is to "move in an energetic or noisy fashion." Just like hustle it denotes, "To move hurriedly in a particular direction." Remember that our goal is not to be lazy or inactive, but to be actively apt, available or ready to serve, while being present in a specific niche. It is best when tied to one's gift and when that gift turns into a skill (ability). One's gift only becomes a skill over time and practice. Solomon said, **"If the ax is dull and its edge unsharpened, more strength is needed, but skill will bring success" (Eclesiastés 10:10 NIV)**. This is where ability and excellence come into play. I'll explain more about this in an upcoming chapter.

CHAPTER 2

When we choose to operate in our true purpose, we become more effective with our time, talent, and energy. Deep down, everyone desires to find that sweet spot—a place where serving others through our gifts becomes a delight, not a burden. Whatever your gift may be, it was never meant for you to keep; it was meant to be shared with the world.

As your gift evolves into a skill through consistent practice and application, it not only becomes more effective, but it can also become a source of income. This is what it means to live at ease within your niche—a comfortable and suitable place in life or work where your abilities thrive.

Even if you're not running your own business but working for someone else, make sure your gift is being used in some form or fashion. That time is never wasted. Your gift is being sharpened into a skill, which will undoubtedly lead to your success—either through promotion in that same space, or through a clear idea to launch your own venture, or both.

As the book of Ecclesiastes wisely states:

> "Sow your seed in the morning, and at evening let your hands not be idle, for you do not know which will succeed, whether this or that, **or whether both will do equally well.**" —Ecclesiastes 11:6 (NIV)

I assure you—your gift will make room for you. Stay faithful, stay sharp, and stay ready.

> **"One's gift is God's provision. The skill you put into that gift is your prosperity." –Carlos Seise**

It's possible for your gift to remain like a dull ax head—ineffective—if it goes unused. But when you begin to use it consistently, that gift sharpens into a skill, which becomes the key to your personal success. This is how your present—your gift—transforms into provision, fulfills purpose, and leads to prosperity.

God never gave Adam a chair—He gave him a tree. The provision was in the tree, but the prosperity was in the potential to craft the chair. Likewise, what you do with what you've been given determines what you'll receive in return.

As Proverbs 22:29 declares:

> **"Do you see a man skilled in his work? He will stand before kings; he will not stand before obscure men." (ESV)**

When we invest time and discipline into our gifts, they develop into skills. These skills position us in a place of confidence and ease—where we can both live well and serve our generation with excellence.

As educator and philosopher John Dewey put it:

"To find out what one is fitted to do, and to secure an opportunity to do it, is the key to happiness."

So, don't neglect the tree (Your Gift). Your future may be hiding inside it.

The phrase "fan into flame the gift of God" from 2 Timothy 1:6 is a powerful exhortation. Paul encourages Timothy—and by extension, every believer—to actively cultivate and stir up the spiritual gifts God has already placed within. These gifts are not to lie dormant; they are meant to be nurtured and exercised.

> **"Therefore I remind you to fan into flame the gift of God, which is in you through the laying on of my hands."**— 2 Timothy 1:6 (ESV)

CHAPTER 2

The Greek word "fan into flame" used here — ἀναζωπυρεῖν (anazōpurein) — means "to rekindle," "to ignite again," or "to stir up once more." It conveys the idea of restoring passion, zeal, or intensity that may have diminished over time. This isn't about starting a new fire, but about strengthening the flame that God has already ignited in you. Notice what the flame is connected to—your gift. Your gift is the spark. And to keep it burning, you need passion. You need to come alive again to what it is that you are gifted to do.

If you struggle to find your purpose, start by identifying your passion—because your passion is tied to your gift. And that gift, when fueled by passion, lights the way toward your purpose with a kind of positively unstoppable momentum.

You are most content, fulfilled, and truly successful when you have entered your sweet place of grace—that place where your passion, gift, and purpose align. That's where you live in flow, serve with joy, and create meaningful impact.

YOUR NICHE

I like to refer to this as our niche. The dictionary defines "niche" as "a comfortable or suitable position in life or employment." It represents that sweet spot we all desire and long to occupy. It frees us from toiling and working excessively, especially in an unceremonious and forceful manner. Have you ever seen someone operating in a role or job position that isn't suitable for them? It's one of the things that frustrates me the most—seeing people outside their sweet spots or doing something they aren't designed or suited to do. It's akin to a trespasser, someone who has entered an unauthorized environment for which they are neither fitted nor have legal permission to be in.

Don't Fall into the Trap of Living Outside of Your Grace. Thus, becoming a busy body.

BEYOND THE HUSTLE

Paul warns, *"We hear that some among you are idle and disruptive. They are not busy; they are busybodies."* (Thessalonians 3:11).

In this passage, the term "busybody" refers to individuals who are not genuinely engaged in productive or meaningful activities but instead meddle in the affairs of others unnecessarily. They are characterized by being idle in their own pursuits while being overly preoccupied with the affairs and concerns of others, often causing disruption and discord. A busybody is someone who interferes in the business of others without a valid reason or invitation, leading to unnecessary gossip, trouble, or conflict.

When you let your gift lie dormant too long, failing to fan it into flame, you risk ending up far from where you truly belong. Many people drift through life because they search for success outwardly, rather than looking inward to their purpose and potential.

People who are far from living a purposeful life may benefit from obtaining a regular job and focusing on basic necessities such as providing for their household and sustaining themselves. Engaging in regular employment can stimulate untapped potential and offer an opportunity to discover something special within themselves, leading to the revelation of their purpose and true capabilities. By actively working and not being idle, individuals can uncover hidden talents, skills, and passions that may guide them towards a fulfilling and purpose-driven life. If you find yourself in this situation, consider immersing yourself in work to unlock the potential for personal growth and self-discovery.

I believe we'll discover that our **niche** is something we are **graced with**, and for most of us it's something we've often overlooked. It's that **sweet spot** that comes naturally — even on days when we feel frustrated, angry, or as if we've woken up on the wrong side of the bed. This niche is what allows us to **flow effortlessly** and **solve the problems around us with ease**.

CHAPTER 2

Take a moment and ask yourself, "What am I graced with?" Grace is a special endowment, in layman's terms. It is also a divine influence upon the heart given to you—a gift or favor you did not earn. You just have it! That is why it says, **"For God's gifts and his call can never be withdrawn" (Romans 11:29, NLT).** Again, YOU JUST GOT IT!

What do others observe in you? Consider that you could be overlooking your gift.

Have you ever encountered someone who exudes a certain quality, prompting others to remark, "This individual has it"? This phrase often reflects an innate ability or exceptional capability that observers recognize. It highlights an individual's unique talent or charisma that sets them apart in a particular context. You came into the world with it, and it cannot be taken away. Therefore, you don't have to search far to discover it. It's within you. It's YOU! This is self-discovery.

Recognizing this should prevent us from becoming cocky, prideful, or boastful. Why? Because our unique niche makes us different, not better than others. It is a natural grace that enables us to flow in a niche that is part of who we are. It's often noticed by others before we even recognize it ourselves—that's how natural it is. This is why we should not think of ourselves more highly than we ought, but rather "think of ourselves with sober judgment" (Romans 12:3, NIV). Why? Because **"we have different gifts, according to the grace given to each of us" (Romans 12:6).** You see, we aren't better; we are just different. Ultimately, we are tapping into our unique selves.

> **"Return to your first works, or else I will come to you quickly and remove your candlestick from its place—unless you repent."** *(Revelation 2:5)*

Your *first works* are not just about chronology—they're about **priority and purpose**. They represent what you were created to do, what flows naturally from you, what you *dominate*. It's the thing you do with ease, with joy, with grace. It's *first* not just because you did it early—but because it sits at the *top* of what you were called and gifted to do.

When you drift from that, you risk losing your influence—your "candlestick," your light, your place of impact. The warning isn't about punishment—it's about alignment. When you walk away from your God-given lane, you dim your own brilliance. But when you return to what you were made for, your flame burns brighter than ever.

There are three ways to lose your candlestick—the very place you were called to shine:

1. Neglect.
   This happens when you know what you're called to do, but fail to do it. The people in Revelation were told to return to their first works—not discover them. They had already walked in their calling but drifted. The flame dies not from ignorance, but from inaction.

2. By having it removed because of unfaithfulness, as a consequence of ignoring the purpose for which it was given.

3. Pride.
   This is when you elevate yourself above your place of grace—thinking you're too good for what you were built for. You outgrow obedience in your own mind, forgetting that the oil only flows where God has anointed. Pride pushes you out of position, and the light goes with it.

In all cases, the result is the same: the candlestick is removed. But the solution is simple—return. Return to what you were made for, where you shine, where grace meets your gift.

Take Elvis Presley— "The King of Rock and Roll." For those who remember, his voice, charisma, and stage presence were

CHAPTER 2

unmatched. He *dominated* music. That was his lane. That was his gift. That was his **candlestick**—where he was called to shine.

But Elvis wanted more. He desperately wanted to be an actor. And because he was so talented, the industry let him do both—they let him act/sing (if that's even a real category), filming him half-performing in half-plotted scripts just to capitalize on his fame. The result? A string of forgettable movies that diluted his impact. He wasn't bad—he just wasn't *graced* for that role the way he was for music.

Elvis didn't fall off because he lost talent. He drifted because he stepped outside his anointing. He left his *first works*.

It's a modern parable: **when you abandon the thing you were born to do, even your success can become a distraction.** Talent can take you far, but only purpose will keep you planted.

To be arrogant is dangerous to our purpose in life. It robs us of our true being. Arrogance means "having or revealing an exaggerated sense of one's own importance or abilities." It comes from a Latin word meaning "presuming." It involves making "claims or pretensions to superior importance or rights," and it is characterized by being "overbearingly assuming and insolently proud."

This is significant: when you feel entitled to a platform, or believe you earned everything by your own merit, you also take on the burden of sustaining it in your own strength.

What begins as a normal zeal or deep desire quickly turns into strain. You start to force what once flowed. You grind to keep up appearances. And eventually, it shows.

It shows on your face—the billboard of the heart. The weariness, the frustration, the weight of trying to maintain something you were never graced to carry.

BEYOND THE HUSTLE

It looks ill-fitting. It feels exhausting. Because it is.

That's what happens when pride moves you out of alignment. But humility brings you back. Back to your lane. Back to grace. Back to your first works—where the burden is light and the oil flows freely.

It is important—*vital*, even—to remember your **humble beginnings**. The place where grace met you. Where your gift flowed effortlessly. Where you were dependent, surrendered, and aligned.

Because when you forget where you started, you risk lifting yourself too high. And what begins in pride must be *sustained* by pride.

As the saying goes, **"What starts in the flesh must be sustained in the flesh."**
When you build in your own strength, you must maintain it in your own strength. That's not only *unsustainable*—it's unhealthy. It pulls you away from *true self-discovery* and into the exhausting trap of performance.

Before long, even being yourself becomes a hustle

This is why the Apostle Paul, one of the most influential writers of the first century, often wrote to his contemporaries with urgency, clarity, and deep conviction. His letters weren't casual—they were purposeful. He reminded believers to return to the core of their faith, to stay humble, and to walk in the Spirit rather than the flesh.

Paul understood the danger of pride, of drifting from one's calling, of starting in grace and trying to finish in self-effort. That's why he wrote things like:

> **"Are you so foolish? After beginning by means of the Spirit, are you now trying to finish by means of the flesh?"** —Galatians 3:3

CHAPTER 2

Paul's writing is a timeless reminder: **Don't forget where you started.** Don't trade divine flow for forced performance. Return to your first love, your first works—where your true identity and calling reside.

He went as far as reminding another group:

> **"Brothers and sisters, think of what you were when you were called. Not many of you were wise by human standards; not many were influential; not many were of noble birth. But God chose the foolish things of the world to shame the wise; God chose the weak things of the world to shame the strong. God chose the lowly things of this world and the despised things—and the things that are not—to nullify the things that are, so that no one may <u>boast</u> before him" (1 Corinthians 1:26-29, NIV).**

There is a reason many of us must hit rock bottom before we truly discover ourselves—it's not accidental. It's intentional. Every story has a rocky chapter, because rock bottom is one of the strongest catalysts for self-discovery. It humbles us. It grounds us. It strips away everything superficial so only what is real can rise.

As I often say: "Whomever God will mightily use, He must first deeply bruise."

Because trials produce character—and it's not gifting, but character, that sustains the gift. Your influence doesn't come from talent alone; it comes from what's been forged in fire.

You are who you are through a God-given grace, and you grow in that grace. You move from grace to more grace, from strength to strength—not by chasing applause or striving to be more, but by becoming more fully yourself. The divine influence on your life reflects what you do naturally—your dominant lane, your first works. And as you steward that gift, you convert it into skill. That's when you begin to thrive: not from effort alone, but from alignment.

Your place of ease is found in *minding your own business*—putting your energy into what you were created to do.

Those who boast, compare, or become haughty often reveal that they've never truly discovered themselves—or have forgotten their humble beginnings. Haughtiness is a symptom of drift. An eagle doesn't compete with a lion—it simply flies. That's what it was born to do. Fish don't boast in the sea; they just swim, because swimming is *natural* in their God-given environment. In the same way, you don't have to force what is real — it flows naturally. *But* to sustain what is fake? That takes constant effort. That leads to exhaustion.

And that's why Scripture reminds us:

> **"God chose the foolish things of the world to shame the wise; God chose the weak things of the world to shame the strong… so that no flesh may glory in His presence."** *(1 Corinthians 1:27, 29)*

Your gift is not proof of your greatness—it's proof of God's goodness.

And when you stay in your lane—when you honor what you were born to do—you don't just *operate*… **You flourish.**

Not by might.
Not by power.
But by grace.

CHAPTER 3

THE UNFORCED RHYTHMS OF GRACE

"Learn the unforced rhythms of grace. I won't lay anything heavy or ill-fitting on you. Keep company with me and you'll learn to live freely and lightly" **(Matthew 11:28-30 MSG).**

"Grace Will Take You Places Hustling Can't." This thought-provoking quote, shared by a realtor friend on her Instagram, captures a powerful truth. She reminds us to in a further comment to **"Thank God for His grace and His mercies, which are new each morning. But still hustle, baby."**

The world teaches us to *grind first* and hope peace follows. But the Kingdom of God flips the order.

We don't start with hustle and try to force flow.
We start by finding our **flow**—our alignment with God's grace, our true identity, and our divine assignment.

Then we hustle.
From clarity, not chaos.
From purpose, not pressure.

This is how grace works:
You receive first, then you respond.
You hear before you move.
You align before you act.

When you operate from flow, your hustle becomes **sustainable**.
You're no longer striving to prove, but flowing to produce.

Just like the greatest example of all—the one who lived in perfect alignment with His life's work—said in John 15:5:

"I am the vine; you are the branches. Apart from Me, you can do nothing."

So the goal isn't to hustle until you burn out, but to *flow until you overflow*.
Find your **Flow first** by staying connected to the Source. **Then hustle.** That's the rhythm of grace.

1. "THANK GOD FOR HIS GRACE AND HIS MERCIES, WHICH ARE NEW EACH MORNING."

It's a reminder that every day we wake up, we're receiving fresh grace and mercy from God. We don't live on yesterday's strength or forgiveness—we're given a daily clean slate.

This is a reference to **Lamentations 3:22–23**, which says:

> *"The steadfast love of the Lord never ceases; His mercies never come to an end; they are new every morning; great is Your faithfulness."*

CHAPTER 3

2. "BUT STILL HUSTLE, BABY."

This is a modern encouragement to **stay diligent, put in the work, and not be passive**, even though grace is available. It's essentially saying:

Yes, God is gracious. Yes, you're covered. But don't use grace as an excuse to be lazy—get up and move. Do your part.

I LIKE TO GIVE THIS A DEEPER MEANING:

Rest in God's mercy, but move with purpose.
Trust Him, but still grind.

Be grateful for the grace, but stay committed to the growth.

It's a spiritual encouragement *with a little edge*—perfect for someone who loves the Lord and still gets things done in accordance to His purpose. Remember: both flow and hustle are essential for extreme productivity.

You need flow to keep you aligned—anchored in purpose, peace, and divine timing.
You need hustle to keep you moving—disciplined, diligent, and intentional with your time and energy.

Flow without hustle can leave you inspired but inactive.
Hustle without flow can leave you busy but burned out. But when you start from flow—from clarity, conviction, and calling—your hustle becomes focused, fruitful, and full of grace.

Flow is your direction. Hustle is your execution.
Together, they make purpose powerful and productivity sustainable.

BEYOND THE HUSTLE

This is how you thrive:
Aligned. Empowered. Engaged.
Not by might, not by striving—but by grace-fueled action.

"This brings to mind the 2005 film Hustle & Flow, starring Terrence Howard — an actor I greatly admire. The story follows a small-time Memphis pimp who dreams of becoming a rapper. Although it's framed as his struggle to break into the music industry, the plot also reveals that he continues exploiting women to finance his dream. The title "Hustle & Flow" plays on that double meaning — hustling on the streets while trying to create a musical "flow."

Once again we see a flipped order: someone trying to reach a new level while still living by an old system. It's a vivid reminder not to be conformed to the world's system but to God's order and way of doing things. It's not "Hustle & Flow," it's "Flow and then Hustle."

In my group discussions at the Self-Discovery Learning Center, I strive to create an environment where participants feel intellectually stimulated — a space that fosters curiosity, reflection, and personal growth.

My goal is to **provoke self-awareness**, challenge participants to **uncover their own purpose**, and awaken a **genuine desire to pursue it**.

We can actually do this while learning to move within a **rhythm of grace**, not a rhythm of grind. Not from a place of pressure or performance. When we find this **flow**—when we align with how God wired us—we stop chasing, and start walking in step with our assignment. To do this properly we sometimes have to train people to regress before they can progress. This is when we can begin to engage authentically, work joyfully, and live **fruitfully**. Fulfillment increases. Striving and toiling decreases. It's like returning to childlikeness— relearning what it means to truly live.

CHAPTER 3

It's exactly what we're invited into by the Master Teacher Himself—Jesus—in **Matthew 11:28–30 (MSG)**:

> **"Learn the unforced rhythms of grace. I won't lay anything heavy or ill-fitting on you. Keep company with me and you'll learn to live freely and lightly."**

This is what it looks like to walk in purpose without pressure—to flow in grace without forcing outcomes.

That's the atmosphere I aim to create:
Safe. Stimulating. Spirit-led.

A space where people don't feel burdened by expectations, but free to discover, express, and grow into who they were created to be—by grace, through grace, and in step with grace.

MY BREAK-DANCING DAYS

The "unforced rhythms of grace" are akin to listening to great tunes that make you bop your head unconsciously. It's more about being than doing when it comes to life and work. A vivid flashback to my breakdancing days illustrates this perfectly. We started a Break Dance Crew called the Rock Sensation Crew in my mid-teens. When the ambience of a dance club is just right, it's usually the music that sets the tone. The DJ plays a crucial role in creating an atmosphere that invites people to dance. I would walk in, merely bopping my head, and eventually find myself surrounded by a circle of people, entertained by the rhythm that carried me along. I would start with popping and locking, then transition into break-dancing, and ultimately freestyle all night.

Freestyling was what captivated the audience the most. It was in those moments that onlookers seemed most entertained. Why?

Because that was where the greatest creativity flowed. Thus, the name "Free Style."

Freestyle typically refers to a form of performance or expression that is done in a spontaneous, unrestrained, and creative manner. In various contexts, freestyle can refer to improvised or spontaneous actions, such as freestyle rap where lyrics are created on the spot, freestyle swimming where swimmers have the freedom to choose their strokes, or freestyle dancing where movements are not choreographed. Essentially, freestyle denotes a sense of freedom and creativity in the way something is done or expressed.

This reflection beautifully captures the essence of spontaneity and creativity in both dance and life. The concept of "unforced rhythms of grace" resonates deeply, emphasizing a state of being that invites both flow and authenticity, much like the experience I had while breakdancing.

When the atmosphere is just right, and the music takes over, it becomes a dance of freedom, where the mind lets go and the body expresses itself. Free-styling, in particular, symbolizes pure creativity—it's unstructured and raw, allowing for **personal expression** that captivates an audience and entertains them.

This idea parallels life and work, where the best experiences often arise from being fully present and engaged rather than rigidly adhering to plans or techniques. Just as I found joy and connection in my dancing, embracing those unforced rhythms can lead to a more fulfilling and dynamic existence. It's a reminder that sometimes, the most beautiful moments arise when we let go and allow ourselves to be guided by the unforced rhythms of life - living from the inside out.

We All Have the Music in Us

CHAPTER 3

"Music is not just something you hear; it's a feeling that resonates within you, waiting to be expressed."

Ken Swift, a fellow breakdancer from the renowned Rock Steady Crew, once said, "Freestyling outdoes technique all the time." True passion can only be fully ignited when we find ourselves in a comfortable and suitable place, wherever that may be. Our greatness emerges from simply being in our place of grace. It is from this foundation that we generate strength and momentum.

Unfortunately, many of us must relearn how to live in this natural state of being. It is the space where we were once influenced and educated, and it is where we must return. From there, we can move from strength to strength and from grace to more grace. Flow, baby!

That's exactly how it is when you're in your niche. You find yourself in an environment that feels comfortable and suited to you—not only in employment and business but in life in general. Often, others can easily recognize when you are operating within your own environment and utilizing your unique gifts. In many cases, people may identify this in you before you even recognize it in yourself.

This is why one of the key questions in my self-discovery questionnaire is:

"WHAT DO PEOPLE OFTEN SAY YOU DO WELL?"

Pay close attention to the consistent compliments, affirmations, and feedbacks you receive. Those aren't just casual words—they're clues. Clues to your natural strengths. Clues to your God-given grace.

Often, we overlook what comes easiest to us, simply because it feels effortless. We assume that if it's not hard, it's not valuable. But that couldn't be further from the truth. What you do well without trying is often exactly where you're most gifted—and where you should be building.

We should focus on building our strengths—the things we already dominate—rather than constantly trying to fix every weakness. Why? Because what you master is what you multiply.

Scripture supports this principle. Proverbs 27:2 (NIV) says:

"Let someone else praise you, and not your own mouth; an outsider, and not your own lips."

Let others speak into your life—and listen.
Their praise may be pointing you back to the very thing God placed inside you from the beginning.

Individuals who have discovered their true selves and found their niche are those who live in the unforced rhythms of grace that align perfectly with who they naturally are and what they are meant to do.

"We have different gifts, according to the grace given to each of us" (Romans 12:6 NIV). We need to discover what we are fitted to do and then be placed in the right environment, allowing us to fully manifest and shine like the bright light of day. That environment is our domain and audience—the space that enables us to express our true selves.

Remember, we are different, not better than one another. Therefore, there should never be a need for arrogance—only confidence. Ultimately, we want to be where we are celebrated, not tolerated.

When the atmosphere is just right and the music takes over, something sacred happens—
It becomes a **dance of freedom**.

The mind lets go.

CHAPTER 3

The body expresses.
And in that moment, especially in freestyle, it's **pure creativity**—raw, unstructured, personal.
It's not about performance. It's about **presence**. It captivates not because it's perfect, but because it's **real**.

This reminds me of a passage I've grown to love:

> "Let your light so shine before others, that they may see your good works and glorify your Father in heaven." — *Matthew 5:16*

Notice it says **your light**—not someone else's.
Your light is personal. It's unique.
It's the way you move, speak, lead, create, serve, and love.

God never asked you to mimic someone else's shine. He asked you to **let your own light shine.**

Like freestyle, your light doesn't need rigid structure—it needs **authentic release**.
It may not look like anyone else's.
It's not supposed to.
That's what makes it powerful.

So don't hide it. Don't edit it to fit in.
**Let it shine—unapologetically.

DRESS HOW YOU WANT TO BE ADDRESSED.

There is nothing worse for me than when people are out of place. I once went out of my way to listen to a speaker who had a great reputation. However, he lost me from the very beginning of his presentation, and it was all because of how he was dressed. His clothes were wrinkled, his pants didn't even fit properly - too baggy, his shoes were old, and his belt had an extra notch poked into it to attempt to fit his skinny waist. To top it off, he wore a dark-colored, old t-shirt under his wrinkled dress shirt.

I know that judging a person solely by their appearance isn't the ultimate measure of what they can bring to the table in terms of information. We all know the saying, "Do not judge a book by its cover." But it made my stomach turn, and it felt to me like he wasn't taking pride in his skill. In fact, he didn't even look comfortable. After giving him the benefit of the doubt—which is always the right thing to do—I was ultimately let down and disappointed. His presentation reflected how he presented himself: off.

Please do not judge me for being harsh; this was my experience with this specific individual. I honestly believed he should have been doing something else.

Today, we have suits and casual attire available in clothing stores in all sizes that are fitted for individuals. This looks, feels, and presents well when showing up for one's assignment or serving one's gift. It's almost synonymous with someone operating in what they are "suited" for. Thus, the word "suited." A suit means "a set of clothes, dress, or attire," while "suited" means "right or appropriate for a specific person, purpose, or situation." Relevancy is one of mankind's main pursuits.

Your gift is just right and fits you. This is how it feels in a room when the person serving is living and operating in his or her niche: comfortable, like a well-fitted glove that requires no strain to put on your hand. Are you in your suited and comfortable place? If so, you will also create an environment that is conducive to your niche.

To "dress how you want to be addressed" goes beyond the attire you wear; it's about doing what you are fitted and suited to do, then securing opportunities to do it, bringing happiness to yourself and your audience. Remember that your audience gets inspired when you let your unique light shine. When you

CHAPTER 3

show up in your zone you inspire an audience to want to be their true selves. That's why we influence more by being in our work, rather than just with our words.

> Even Partners are supposed to the right FIT,
> NOT just the right LOOK.

Partners are also suited for us.

Both business partners and life partners should be well-suited for us. (Life and Work) The LORD God said, **"It is not good for the man to be alone. I will make a helper <u>suitable</u> for him" (Genesis 2:18).**

When entering into business with others, it is important to consider that those individuals should bring something to the table that complements the overall vision of the organization—whether it be the right abilities, skills, talents, or areas of expertise. I have always thrived in business partnerships when others possessed what I lacked.

Proficiency + Passion = Purpose.

Similarly, when choosing a mate or life partner, we should focus not just on love but on finding the right fit for our niche. We marry because of purpose over love. It's not about the right appearance; it's about compatibility and how well two can complement each other.

So, we choose not just out of love but from within our niche—not about the look, but more about the fit! Is he or she a right fit for you?

> Can two walk together, except they be agreed? (Amos 3:3 KJV).

I usually tell people to use like and chemistry to guide the initial introduction. After that, let the interview process take over.

GIFTS OF GRACE

"Are you tired? Worn out? Burned out.... Walk, Work, and Watch"

There are a lot of people living unauthorized lives. In other words, they haven't found their environment. Every day, people find themselves somewhere other than their own place of grace. They have been convinced either by themselves or someone else to be out of place and be okay with it. Constantly trying to fit into an environment that's not for you can leave one burned out, worn out, exhausted, and tired. We call this toiling.

This is the very thing the young Jewish Carpenter of the First Century described when he said, *"Are you tired? Worn out? Burned out on religion? Come to me. Get away with me and you'll recover your life. I'll show you how to take a real rest. Walk with me and work with me – watch how I do it. Learn the unforced rhythms of grace. I won't lay anything heavy or ill-fitting on you. Keep company with me and you'll learn to live freely and lightly"* (Matthew 11:28-30 MSG).

Here is a comparison between a person who toils and a person who lives at ease:

The person who toils is constantly striving, pushing themselves to fit into a mold that was never meant for them. They feel out of place, exhausted from trying to be someone they are not. Their days are filled with stress, frustration, and a sense of never truly belonging.

In contrast, the person who lives at ease moves through life with a sense of peace and contentment. They have found their place of grace and feel comfortable being their authentic self. Their days are filled with joy, fulfillment, and a deep sense of belonging.

While the person who toils may feel lost and weary, the person who lives at ease radiates confidence and inner peace. They have embraced who they are and have found harmony in their environment.

Ultimately, the choice between toiling and living at ease is about finding your true self and honoring that authenticity. It may require courage and self-reflection, but the rewards of living authentically are immeasurable.

> ***"If good people barely make it, What's in store for the bad? So if you find life difficult because you're doing what God said, take it in stride. Trust him. He knows what he's doing, and he'll keep on doing it." (1Peter 4:18-19 MSG).***

Both the person striving to live according to the Manufacturer's design—that is, God's intent—and the one who is alienated from the life they were meant to live will face challenges. No one is exempt from trials, tribulations, or tests. These experiences are not punishments but essential tools for shaping our character.

Even those who live at ease, in their niche, are not immune to the challenges and difficulties that life may bring. However, when they encounter obstacles, they are better **equipped to** navigate through them with grace and resilience, drawing strength from being in alignment with their true selves.

On the other hand, for those who are outside of their place of grace, the struggles may be even more overwhelming. They face an uphill battle, constantly trying to fit into a space that does not align with their authentic self. The effort to conform and please others will lead to a sense of disconnection, burnout, and inner turmoil.

If even marrying someone well-suited to you—aligned in purpose, values, and faith—still brings challenges, then why would anyone choose to build a life with someone who isn't? Why step into a covenant with someone outside your God-given niche, becoming unequally yoked, and invite unnecessary strain into what is already a sacred and stretching journey?

As the scripture in **1 Peter 4:18 (MSG)** reminds us, *"If good people barely make it, what's in store for the bad?"* This serves as a powerful reminder that even those who are living authentically and, in their element, may face difficulties, highlighting the even greater challenges that await those who are living inauthentically.

It is important to heed this wisdom and strive to find our place of grace—our sweet spot in life. By embracing who we truly are and aligning ourselves with our values and passions, we can navigate life's challenges with greater ease and authenticity. Don't struggle unnecessarily by trying to fit into a space that is not meant for you. Embrace your true self and find your place of belonging, allowing only those who also belong there to join you in your sweet spot!

MAN, NOT MADE FOR RELIGION

"Religion is the opium of the people."- Karl Marx,

Back to our chosen passage for this chapter. Let's take a closer look at it through this unique and refreshing translation:

> **"Are you tired? Worn out? Burned out on religion? Come to me. Get away with me and you'll recover your life. I'll show you how to take a real rest. Walk with me and work with me—watch how I do it. Learn the unforced rhythms of grace. I won't lay anything heavy**

CHAPTER 3

or ill-fitting on you. Keep company with me and you'll learn to live freely and lightly" (Matthew 11:28–30 MSG).

From our discussion, we can conclude that being tired and worn out is often the natural result of toiling—of living outside of our intended design.

Jesus, the young Jewish carpenter, addressed something much deeper than just physical fatigue. He spoke to a spiritual and emotional exhaustion—especially among people burdened by religion. Notice the question: "Burned out on religion?" He wasn't speaking against faith itself, but rather the heavy-handed traditions, rules, and systems that had replaced relationship with ritual. These were people going through all the motions their ancestors passed down—motions that no longer breathed life. They were operating far outside of their natural, God-given environment.

The result? Life no longer felt free. It felt forced. Heavy. Ill-fitting.

They weren't living in rhythm with who they were created to be. Every day felt like a chore. Like survival. And the crushing weight of religion—something that was meant to draw them closer to God—was actually pushing them further from their own identity and joy.

Then Jesus gives the invitation:
"Come unto me, all you who are weary and heavy-laden..." (as another translation renders it).
It's a call not just to rest, but to recovery.

"Get away with me and you'll recover your life."

This is the call to return—to come back into alignment with grace, into the environment where we were always meant to thrive.

Jesus isn't offering another rulebook. He's offering relationship, rhythm, and rest.

The call is also for him to, **"show you how to take a real rest"** and live again by, **"Walking with him and working with him – watching how he does it."** This way we would all **"Learn the unforced rhythms of grace."** He promises that he **"won't lay anything heavy or ill-fitting on you."** And ultimately, if we **"Keep company with him we'll learn to live freely and lightly"** *(From Matthew 11:28-30 MSG).*

It was Karl Marx's celebrated dictum that still resonates, "**Religion is the opium of the people.**"

The phrase "burned out on religion" is loaded with meaning—and it invites us to pause and consider what Jesus was really addressing.

Religion, at its best, is meant to be a pathway to connection: with God, with truth, with purpose. It often arises from a deep desire to know something greater than ourselves. This pursuit can lead to rich exploration, honest questions, and transformative discovery. But if we're not careful, the search itself can become exhausting.

When religion becomes more about rule-keeping than relationship, more about performance than presence, it becomes a weight rather than a wellspring. People can end up so consumed with trying to get it right that they miss the invitation to simply be with the One who already made things right.

That's how burnout happens.

You can spend years seeking meaning, yet never stop long enough to receive it. The journey becomes a loop of striving rather than a rhythm of grace. The search, ironically, can become a form of escapism—always reaching, never resting. Always doing, never dwelling.

CHAPTER 3

But Jesus offers a different way. He says:

"Walk with me and work with me—watch how I do it. Learn the unforced rhythms of grace."

This isn't an invitation to abandon the search for meaning—it's a call to rediscover that the very meaning we're chasing is found in Him. Not in rituals. Not in religious performance. But in relationship.

To avoid spiritual burnout, we must learn to seek without striving and grow without grinding. True rest isn't found by stopping the search, but by shifting how we search—moving from anxious effort to Spirit-led rhythm.

The key is balance: between seeking and settling, between movement and stillness. Between asking big questions and receiving small moments of grace.

Because sometimes the most sacred revelation isn't found in a breakthrough—it's found in a breath.

Religion is associated with the concept, "to search." It can be a never-ending search that keeps people numbed in the search itself and not the end.

> **"Religion is the worship of a Deity through a set of beliefs, expressed through rituals, customs, and rites, producing a sectarian distinction and a unique group of people." –Myles Munroe**

The young carpenter named Jesus was incredibly controversial in His time—and for good reason. He disrupted the religious norms of the first century, not by rebelling for rebellion's sake, but by calling people back to their original purpose. And that purpose wasn't rooted in religion. No wonder the religious leaders of His day wanted Him silenced.

His message was revolutionary:

> **"I won't lay anything heavy or ill-fitting on you. Keep company with me and you'll learn to live freely and lightly." (Matthew 11:30 MSG)**

Where religion tends to pile on pressure—systems, rituals, and traditions—Jesus offered something radically different: relationship. Religion required jumping through hoops; Jesus invited people to walk with Him. Religion placed a yoke on people's necks; Jesus promised rest for their souls.

He came to break the hustle, not bless it.

The systems of His day demanded performance. But Jesus taught that purpose flows from presence—not performance. He wanted His followers to stop striving, stop toiling, stop trying to manufacture results on their own. He was calling them out of the rat race of doing and into the sacred rhythm of becoming.

That's why His message still speaks to us today.

Psalm 46:1 reminds us of this divine availability:

> **"God is our refuge and strength, a very present help in trouble."**

The word "present" is key. It means God isn't distant, detached, or waiting for you to clean yourself up before He steps in. He is here—now. Involved in the grit and grind of your everyday life. He's not just for the "sweet by and by," but for the "sour here and now."

His presence isn't reserved for the temple, the pulpit, or religious rituals. It's available in traffic, in grief, in doubt, in dinner prep, in deadlines.

CHAPTER 3

This is the life Jesus was offering: not a religious checklist, but a relational connection that frees us from the burden of trying to be enough on our own.

WHAT IS THE KINGDOM?

Jesus came not to intensify the search, but to end it—to freely give us access to His culture, His presence, and His leadership. But this Kingdom reality isn't forced; it's offered to "whosoever wills."

Unlike religion, which often centers on systems, rituals, and requirements for membership, Jesus offers something far greater: the full privileges and benefits of a different world—a Kingdom. Just as citizens of a country inherit rights, protections, and benefits, so too do we, as Kingdom citizens, receive access to a superior government with divine benefits.

Though this Kingdom is unseen, it's more real and lasting than the visible. Jesus declared:

> **"Do not be afraid, little flock, for your Father has been pleased to give you the Kingdom." (Luke 12:32 NIV)**

That's not religion. That's inheritance.

Religion requires entrance into man-made systems. But the Kingdom is a culture—a living expression of Heaven's rule—extended to us through citizenship:

> **"But our citizenship is heaven. And we eagerly await a Savior from there, the Lord Jesus Christ."(Philippians 3:20 NIV)**

Jesus made it clear: this Kingdom isn't distant or merely symbolic.

"The Kingdom... is not something that can be observed, ... because the Kingdom of God is in your midst."(Luke 17:20–21 NIV)

> **"May Your Kingdom come... on earth as it is in Heaven." (Matthew 6:10, paraphrased)**

Why can't it be observed in the typical way? Because the Kingdom is a lifestyle—a culture made visible only through the lived expression of purpose. You begin to see it as you walk it out. As Jesus put it:

> **"Let your light shine before others, that they may see your good deeds and glorify your Father in Heaven."(Matthew 5:16 NIV)**

We were created to live freely under the governing influence of Heaven's King, right here on earth—to express His intent, will, and design for our lives now, not just someday.

This is how we live out our true selves, made in God's image. This is how we step into our divine purpose—a purpose that's often the very thing we'd naturally love doing... because we were wired for it.

RELEARNING BY UNLEARNING

Jesus said:

> **"Take my yoke upon you and learn from me, for I am gentle and humble in heart, and you will find rest for your souls." (Matthew 11:29 NIV)**

Learning the "unforced rhythms of grace" means relearning who you are—but it also means unlearning what religion and society have falsely laid on you.

CHAPTER 3

He was never trying to make people into something they weren't. He came to draw out what was already there—what God had placed inside from the beginning. His goal was to reintroduce people to themselves and guide them back to that original place of rest and identity.

> **"The purpose in a man's heart is like deep water, but a man of understanding will draw it out." (Proverbs 20:5 ESV)**

Jesus was that man of understanding. And He still is. He came to pull out the trapped self in each of us—the version of you that's been buried beneath layers of religious expectation, cultural comparison, and internalized limitation.

And this still holds true today. If you want to find your purpose, surround yourself with people of understanding who know how to pull the real you out. And if you're alone? Start this journey within the pages of this very book. Because...

> **"The greatest discovery in life is self-discovery. Until you find yourself, you will always be someone else. Become yourself." – Dr. Myles Munroe**

HUMILITY: THE GROUND FOR GROWTH

To truly discover who we are, we must become humble—not in a performative way, but in a deeply human way.

The word humble comes from the Latin humus, meaning "earth" or "ground." It's where we also get the words human and humanity. To be humble is to be grounded—to be real. And strangely enough, in our world of curated images and performative identities, we must relearn how to simply be... human.

Humility is not self-deprecation. It's authenticity. It's freedom from pretense, posturing, and comparison.

We'll continue from here in the upcoming chapters. Also, stay tuned for an upcoming book on God's Kingdom, where we will explore in greater detail how to enter into it by understanding the message and the original intent of God for the earth and for mankind.

Stop trying to keep up with the Joneses. Stop measuring yourself by external standards. Instead, understand who you are, what you're wired for, and where you thrive. That's not selfish—that's stewardship.

> **"... for I am gentle and humble in heart, and you will find rest for your souls." (Matthew 11:29 NIV)**

SO, HOW DO WE START TO DISCOVER OUR PURPOSE?

First, understand this: your purpose isn't far off. It's not unreachable. It's not reserved for the elite. It's already in you.

You don't need to earn it—just unearth it.

And that begins by drawing close to the King, letting go of the yoke of religious striving, and embracing the lifestyle of the Kingdom. Only then can you walk in the "good, pleasing, and perfect purpose of God" (Romans 12:2, paraphrased).

CHAPTER 4

PROVOKING PEOPLE TO PINPOINT AND PURSUE THEIR PURPOSE

The greatest tragedy in life is not death but living a life without a purpose. – Myles Munroe

YOUR PERSONAL SUCCESS STARTS WITH YOUR PURPOSE

In this chapter, I want to begin by sharing a few personal experiences—real moments and lessons that have shaped my understanding of purpose. Before we dive into practical steps you can take and apply to your own life, I want to help you understand why purpose matters so deeply—why it is the true starting point for personal success.

So, let's ask the question:
Why purpose? What is it really?

Purpose is original intent. It's the reason something was created, designed, or brought into existence. Everything created—every invention, every design, every person—exists for a reason. And when something operates outside of its purpose, frustration is inevitable. But when it functions according to its intended design, fulfillment flows.

The same is true for you.

You were created with intentionality. You are not an accident. You carry within you the blueprint of a purpose that was encoded by your Creator before you were even born. And discovering that purpose—living from it, not just toward it—is the key to finding lasting meaning, peace, and impact in your life.

> "PURPOSE IS THE SOURCE OF FULFILLMENT. UNTIL PURPOSE IS FOUND, OUR OWN EXISTENCE HAS NO MEANING. PURPOSE IS ALSO THE ORIGINAL INTENT FOR THE CREATION OF A THING, THE END FOR WHICH THE MEANS EXIST, THE VERY CAUSE FOR A CREATION OF A THING, THE DESIRED RESULT THAT INITIATES PRODUCTION, THE EXPECTATION OF THE SOURCE, THE OBJECTIVE FOR THE SUBJECT, THE ASPIRATION FOR THE INSPIRATION."
>
> –DR. MYLES MUNROE, PURSUIT OF PURPOSE

Purpose is so important that it captured the attention of millions around the world through the bestselling book *The Purpose Driven Life* by Rick Warren. Released in 2002, it became one of the fastest-selling nonfiction books in publishing history, selling over 30 million copies within its first five years. To date, it has sold more than 50 million copies and has been translated into over 85 languages. Its global impact is a clear sign that people everywhere are searching for meaning, direction, and a deeper understanding of why they were created.

CHAPTER 4

Why is the topic of purpose so important in today's world?

1. **People are Searching for Meaning**

   In a world filled with noise, distractions, and uncertainty, people are desperate to know why they exist. Purpose offers clarity.

2. **Purpose Grounds Identity**

   Without purpose, people often tie their worth to careers, relationships, or possessions—things that can fade. Purpose gives lasting identity rooted in meaning, not performance.

3. **It Brings Direction**

   Purpose acts like a compass. When you know where you're going, it's easier to say "no" to distractions and "yes" to the right opportunities.

4. **Mental and Emotional Health**

   Many struggles with depression and anxiety are linked to a lack of direction. A sense of purpose gives people something to live for, work toward, and hope in.

5. **God-Planted Desire**

   As Rick Warren and Dr. Myles Munroe both emphasized, the desire for purpose is not man-made—it's God-given. It's a divine pull to align with the Creator's plan.

A GOD OF PURPOSE:

It is imperative to know, first and foremost, that our Creator is a God of Purpose. He already had an intent for everything and everybody He created. When that purpose isn't known, abuse or "abnormal use" become inevitable. It states of old regarding Him (Our Creator),

> "*I make known the end from the beginning, from ancient times, what is still to come. I say, 'My purpose will stand, and I will do all that I please'" (Isaiah 46:10).*

The concept of God as a God of purpose is evident throughout the scriptures. Here are a few examples of verses that highlight God's purpose and intentionality:

1. *"For I know the plans I have for you," declares the Lord, "plans to prosper you and not to harm you, plans to give you hope and a future." (Jeremiah 29:11).* Here we see the emphasis of God's specific plans and purposes for everyone's life.

2. *"In him we were also chosen, having been predestined according to the plan of him who works out everything in conformity with the purpose of his will." (Ephesians 1:11).* Here we see how this verse underscores God's sovereignty and the fulfillment of His purpose through His will.

3. *"And we know that in all things God works for the good of those who love him, who have been called according to his purpose." (Romans 8:28).* Here we see how Paul reassures believers that God's purposes are ultimately for their overall good and His glory.

CHAPTER 4

4. *"Many are the plans in a person's heart, but it is the Lord's purpose that prevails." (Proverbs 19:21).*

This verse emphasizes the sovereignty of God's purpose over human plans and actions.

These verses, among others, demonstrate that God is a God of purpose who has specific plans and intentions for His creation and works all things according to His will.

You will learn that everyone has a why and it is key to find that why to embrace your personal success. You will also learn that you won't have to go very far to discover it either.

Let's look at *Proverbs 19:21 more in-depth.*

> *"Many are the plans in a person's heart, but it is the Lord's purpose that prevails." (NIV)*

Another Translations says,

> *"Many are the plans in the mind of a man, but it is the purpose of the Lord that will stand." (ESV)*

It's firm that if our Creator is a God of Purpose and here, we read that His purpose will stand. *"My purpose will stand".*

1. *Stand - refers to remaining firm, unwavering, and steadfast in the face of challenges or obstacles.*

2. *Prevail - as read in the first translation, means to triumph, succeed, or overcome difficulties or opposition. It conveys the idea of emerging victorious, achieving one's goals, or seeing one's purpose fulfilled despite challenges or setbacks.*

Can something (or someone created) outdo its Creator? ...and He adds from Isaiah 46:10, "*I will do all that I please.*"

When something stands, it remains steady in an upright position and is supported. The word prevail also speaks loudly in this context. When something prevails, it proves more powerful than opposing forces. Plans in the hearts and minds of people that are not congruent with what they were created for often become opposing forces. These can show up as ideas, cultural pressures, or even well-meaning suggestions—like a career path or a picture of what you think your future should look like.

To truly discover one's purpose, one must seek deep. The original intent for which you were created—what you once saw in your heart as vision—may have been clouded over time by unauthorized opinions from others or even good ideas that aren't aligned with the real you.

For many, this book may become a journey of reprogramming your thinking, or an assignment in unlearning, before any healthy preprogramming can begin.

Purpose, again, means original intent. And you are an original. Your purpose was established at birth—unique, unrepeatable, and specific. The end was already determined at the very beginning, revealed in the form of your purpose.

Each one of us, among nearly 8 billion people on earth, is a distinct, one-of-a-kind individual. And every single one of us was created with and for a reason. You exist because there is a problem or need on earth that you—through your unique gift, niche, and calling—were predestined, equipped, and qualified to solve.

You were born for a purpose and nothing can change that. It's no wonder that "***The gifts and the calling of God are irrevocable***" ***(Romans 11:29 ESV).***

CHAPTER 4

LIVE INDEPENDENTLY OF THE GOOD OPINIONS OF OTHERS

"Don't let the excitement of youth cause you to forget your Creator. Honor him in your youth before you grow old and say, "Life is not pleasant anymore." (Eclesiastés 12:1 KJV).

Abraham Maslow defined self-actualization as "being independent of the good opinion of others." It's okay to listen to the opinions of others, so long as we make a conscious choice not to adopt them, especially if they don't line up to who we are. This includes what many folks we look up to are telling us. Sometimes we must go as far as "breaking up" with our parents to self-actualize and live OUR Full purpose. You have no idea how fully aware I am of this reality.

That's why I believe what the Wise King Solomon stated in ***Ecclesiastes 12:1 (NIV), "Remember your Creator in the days of your youth."*** He was telling us to protect ourselves from what follows youth. It could read something like this, 'Remember what you were created for in the days of your youth. Stick to that and do your best not to get educated out of it. Do not let the excitement of your vibrant youthful years cause you to forget your Creator and what you were created for. Believe in your dream. Always keep your authentic vision in front of you.' I believe that our dreams and purposes are very vivid and clear in these tender years between 8-12 years old or, for many of us, that period between childhood and adulthood. Even children believe with untainted faith that we all have been called to change something or contribute toward something greater than ourselves. We need to **'become like little children again' so we will experience our purpose. (Matthew 18:3)** My job is to bring you back to your youthful golden years but with intent.

It is mostly after these years of youth that we start getting educated out of ourselves and end up needing to reeducate ourselves, or renew our minds, back into our Original Intent. It is after these years, and sometimes even during them, that we struggle the most with our identities. On many occasions, no thanks to the people around us – including our parents – we get stuck where we weren't intended to be, because of these influences that do not help. Thus, forcing us to end up where we have no pleasure in being, let alone any business in being or with any real meaning to it. Now we end up on our own, trying to figure it out in a process called Self-Discovery, which is really getting back to who we were originally intended to be and doing what will leave the greater impact on our generation and generations to come. That's what we'll focus on in this book.

I love the second part of this verse from the Wise King Solomon. It states, ***"...before the days of trouble come and the years approach when you will say, 'I find no pleasure in them'"—(Eclesiastés 12:1 NIV).*** The years ahead are a test. Parents and others can only truly assist if they take the time to carefully observe and study who their children are naturally becoming. The real challenge often arises after childhood, when we begin to adapt to competing alternatives that pull us away from our true selves. Interestingly, some of the greatest setbacks—and even traumas—can occur as early as the tender ages of 7 and 8. These early experiences can significantly shape, shift, or suppress one's sense of identity and purpose.

We have an acre enemy of potential who is trying everything in his power for you not to flourish. Ultimately, putting us in a place where there is no pleasure in it for us. Pleasure in this sense is that feeling of happiness, satisfaction, and enjoyment. Depression, anxiety, and frustration are often the results when we are living someone else's dreams and vision, and not our own, or being simply stuck.

CHAPTER 4

A STROLL THROUGH THE PARK

I remember discussing this topic on an occasion in a park with one individual, while being overheard by another individual, the primary man's best friend. At the end of my conversation with the first gentleman, the other gentleman (overhearing) came to me and asked, "What would you tell me, a 65-year-old retired architect, who built some of the most prestigious buildings and communities in Southwest Florida?"

He mentioned one of the communities to me, which I was very familiar with, since I was also a resident in Southwest Florida at the time. Rather than speaking with pride about his accomplishments, he spoke to me as a person in rage and regret, as if his whole life had been taken away from him or passed him by. Although he was a 65-year-old retired architect, he had to admit that it was never his career of choice. Architecture was a path his parents imposed upon him because his dad was also an architect.

I was just becoming familiar with this topic on purpose, but I was able to recognize that part of my own purpose was helping other people pinpoint their purpose. I was so passionate at that time and still am when discussing this topic with others. However, even though I recognized this as my purpose or life assignment, I must be honest. I was in shock to hear this older man ask me, "What do you have to tell someone like me?" I assumed that most successful people have tapped into theirs.

In other words, he wanted an answer from me right then and there, and the pressure was on. I could have defaulted to the many excuses we use when we doubt our purpose. "Who am I? Why me in directing this older professional man? What knowledge do I have? Why would anyone listen to me about anything?"

Thankfully, that did not happen. Instead, I was in my zone and trusted I was equipped for this assignment specifically. I briefly looked up to Heaven and responded, as if I trusted in my endowed grace and gift. I started, "Number one, as long as you are alive, your purpose has not ended. Number two, there is no time wasted with God. He can restore the years that the cankerworm has stolen, so to speak…or years that have seemed lost." I added, "Let's get to doing what we were born to do, even at this age, and especially help the youth in this generation to not make the same mistakes we made" by being independent of the good opinion of others and not living other people's dreams.

I continued and then asked him, "What was it that you envisioned yourself doing from the age of seven? Or even ages 8–12?"

His answer came very quickly, as if it had been marinating in his heart since he was seven years old. "I wanted to be an evangelist," was his blunt reply.

This gentleman retired from something he had no interest in doing. I immediately learned first hand that being successful in the wrong assignment equals failure. But our failures turn into successes, if we learn from them and move on. I directed him along these simple lines of discussion that needed not be too lengthy.

Through a very unusual setting, I happened to meet his wife, the Sunday morning following our encounter. The first man's wife was there as well. These men were best friends. They were so happy to meet me, and it wasn't planned at all. I happened to visit their church, and we ran into each other in the lobby. The first gentlemen insisted that I meet both of their wives, who were sitting together in the pews, before the service began.

The second individual's wife, the 65-year-old retired architect, said something I will never forget. "My husband isn't the same. He has not been able to sleep after your conversation with him." It was the Monday afternoon prior to that Sunday. She then added, "Thank you very much!"

CHAPTER 4

I'm aware that, sometimes, all one is called to do is stimulate the mind for the recipient to act. Sometimes, **"A word aptly spoken is like apples of gold in settings of silver." (Proverbs 25:11 NIV)** The right word shown stimulates dormant ideas that turn into action. These actions, in turn, become habits toward a journey and destiny of purpose. Sometimes this requires getting your whole world turned upside down.

I know we say, "Happy Wife, Happy Life!" But, what about when a man finds his rightful happy place? Imagine what can happen to our world, not just his life. Imagine what a suitable wife works with when a man finds himself and his purpose. Her industrious qualities awaken and emerge. She has something to incubate and cultivate (Proverbs 31). A seed of potential in the right soil and the world is ripe for change. Purpose prevails over every good agenda that isn't just right for you. So, you ought to align yourself with your purpose!

THIS IS MY NICHE!

During this time and thereafter, I would speak in all types of settings: businesses, schools, churches, home groups, and especially one-on-one as a personal coach. The results were shocking to me. People started making drastic decisions and changes in their lives. There were businesses and churches that I have spoken at, where peers and employees left to follow their dreams and pursue their purpose. They affirmed that the environment wasn't right for them or conducive for their passion and growth.

> **"If where you are at isn't what you saw, then where you're at is temporary." (Unknown)**

There comes a time when you must move on!

BEYOND THE HUSTLE

One specific place comes to mind. The CEO of a medical imaging company invited me to speak to his employees in Sarasota, Florida. When some of the employees asked for me to come back, the owner responded that he couldn't afford for me to come back and speak at his company.

"What happened?" I asked, a few months later when I saw him at a birthday party.

He responded, "After you spoke to our staff, my future son-in-law, who I made manager of my company, left to follow his purpose and dream."

"How old is he?" I asked.

"20 years old." He replied.

"Wow! That's awesome! He is about to marry your daughter and had the courage to leave your business to ensure that he remains in his own lane?" I continued, "That's a blessing! How's he doing now?"

"He enrolled in graphic design and videographer school, saying that was always his passion and what he envisioned himself doing."

I concluded, "You should be proud of this, because your son-in-law's true success is in his dream, not yours. He came back into his lane and started making the right adjustments toward his vision for his life."

He drove around the block of his father in law's house numerous times because knocking on his door to tell him that he was about to leave him to launch into his own vision. It was very uncomfortable for him. He finally did it.

CHAPTER 4

I have to say, even though I will probably never be invited there again, I am so happy that I made a difference in that young man's life. I could say that I felt bad for causing a huge discomfort in that CEO's life but that'd be a lie – I really loved it! Our deepest desire is to discover our purpose, and his future son-in-law chose to pursue his purpose. That is worth celebrating for me.

Did you know that his son-in-law, along with his wife, now owns one of the top 10 largest companies specializing in wedding videography nationwide? Their company films weddings worldwide, catering to clients across Europe and producing content for various events, including extravagant weddings for celebrities. Initially charging $5,000 per event, they have now elevated their prices to six digits, reaching up to a million dollars for unique events. Recently, their work was featured in VOGUE Magazine as one of the top 10 companies globally. This is exactly what this 20-year-old envisioned when he sat in that session at his father in law's Imagining Center while working as his manager.

We aren't preachers, but problem solvers and perspective adjusters

There have been multiple young people I have helped get back into their lane or at least provoked them to pursue their purpose. Dr. Myles Munroe, often told us, his students, that we weren't preachers, but perspective adjusters. I added, also, problem solvers. We don't impose, but influence. These words have certainly affected the way I approach conversations with others, especially when discussing their purpose or the topic of purpose generally. I've learned that **"we cannot force someone to hear a message that they are not ready to receive, but we must never underestimate the power of planting a seed" (Dan Nielson, author of "Be an Inspirational Leader").** This quote and message support and speaks to both sides: The speaker and the listener.

This kept on happening everywhere I went. Like a Sower, I just kept on sowing seeds and the results were amazing.

"PROVOKING PEOPLE" BECAME PART OF MY MISSION STATEMENT

It was at this time that I confirmed my mission statement from here on out was going to be, "Provoking People to Pinpoint and Pursue Their Purpose."

According to the dictionary, "provoke" means to "stimulate or to give rise to a (reaction or emotion, typically a strong and unwelcome one) in someone." It also means "to stimulate or incite (someone) to feel or do something, especially by arousing anger in them." Ruffling feathers usually entails all the above. Stimulating a new way of thinking is really the goal, because I'm not in the business of manipulating behavior but instead influencing thinking. However, sometimes this entails getting people angry because they are being reminded to come out of their comfort zones, preconceived notions, and previous way of thinking. We need to have our minds renewed to our Original Intent, what we were primarily created for. This means we go back; we regress before we can progress.

My life has been interesting and amazing since I grasped my message and assignment. The greatest clarity and my mission statement came at a time right smack in the middle of my years when I lost a good job and parted ways with a company that gave me a good income for 7 years. After that time, I went into a quiet place to ask the question, "Now what? What is this next phase of life supposed to bring me?" I specifically asked God, "What's the next phase for me?" I've always believed that a job is really just a phase of education—at a company's expense. I sensed there was a new level of learning and growth ahead, but I had no idea where it would come from or how I would step into it. Up until that season, my life had been absolutely amazing. Every job

CHAPTER 4

I had came at just the right time. Each one provided exactly what I needed to prepare me for the next. Little by little, I was unknowingly building the foundation for what would become my ultimate life assignment. A job, many times, is what you use to take in an income—but your purpose, your life assignment, is where you begin to give out and make a true impact. This is where the principle "It is more blessed to give than to receive" truly comes into play. Purpose isn't just about what you gain; it's about what you give, how you serve, and the difference you make. "***Freely you have received, freely give." (Matthew 10:8 NIV)***

This is where the principle "It is more blessed to give than to receive" comes into focus. In Acts 20:35 (NIV), Paul reminds us of the bigger picture: "***In everything I did, I showed you that by this kind of hard work we must help the weak, remembering the words the Lord Jesus himself said: 'It is more blessed to give than to receive.'"*** Purpose isn't just about personal gain; it's about meaningful contribution—serving others, helping the weak, and pouring out what's been placed within you for the benefit of those around you.

Therefore, every job you have should be viewed as an opportunity—not just to make a living, but to work diligently with your hands, providing for yourself and your household, and ensuring that your labor is profitable. Within this phase, two things are happening simultaneously: you're stirring up the potential for what you could be doing at your next level of influence, and you're gaining hands-on education—at the company's expense—all while earning an income. Each role is a classroom, and every assignment is preparation for your greater purpose.

That's why **Colossians 3:23-24 (NIV)** also says, **"Whatever you do, work at it with all your heart, as working for the Lord, not for human masters, since you know that you will receive an inheritance from the Lord as a reward. It is the Lord Christ you are serving."**

When I received this insight of helping people find their purpose, some of the first words to cross my mind were from **Romans 8:28 KJV, *"And we know that all things work together for good to them that love God, to them who are the called according to his purpose."*** Notice that loving God and putting this love for Him first is key, but not a 100% guarantee in experiencing success in one's life assignments.

There are a lot of people close to the Source (God), they have all the information necessary and are right in front of the Fountain of Life. They say they love God but haven't yet obeyed Him. They are still lost in a sense. Why? Because they lack tapping into the purpose for which they were created. God is obligated to His purpose and His people who are living in it. Just like a great manufacturer is obligated to provide warranty, service and follow up for the products it creates. The best parts are also available from that manufacturer, when something malfunctions or breaks down. Know your purpose and you won't miss out on all the resources you need to fulfill it. A manufacturer's Great Name is tied to the product it produces and therefore obligated to perform. Same is true toward you, when you're moving toward your "why." ***"He restores your soul: He leads you in the paths of righteousness ... all for His name's sake" (Psalm 23:3 Paraphrased). His brand, name and reputation are tied to the very intent He created you, the crown and joy of everything He created.***

MY INVITE AS A RADIO SHOW GUEST

I remember an important lunch meeting with Trista Sue, a mentor and advisor of mine at the time, Dr. Rick Kendell and his wife. After getting to know me a little, Dr. Rick told me that I was going to ruffle the feathers of many leaders, but afterwards many of the ones whose feathers I ruffled would ask me to assist them in seeing how I see. I guess it was because of what he observed in our conversation.

CHAPTER 4

Right after that lunch meeting, I was invited to a live radio station to speak on various topics. I didn't even know what the topics were going to be about. The host who invited me was a well-known overseer and pastor of many churches, and he himself was from Central Florida. We just bumped into each other at a local mall, and immediately he invited me for the next morning. In my excitement with this view of self-discovery and purpose, I was literally contradicting almost everything he was saying over the air. Even though I was flowing with answers to the questions I was asked, I was shocked at how far this leader was from this perspective of mine, which is really truth. Phone calls started coming, and I felt like I was in my zone. It went very well, but I didn't quite feel he was on the same page as me. It was strange, and many times I felt like I should hold back and not speak my mind or tell the truth because I wasn't sure how he would take it. I was happy and uncomfortable at the same time.

Later that afternoon, I decided to call the host and apologize just in case I offended him. I guess I was second-guessing myself. I started believing the age-old excuse of, "Who am I to educate him or teach him something new?" After all, he's way more qualified than I am. After much hesitation, I finally got the courage to pick up the phone and dial.

I started my conversation with him like this, "Pastor _____, you do know that I respect and honor you, right? Also, you know that you are one of those figures who can correct me at any time, right?" I added, "I am always open to your advice and suggestions about almost anything you feel I need help with." Then I continued, "Just in case I offended you in anything I said this morning..." I didn't have time to finish my statement, because I was immediately interrupted by him.

"Stop right there." He exclaimed, "It is four p.m. and this is the time I usually take my afternoon nap. I'm not able to do so, because of everything you said on the radio station. I can't rest. All I have to say is that what you had to say was very interesting."

BEYOND THE HUSTLE

After he said this, I remembered all the words Dr. Rick Kendell had said at our lunch meeting, "You will ruffle a lot of feathers. After that (approximately six months), some of these leaders will ask you to help them see the way you see." Well, that was also the case. Not just him, but many well educated and competent leaders were doing just that. Do you know that at the very moment he finished speaking, I heard as if it were a voice say to me, "Don't ever apologize for speaking the truth."

When I hung up from that phone call, I recognized that our greatest enemy is self-doubt. Here I was recognizing that my purpose is helping people pinpoint and pursue their purpose. At the same time, I was doubting my own purpose and mission, because there was a chance I could have offended somebody. Well, the truth will do that occasionally. Expect that and more when you are adjusting perspectives through your gift.

The young king David experienced this as he expressed it in Psalms 119:99. Here are two versions of this this verse:

1. New International Version (NIV): "I have more insight than all my teachers, for I meditate on your statutes."

2. King James Version (KJV): "I have more understanding than all my teachers: for thy testimonies are my meditation."

These passages express the idea of gaining wisdom and insight through meditation on God's precepts.

Be the wiser person in the room by first meditating on, internalizing, and digesting the information. After all, you cannot impart what you do not first possess.

We should never have to apologize for being ourselves when we are walking in our purpose and executing within our life assignment. This is our platform for how we make the truth known, and truth sometimes stings. Ultimately, it should be **"Blessed**

CHAPTER 4

is he who is not offended because of Me" (Matthew 11:6), not the other way around. Truth means "original intent." When we are confronted by truth, we are being invited—sometimes even provoked—back into alignment with who we were truly created to be: our authentic selves. Truth and purpose are synonymous. They both point to original intent. For some of us, the journey back can feel unsettling, especially if we've been away from that place for a long time. But it's also freeing. It's a call to return—to come back to who we were before the noise, before the fluff, before the well-meaning but misaligned opinions of others shaped our direction. Truth doesn't just expose; it restores. It draws us back to purpose.

HELPING COMPETENT LEADERS DISCOVER THEMSELVES, THEIR VALUE AND HOW TO IDENTIFY THEIR PERSONAL PURPOSE…" (PART 1)

And from this moment on, I've had numerous people, already trained and advanced in their fields (some in religious circles), secretly call and ask to meet with me so I can assist them in getting back to the original message and their purpose, many of them having swerved from it at the time. I loved every minute of these meetings and deep conversations. I understood why I was in Naples, Florida for 4 years, learning the important message of the Kingdom of God, which we will discuss in an upcoming book, focusing on purpose, potential, and vision. Yes, apart from learning about leadership, purpose, and vision, I gained an education in the most important message of all – the Kingdom of God and of Heaven. It took a lot of unlearning before I could understand it too. Now, I've been teaching leaders how to do the same. It only works when they are willing. Those not yet ready would need a little provoking and mainly seed-sowing until they are ready. Remember, the student ultimately determines the topic and many times, the timing. They must be prepared for the right instructor to come along.

I wondered why these competent people were coming to me. I learned that these doors of opportunities that present themselves and that align with your area of service, strength, and gifting shed light on your very purpose. Do not underestimate those doors of opportunities that give you moments to practice your life's ultimate assignment. Do it with all your might and to the best of your ability.

"Competent" means having the necessary abilities, knowledge, or skills to perform a task or job effectively and successfully. It refers to being capable, skilled, proficient, or qualified in a particular area of expertise. A competent individual demonstrates the capacity to handle responsibilities, complete tasks with proficiency, and achieve desired outcomes in their field of work or study. Note that most competent people, when they are living their lives with order attract resources. I learned that God doesn't bless good people, but He blesses good stewards who are competent in their area of expertise.

In Naples, FL I practiced my assignment with people who were successful, and many successful in areas that weren't suited for them. Being successful in something outside of what truly matters to you in life can equate to a form of failure. Finding your sweet spot is key to your personal success.

"...IN ORDER FOR THESE COMPETENT LEADERS TO GO BACK INTO THEIR SPHERE

CHAPTER 4

OF INFLUENCE AND IMPACT IT WITH THE RIGHT MESSAGE, IN THE RIGHT METHOD." (PART 2)

BE C.O.C.K.Y

Thank God I had an overseer prepare me for this, by positively speaking into my life. A key for one's success is to position yourself and surround yourself with people who believe in you. Whether those are small meetings over lunch, dinner, a glass of juice, coffee, or tea. Even a mastermind group that you join, where you can also be accountable to others. Always seek them out. **Wisdom is the principal thing in life and with all you're getting, don't forget to get understanding. (Proverbs 4:7)** This principle protects us against self-doubt, fear, and especially frustration. It Creates Confidence!

Zig Ziglar once said that F.E.A.R. has two meanings, **"Forget Everything and Run' or Face Everything and Rise. The choice is yours."**

Zig Ziglar's quote about F.E.A.R encapsulates the dichotomy of fear and how we respond to it. To conquer fear and nurture self-confidence, you must face your fears and consistently rise above them by moving on through them. This process is essential for **adding value to your gift by honing it into a skill**. Your success is intricately tied to your skills—because skills are simply **refined gifts**, sharpened through discipline, time, and intentional development.

If you are called to speak in front of crowds and are afraid of standing before a number of them, try first to speak to smaller crowds. Build your confidence.

You will attract the proper resources, including encouragers, mentors, and teachers for your assignment. Even other people need to be the right fit for your personal purpose and vision.

When we find our purpose, all things begin to line up and work together for that good. The right folks continually coming into your life are opportunities and signs that reveal your calling or assignment as well. Don't ignore them.

> **"Our deepest desires, natural and spiritual talents, and constant doors of opportunities reveal God's purpose and dreams for our lives." (Unknown)**

God is truly on your side since He's more invested than you are to make sure you get it right. After all, He so loved the world, the very place you are called to influence, that He sent his Son to work on the minds of 12 men that He might send them out to change that world. They needed to be with their leader first.

"And He appointed twelve [disciples], so that they would be with Him [for instruction] and so that He could send them out to preach [the gospel as apostles—that is, as His special messengers, personally chosen representatives]". (Mark 3:14 AMP). A unique Afterwards, it says, "that He could send them out..." You need to be sent to your sphere fully equipped and empowered.

Again Jesus said, "Peace be with you! **As the Father has sent me, I am sending you.**" (John 20:21).

That's right—God will never expose you to something He doesn't intend to bring you through. If certain people show up in your life, be open and sensitive to their presence. Take time to discern who you're meant to follow, and be willing to learn from your unique experiences and God's leading. If God is with you, no one can stand against you.

This is how you become C.O.C.K.Y, by "Concentrating on Confidence, & Knowing Yourself!"

CHAPTER 4

THE TEACHER APPEARS WHEN THE STUDENT IS READY

I was privileged to learn from one of the best teachers of our time. That's my belief. And, for the record, everyone learns from someone, but we can choose who we learn the most from in terms of lessons and instructions. Most of the time, that learning is usually for a season. It was very convenient and suitable for me to learn from the late Dr. Myles Munroe. This period lasted a little over four years before he passed away on November 10, 2014. His message fueled my vision and personal purpose, shaping where I saw my future and assignment taking me. I was privileged to be next to him on numerous occasions, even until three a.m., many times. There was so much wisdom flowing out as he opened his mouth to teach in hotel lobbies and other places like green rooms, and even in the comfort of his own home. Along with the many lessons taught at seminars and leadership classes we attended. He would say that when we have the right information, we aren't just preachers; we are perspective adjusters empowered to help people see. After all of this, we had opportunities to be trained and see firsthand how he did it in speaking settings, etc., as he allowed us to travel with him. Now, this was the icing on the cake. I would see how mature people from the audience would make statements like, 'What do I do now? I must start all over again from the beginning.' This marks the beginning of transformation for them through mind renewal, if they stick with it. Remember, it's regressing and then progressing."

Wisdom in action is when we help others see, without imposing our information or our conviction on them. I guess it's true, as he would say, "The hunger of the students determines the topic of the teacher." When the information is drawn out of us, we feel we're in that right, suitable place. The environment is right and ripe, because of the anticipation of the students.

Finding this suitable place in life and in employment (especially in life) is so key, we need to stay around the right people to be nurtured. Remember the words from the Young Jewish Carpenter? "Watch how I do it. Learn the unforced rhythms of grace." (Jesus) "Hear how I do it" is teaching. "Watch how I do it" is training. We were privileged to be bother taught and trained.

"Even though we have 10,000 instructors, we don't have that many fathers," (1 Corinthians 4:15 KJV). A father is one who cares for and encourages the development and growth of his family. Nurturing from the right father (leadership figure) doesn't only get information in your head, but wisdom, life, substance, and experience in the core of your being. This is when you get it! As Dr. Munroe used to tell us, **"Leadership isn't taught, but caught!"** Get it?

The right mentor, or person you get your information from is key, because it should be someone who has already gone through where you are going or want to go. It's someone who can impart what he/she has possessed. You don't only get knowledge, but fuel (in the form of inspiration, passion and wisdom) to get through your hurdles and obstacles of your progress. It's like passing the baton. We'll discuss the importance of a mentor, coach, and nurturer while defining your vision for your purpose in a later chapter.

In those moments I had listening to Dr. Munroe, I wouldn't want to sleep. Instead, I would continue to fuel myself, by expounding on the information I'd just heard. He stood with us for those long hours, because we would ask more questions. I too, expressed the same emotion as the early students of the First Century when they talked about their leader and teacher, *"Were not our hearts burning within us while he talked with us on the road and opened the Scriptures to us?" (Luke 24:32 NIV).*

A good mentor would not just give you information but teach you understanding insight. Open things up that are concealed.

CHAPTER 4

Ultimately, wisdom on how to apply the principles learned secures our success in learning and training others. Dr. Munroe would invest long hours of hands-on training, because he wanted to make sure his mentees were well equipped to take the baton of leadership he was passing on to them.

After I got my personal revelation on this message of PURPOSE in 2010, I went to Southwest Florida, where I stayed for a while under the leadership of Trista Sue and The Naples Embassy Group, an Education Center for Self-Discovery and Leadership Training. Like I said in the Dedication of this book, she was the one who introduced me to Dr. Myles Munroe. There we would get educated, sharpen our gifts, and build on our knowledge for the next four years under his leadership and training seminars. We learned and immediately imparted to others what we were learning, by inviting others to get the information we were receiving. We did this at her hotel—the Bayfront Inn—in lovely Naples, Florida. This was fun!

Dr. Myles Munroe was known in his early years as Mr. Purpose because he too was possessed with the topic of helping people discover their purpose. Mine was right along those lines, right before knowing him. Immediately right after I got my revelation on purpose, I was introduced to him. I'm a believer that when you pinpoint your life assignment and pursue your passion and dream, God has a way of connecting you with a coach or mentor figure who can help you get to your calling more successfully. **Zig Ziglar** has an excellent quote regarding mentors, **"A lot of people have gone further than they thought they could because someone else thought they could."**

Dr. Myles Munroe told me in a meeting at his house just months before passing that he would forward this book for me. Sadly, he's not around to give me that privilege. He also gave me permission and his blessing to use what I've learned from him to train others. He told me I could put it in curriculum form, books, or whatever other means I could use to get the message out.

That is why you'll probably see a lot of his quotes and comments used throughout this book.

People more experienced than you should help you toward the process of self-discovery and fulfilling your assignment. You should seek this out before the actual assignment. That's simply a great way of playing it safe. The first thing to do is pinpoint your purpose. Secondly, be ready to pursue it with passion. Thirdly, find a mentor figure, someone with experience and knowledge in the area you are heading in. Don't be a lone ranger. There are others who have been there before you and you can easily be spurred into your good work through the help of others.

Lastly, Dr. Munroe invited me to that final trip he made in 2014. It was to Africa first and then to the Bahamas. He stated, "Roberto, this trip will be good for your learning and training. Come with me and afterwards we'll fly together to the leadership training in Freeport, Bahamas. You'll fly with me in my private jet."

I responded, "The next trip. Not this one." I didn't feel quite ready for that one. Things in my life did not seem right for me to take such a long trip. It was too soon for me, at least it was how I felt at that time. That was his last trip. The plane didn't make it to Freeport. It crashed right before landing. It was a very sad day for a lot of us. It was also a huge loss for one of our generation's great generals. I immediately thought of this passage when this transpired, **"Unless a kernel of wheat falls to the ground and dies, it remains only a single seed. But if it dies, it produces many seeds" (John 12:24 NIV).** I believe he produced many seeds through the lives of those he both taught and trained. Now, it's their turn to go and do their part. This is the cycle of life. Leaders train leaders. We help competent people (leaders) impact their sphere of influence with the right message, in the right method.

True leadership is ultimately what happens in one's absence, not in their presence.

CHAPTER 4

The right people create an environment that's safe and conducive for one's growth in their life's work. Even by allowing you to come alongside of them to be trained and get instruction. Do not take these for granted. These are golden opportunities. ***"And let us consider one another to provoke unto love and unto good works: Not forsaking the assembling of ourselves together, as the manner of some is; but exhorting one another: and so much the more, as ye see the day approaching" (Hebrews 10: 24,25 KJV).*** It's like looking after one's own safety first.

> **"The safest place on earth is in community and under authority." – Dr. Myles Munroe**

CHAPTER 5

YOUR PURPOSE IS FOUND IN TWO PLACES

"Everything in life has a purpose. Everyone on this planet was born with, and for, a purpose. It is this purpose that is the only source of meaning. Without purpose, life is an experiment or a haphazard journey that results in frustration, disappointment and failure. Without purpose, life is subjective, or it is a trial-and-error game that is ruled by environmental influences and the circumstances of the moment. Likewise, in the absence of purpose, time has no meaning, energy has no reason and life has no precision. Therefore, it is essential that we understand, and discover, our purpose in life, so that we can experience an effective, full and rewarding life." (Excerpt from "*In Pursuit of Purpose*," Dr. Myles Munroe)

When a manufacturer creates a product, that product is designed with a specific purpose. The purpose is first conceived in the mind of the inventor and then built into the product itself.

As an example, the purpose, intent, and hidden capabilities of our smartphones are built into the device itself. These phones were invented to solve problems. The invention of the smartphone made it possible for both the tech-savvy and the tech-illiterate to use them effectively with remarkable simplicity. Anyone who experiments with a smartphone long enough will discover its hidden capabilities and come to this conclusion on their own.

If you think a phone is only good for making calls, you'll soon realize you're missing out on a wealth of additional functions and apps. Smartphones allow us to take pictures and videos, manage to-do lists and calendars, navigate maps, send emails, FaceTime, stream music—the list is endless. Today you can literally run an entire business from your device. With new apps being released daily, many younger users are tapping into these capabilities even more than previous generations.

This leads me to a key point: **purpose is always found in two places—first in the mind of the creator, and second in the product itself.**

That said, I would like to submit the idea to you in which purpose is found in two places.

1) PURPOSE IS INHERENT.

Purpose is built into the product itself. It already exists as a permanent, essential, and defining attribute — not something added later, but something designed from the start.

Most of us instinctively look inside something to understand it. When we buy a new product, we tear open the box, peel away the plastic, and start trying to figure it out for ourselves. In the same way, the excitement we show when exploring material products is the same excitement we ought to have about our personal lives.

CHAPTER 5

Purpose isn't something we invent; it's something we discover. Each of us already carries a God-given purpose — an original intent designed into us from the beginning.

Remember the niche we talked about earlier, your sweet spot? Purpose is something that is inside each one of us. It correlates with most of what we already carry on the inside of us as it relates to our capabilities, gifts, passions, talents. That's why it stated centuries ago, **"According to his power that is at work within us." (Ephesians 3:20 NIV)** This ability remains dormant when it is suppressed, undiscovered, or left untapped, preventing its full display for all the world to see. You are equipped for your purpose.

In the context of the passage "According to his power that is at work within us," the term "power" refers to the divine strength, energy, and capability that God provides to believers to accomplish His will and purposes, which is also your true intent. It signifies God's supernatural ability and authority that empowers individuals to carry out their spiritual calling, activate their gift, and live according to His plan.

In Greek, the word for "power" in this context is "δύναμις" (dynamis), which denotes strength, might, or miraculous power. It signifies a powerful and active force, particularly in the spiritual realm, indicating that we are empowered and sustained, even in moments of weakness. This concept provides us with renewed strength and energy, akin to a second wind, to persevere and thrive.

Let's go back to smart phones for a moment. You can pick up a smart phone and use it as a paperweight. That is obviously not at all the purpose of a smart phone. If you put it in the hands of the wrong person, a child for instance, they can turn around and use it as a toy submarine and submerge it into water.

Though some of these devices are waterproof today, they were not originally intended for underwater usage. Alternatively, a child can tie a rope around the phone and drag it across the ground as if it were a toy car with no wheels, obviously. This is considered abuse or abnormal use of the device, which leads me to say, when we do not know the purpose of a thing, we naturally abuse it. We use it in an abnormal fashion.

"When the purpose of a thing is not known, abuse is inevitable."- Myles Munroe

How can we not abnormally use or abuse our lives? When we understand our purpose and move in its direction, carrying out exactly how are were designed to live. Living from the inside out. How do you **tap** into a product's full potential? Both business partners and life partners should be well-suited for us. (Life and Work) How do you understand the entire purpose of its existence? Can you experience the entire purpose of your existence?

Similar to a product, your purpose can be uncovered and solidified from two sources: within the product itself and within the mind of its creator. To ensure that you are in harmony with your purpose, thriving in your unique strengths, and fully engaged in your specialized niche with minimal distractions, you must access this inherent privilege we all hold - Your Original Intent, derived from two sources that will always align.

There are many individuals who don't yet have a personal relationship with the Manufacturer, yet they still live out much of their purpose and exercise a significant portion of their potential according to their giftings. I suppose God ultimately blesses **managers**—those who steward well what He has deposited within them. After all, He calls us to be **good stewards** of the resources, abilities, and opportunities He entrusts to us.

As a result, **resources and opportunities tend to follow the good stewards** more than anything else.

CHAPTER 5

This is why believers are encouraged to do this. ***"Each of you should use whatever gift you have received to serve others, as faithful stewards of God's grace in its various forms." (1 Peter 4:10)***

If you are a believer and are not using your gift or fulfilling your purpose, you can be considered a wasteful servant—and one thing we can be sure of about God is that He does not tolerate waste.

This example is given to us in the parable of the talents that were given to a servant who poorly managed his portion.

> ***"His master replied, 'You wicked, lazy servant! So, you knew that I harvest where I have not sown and gather where I have not scattered seed? Well then, you should have put my money on deposit with the bankers, so that when I returned, I would have received it back with interest. "'So, take the bag of gold from him and give it to the one who has ten bags. For whoever has will be given more, and they will have an abundance. Whoever does not have, even what they have will be taken from them. And throw that worthless servant outside, into the darkness, where there will be weeping and gnashing of teeth.'" (Matthew 25:26-30)***

We can conclude that it is possible for individuals to fulfill a significant portion of their purpose and make a meaningful impact in the world—even without a direct relationship with their Creator. This underscores the importance of being good stewards of the resources and opportunities entrusted to us. Demonstrating responsibility and faithfulness in managing what we have reflects both integrity and a deep respect for what we've been given.

Therefore, in the next chapter we will study more on how to define your Purpose by Studying YOU - the product made in the Image and Likeness of an Awesome Intentional God.

2) PURPOSE IS INTENTIONAL.

Purpose exists in the mind of its Manufacturer. There is a **plan** and a **destiny** designed for the future — nothing about it is accidental.

We can tap into a product's full potential and purpose when we **seek the mind of its inventor or creator**. Within the mind of the inventor or manufacturer exists a plan or goal for the product — this is known as its **original intent**.

This is how it works with products that we purchase in the department store, but it is also how we are designed. To ensure we excel in our self-discovery process and fulfill our purpose, it behooves us to go to the throne, not just to the phone. We can and should take advantage of the privilege we have been given to access the manufacturer, our Creator and Lord, directly. While we may seek guidance from others (the phone) initially, we have the warranty and privilege to go directly to the manufacturer (the throne).

The writer to the Hebrews said, *"Let us therefore come boldly to the throne of grace, that we may obtain mercy and find grace to help in time of need." (Hebrews 4:16 NKJV)*

Paul, the writer to the believers in Rome said, *"Therefore, having been justified by faith, we have peace with God through our Lord Jesus Christ, through whom also we have access by faith into this grace in which we stand, and rejoice in hope of the glory of God." (Romans 5 :1–2 NKJV)*

When we seek to understand a product's full potential and intent, we often need to delve into the mind of its inventor or creator.

CHAPTER 5

The creator's original intent reflects their vision, purpose, and goals for the product they have designed. By aligning with the original intent behind the creation of the product, we can unlock its true value and maximize its effectiveness.

GOD IS A GOD OF PURPOSE:

It's important to first and foremost understand that God is a God of Purpose.

> *"I make known the end from the beginning, from ancient times, what is still to come. I say, 'My purpose will stand, and I will do all that I please.'" (Isaiah 46:10).*

What can we learn from this passage alone.

- God reveals the end (the finished purpose) before the beginning.

- God starts with the conclusion (your purpose) and then backs up to begin your life.

Your life is unfolding according to what God already saw—and settled—in His mind. Knowing the purpose of a thing allows us to use it frustration free.

DO YOU WANT GOD'S ATTENTION, OR DO YOU WANT GOD'S INTENTION?

God's attention refers to seeking God just to get noticed- often tied to emotional moments, temporal needs, or surface-level worship.

God's intention refers to aligning to His purpose, His will, and His destiny for your life -walking in what He destined you to be and do.

This is where we, as believers, need to seek God for His purpose, not just His provision; His heart, not just His hand. Too often, we approach God only for what He can do for us, rather than for who He can be in us.

> "You will seek me and find me when you seek me with all your heart." (Jeremiah 29:13 NIV)

The term "heart" refers to the innermost core of a person's being—the seat of their emotions, desires, and intentions.

Seeking God with all your heart involves a deep, sincere, and wholehearted pursuit of a relationship with God, aligning one's desires and intentions with God's will, and demonstrating genuine commitment and devotion to Him. This authentic seeking of God leads to a profound encounter with Him and a deeper understanding of His plans and purposes for one's life.

And I call this the universal promise for all:

***"To all who ask—it will be given. To every seeker—you will find. And to all who knock—the door will be opened."* This is not mere encouragement; it is a divine guarantee. It is the universal promise of Heaven: that the heart in pursuit will never go unanswered. For the soul that truly seeks attracts its answer—just as the ready student draws the appearing teacher. God responds not to passivity, but to pursuit.**

(Matthew 7:7–8, paraphrased and expanded)

God responds to a desire to know, not merely a need to know. His revelation is drawn to hunger, not just necessity.

CHAPTER 5

Failure to recognize and honor the original intent behind a product can lead to inevitable challenges and limitations. When individuals or users deviate from the intended purpose of a product, they may not fully utilize its capabilities or experience the intended benefits. This misalignment can result in inefficiencies, reduced effectiveness, and missed opportunities for growth and development. Recognizing and honoring the original intent behind a product is essential for realizing its full potential and achieving optimal outcomes. This is guaranteed in the mind of the Creator.

THE MANUAL

The iPhone was designed by the late Steve Jobs. Though he is no longer with us, he and his company left behind an instruction manual for each Apple product. Many of us never read these manuals until we discover a feature that interests us and want to learn more—or until something goes wrong, prompting us to research and find a solution.

A manual is a book of instructions, especially for operating a machine, product, or learning a subject — essentially, a handbook. Its purpose is to bring out what has not yet been seen in a product, and by extension, in us — God's intentional creation. When others witness you living as your full, authentic self — expressed through your unique gifts and good works — they are drawn to what you have: individuality. In the same way a product reveals the design and intent of its manufacturer, our lives reveal the work of God's hands. This, in turn, compels others to seek out the Manufacturer: God.

I have always believed that the most effective way to influence others is not merely through words but through the power of your personal work—the visible expression of your purpose.

Matthew 5:16 (The Passion Translation) says,

> *"So don't hide your light! Let it shine brightly before others, so that the commendable things you do will shine as light upon them, and then they will give their praise to your Father in heaven."*

This verse reminds us that when we live out our God-given purpose, our actions become a light that draws others toward Him.

The King James Version says, "Let your light so shine before men, that they may see your good works, and glorify your Father which is in heaven."

It's always works over words. It's like showing others how you (the product) operate or work. That is what light means, "knowledge." When you live out your purpose, it carries an influence so strong that it naturally leads others through you and directly to the Source—your Father in heaven. They're drawn in because, for once, someone is showing them how the "product" truly works—when it remains in direct relationship with its Manufacturer.

The word translated as "commendable things" can also mean deserving of praise. That's because walking in your purpose and using your gifts is an act of good stewardship. And stewardship—when done faithfully—attracts the right audience: people whose hearts, mouths, and lips are ready to praise what God is doing through you.

You were made to attract—not for your glory, but so others would see His.

Definition of "Manual" (as in an instruction manual)

The manual, being a guidebook or handbook, also provides not just instructions on how to operate or assemble products, but also how to troubleshoot a product. It is designed to give

CHAPTER 5

step-by-step directions in a structured and detailed manner, ensuring the user understands how to use a device, system, or tool correctly.

Etymology: Latin Origins

Latin: "Manualis" (from "Manus")

- The word manual comes from the Latin word "manualis," which means "of or belonging to the hand."
- It is derived from "manus," meaning "hand."
- In Roman times, something manual is referred to something done by hand or a small, hand-held book.

Isn't it amazing that we are the very workmanship of the hands of an intentional God who doesn't miss a beat? The word workmanship means "masterpiece." God is a Master Craftsman, and you are His product—carefully shaped with purpose, precision, and love.

And like any great artisan, He provides a manual—His Word. The Bible is not just a book; it's the blueprint of your design. When you follow its instructions, you're aligning with the hand that made you. Every command, every principle, and every promise is part of His ongoing craftsmanship in your life. The more you walk in the manual (aligned with it), the more His masterpiece in you is revealed.

> ***"For we are God's masterpiece (workmanship). He has created us anew in Christ Jesus, so we can do the good things he planned for us long ago." (Ephesians 2:10 NLT)***

You were designed with purpose in you. It's wired into your makeup.

Also, **Psalm 8:5** is a powerful and deeply meaningful verse expressing this finished work - mankind, from a Master Craftsman.

> *"For You have made him a little lower than the angels, And You have crowned him with glory and honor." (NKJV)*

Being crowned with glory and honor means God bestowed upon humanity a royal identity. "Crowned" signifies authority, rulership, and worth. "Glory and honor" speak of the divine nature, purpose, and responsibility God gave to humans—to reflect His image, steward creation, and live in relationship with Him.

We were created with intentional greatness—set just beneath God, wearing a crown of purpose, dignity, and divine calling. You're not ordinary. You carry the weight of glory and the honor of heaven's intention.

MADE AND CREATED WITH PURPOSE

Mankind was both **made** and **created**, and this distinction is important in understanding purpose and identity.

1. "Created" – Hebrew: Bārā' (אָרַב)

    - Found in **Genesis 1:1** – *"In the beginning God created the heavens and the earth."*

    - This word means:

    To create something out of nothing—a divine act only God can perform.

    It refers to bringing forth something that never existed before.

CHAPTER 5

> "In the beginning God created the heavens and the earth." (Genesis 1:1)

In reference to humanity:

- **Genesis 1:27 – "So God created man in His own image..."**

    This refers to the spiritual aspect of mankind—our essence, identity, and image-bearing nature.

    This is when man was created in the image of God—a spirit being.

2. "Made" – Hebrew: ʿĀśāh (הָשָׂע)

    - Found in **Genesis 1:26 – "Let Us make man in Our image, according to Our likeness..."**

    - This word means:

    To form from pre-existing materials—to build, fashion, or accomplish something.

    In reference to humanity:

    - **Genesis 2:7 – *"Then the Lord God formed man from the dust of the ground..."***

Here, the word for "formed" is Yatsar (רַצָי), but it still implies working with existing materials—God is now shaping the body of man from the earth.

Two things to consider here is that we were in God's mind and created before anything was done (His mind - intent, purpose and will) and then we were formed (fashioned and made form the dirt for a purpose in the earth) - for a time such as this.

This is important to understand the power of God's earthly legal agents - Humans.

The emphasis is that:

- Man was created (bārā') as a spirit in God's image (Genesis 1).

- Man was made ('āsāh) as a body from the earth (Genesis 2).

- So, man is a spirit, who lives in a body, and possesses a soul—a triune being.

Humans are the legal agents to carrying out God's dominion mandate for earth, colonizing it for heaven's sake. *"Then God said, 'Let Us make man in Our image, according to Our likeness; let them have dominion over the fish... birds... cattle... and over all the earth...'" (Genesis 1:26 NKJV)*

- God is Spirit, and the legal authority to operate on Earth was given to humans in a body.

- This is why God gave mankind dominion—not ownership, but management authority.

- Because of that, God works through man to carry out His will on Earth.

- This is also why prayer is essential—it's man giving Heaven permission to interfere in Earth's affairs. This signifies that we are fully covered, even as we seek help in establishing His intent, and ours (when aligned with His), for earth.

The original Hebrew word for "dominion" Genesis 1:26 is:

CHAPTER 5

"Radah" (הָדָר) – Hebrew which means

- To rule
- To reign
- To have sovereign authority
- To govern or manage with responsibility

It does not mean to dominate in the sense to oppress. Rather, it speaks of kingly authority exercised with wisdom, stewardship, and alignment with God's will.

It is "Sovereign authority. Kingdom rulership. The right to govern or control."

Dr. Munroe consistently taught us that when God said in **Genesis 1:26, "Let them have dominion…"**, He was assigning kingdom leadership to mankind—not domination over people, but rulership over the Earth and its systems.

Here are some principles on this teaching:

1. Dominion is not ownership, it's stewardship.

    God owns everything; humans were given the responsibility to manage creation on His behalf.

2. Dominion is a kingdom term, not a religious one.

    It reflects the concept of a king delegating power to a representative—a governor or ambassador.

3. Dominion is at the heart of purpose.

> You were created not just to exist, but to **rule in your area of gifting**—your domain.

4. Dominion requires a body.

   God gave dominion to mankind in physical bodies, which is why legal authority on Earth is tied to being human.

Dominion is the God-given right to rule, govern, and manage the Earth as Heaven's representative.

Humans are crowned with glory and honor and assigned dominion. We are Heaven's ambassadors, Earth's stewards, and carriers of divine intention.

When Scripture says in Ephesians 2:10, "For we are His workmanship, created in Christ Jesus for good works...", the word "workmanship" comes from the Greek word poiēma, which can be translated as masterpiece, work of art, or poetic expression.

So yes—we are the masterpiece or artwork of an intentional Creator. That means:

- We are intentionally designed with purpose and precision.
- Nothing about us is accidental.
- Our gifts, passions, and even our personalities are woven into our design for a reason.

Discovering your purpose is really about uncovering what the Creator already placed within you.

We also have a **manual** (the Bible) to ensure we get it right. It is not a devotional book, as many of you treated as such. But rather is it a powerful tool, a guidebook or handbook that provides instructions on how to operate, understand your full value,

CHAPTER 5

and even troubleshoot our lives, reset ourselves to ensure we are living to our fullest potential, not just experimenting through life. This is why we become born again or restart our lives to make all things new.

"***This means that anyone who belongs to Christ has become a new person. The old life is gone; a new life has begun!" (2 Corinthians 5:17)***. Even when we sin, meaning "missed the mark", through the power of forgiveness, we can come right back and feel as if we have not missed a beat.

This shows us just how much God is commitment to filling the earth with His nature, values, and presence—His culture. It supports the idea that we, as His earthly agents, are part of that divine agenda to extend heaven's influence on earth.

> **"For the earth will be filled with the knowledge of the glory of the Lord as the waters cover the sea."**(Habakkuk 2:14, NKJV)
>
> *"If we confess our sins, he is faithful and just and will forgive us our sins and purify us from all unrighteousness."* **(1John1:9 NIV).**

By constantly going to the **manuel** and learning the principles from it we can secure our purpose and God's very plan for our life. The key is to learn the principles, not just the stories. Even the Old testaments stories are supposed to instruct us in every area of life. The statement that "the Old Testament was written for our learning" is supported by the scripture in Romans 15:4, which states that "everything that was written in the past was written for our instruction, so that through endurance and the encouragement of the Scriptures, we might have hope". Do you see how this handbook is constantly providing instruction?

"Whoever heeds instruction is on the path to life, but he who rejects reproof leads others astray." (Proverbs 10:17 ASV)

We can do this, but we must do so by faith. *"For without faith it is impossible to please God." (Hebrews 11:6).*

Heeds to *Instruction* = "Musar" (מוּסָר). Meaning:

- Discipline
- Correction
- Chastening
- Moral instruction

It is not just "teaching" as in giving knowledge — musar refers specifically to corrective training, the kind of instruction that shapes character through correction, discipline, and guidance. Instructions, just like following the instructions of a manual, lead you into the path He has purposed for you.

1. PROVERBS 3:5–6 (NKJV)

"Trust in the Lord with all your heart,

And lean not on your own understanding;

In all your ways acknowledge Him,

And He shall direct your paths."

- Submitting to God's wisdom leads you into the path He has purposed for you.

CHAPTER 5

2. JOSHUA 1:8 (NKJV)

"This Book of the Law shall not depart from your mouth, but you shall meditate in it day and night, that you may observe according to all that is written in it. For then you will make your way prosperous, and then you will have good success."

- Following God's instruction (His Word) results in success and fulfilling destiny.

3. PSALM 32:8 (NKJV)

"I will instruct you and teach you in the way you should go;

I will guide you with My eye."

- God's instruction is a personal guide to walking in your unique purpose.

4. 2 TIMOTHY 3:16–17 (NKJV)

"All Scripture is given by inspiration of God, and is profitable for doctrine, for reproof, for correction, for instruction in righteousness,
that the man of God may be complete, thoroughly equipped for every good work."

- The Word equips you to be complete and ready to fulfill every good work—your divine assignment.

Submitting to God's Word is the training ground for stepping fully into your God-given purpose.

MANUAL AND EMMANUEL

Finally:

- In Latin: Manualis → "Belonging to the hand" (from manus = "hand").

One Last Thing Relating to Its Meaning:

Manual and Emmanuel look and sound very similar, but they have different origins and meanings.

1. "Manual" vs. "Emmanuel" We are privileged to have both Emmanuel and the manual. Though the words sound alike, they are not the same. Each carries something unique for us to understand about the nature of God and about our own purpose.

Emanuel refers to the presence of the Creator who promises to be with us all the way to the end. The Hebrew expression is "Immanu El", which literally means "God with us."

This is first prophesied in Isaiah 7:14 and fulfilled in Matthew 1:23: "They will call him Emmanuel — which means 'God with us.'"

Emmanuel means "God with us" — the living presence of God. The manual is practical —focused on guidance, instruction, hands-on application, and applying the principles we've learned Together they show us that God not only gives His presence (Emmanuel) but also His principles and instructions (manual) so we can live out our calling effectively. Sometimes we even have the privilege of sensing that presence with us, and it is marvelous. But we don't always feel it. Many times we only have His Word — implying that, feeling or no feeling, we must still apply the principles in challenging situations. **This is God enabling us to walk by faith, for without faith it is impossible to please Him (Hebrews 11:6)**.

CHAPTER 5

While manual (Bible) gives instruction, Emmanuel (Jesus) gives us connection. In him we are supposed to have it all down packed - everything we need to carry out our purpose: **He isn't just the Word written - He is the Word made flesh (John 1:14)**.

To a large degree, we have no excuse for not fulfilling our God-given purpose on earth. We've been equipped with everything we need—identity, intention, gifts, and grace—to carry it out.

This truth is magnified in the words of Jesus, who perfectly fulfilled His assignment: **"I glorified You on earth by finishing the work that You have given Me to do." (John 17:4, TLV)**

Jesus didn't just come to save us—He came to model what it looks like to live a life of purpose, stewardship, and obedience. And if He could finish the work the Father gave Him, so can we—because the same Spirit that empowered Him is now at work in us.

This teaches us that we aren't just called to worship, but to work. He gave us His presence to live a practical life of purpose. Not only was Jesus the Word, but was the Word made Flesh. He embodied God's mind, will and nature. He brought God's invisible truth to visible form.

"In the beginning was the **Word**, and the **Word** was with God, and the **Word** was God." (John 1:1 NKJV)

"And the **Word** became flesh and dwelt among us, and we beheld His glory, the glory as of the only begotten of the Father, full of grace and truth." (John 1:14 NKJV)

What does "The Word made flesh" mean?

1. Jesus is the embodiment of God's mind, will, and nature. You too must activate this.

- The Greek word "Logos" (Word) means the divine expression, logic, or reason of God. God had an IDEA that was finally expressed with clarity through the work and life of His son Christ. You too must express the very reason for which you came to your generation for a calling way higher than you can imagine. You are not here to make a paycheck; You're here to make an impact that last. We must get God's big idea and express it from our two legs, by living our purpose.

Christ was the **firstborn among many brothers and sisters** (Romans 8:29), meaning He set the pattern for a new kind of humanity—sons and daughters who would walk in the same Spirit, the same authority, and the same purpose. He didn't just come to be admired; He came to be followed. As the firstborn, He is both our example and our access point. His life, death, and resurrection opened the door for us to become children of God—restored to purpose and reconnected to our original design and intent.

> "For those whom He foreknew, He also predestined to be conformed to the image of His Son, so that He would be the firstborn among many brothers and sisters." —Romans 8:29 (NASB)

- Jesus wasn't just speaking God's Word—He was the full expression of it. When you find your work, purpose you'll be able to express God's intent.

2. He brought God's invisible truth into visible form. This is where you will need to be practical about your business for earth. Not just worship but roll up your sleeves and work.

- What was eternal and spiritual became tangible and physical. We shouldn't over spiritualize things. Bring yourself down to earth where you are called to influence.

CHAPTER 5

- In Him, the character, will, power, and truth of God became touchable, relatable, and knowable. Choose simplicity over superfluity.

3. He didn't just deliver the message—He is the message. Your work will always speak louder than your words. "Preach the gospel at all times. If necessary, use words." (St. Francis of Assisi)

- Every action, word, and miracle Jesus did was a manifestation of God's Word in motion. He said, ***"Very truly I tell you, whoever believes in me will do the works I have been doing, and they will do even greater things than these, because I am going to the Father."*** **(John 14:12 NIV)**

So, when we say:

Jesus was not just a word from God— **"He was the Word made flesh,"**

We're saying He is the living blueprint, the physical revelation, and the embodied truth of God's heart and purpose. He was God's Expressed Idea, what God purposed for earth was seen clearly in what he came to both say and do.

When we do God's purpose, we reveal God presence in a practical and peculiar way.

EMMANUEL = GOD WITH, IN AND FOR US.

We too have the greater one in us as it states, "***Greater is he that is in you, than he that is in the world" (1 John 4:4).***

This denotes that there is far more to us than the naked human eye can see. There's a saying that much of what we see in our world has been accomplished with only limited power. But by connecting and tapping into the GREATER ONE within us, we can do exploits—greater things than what we are presently experiencing.

We are powerful, equipped with intrinsic power from above as well as an external power: to adhere to the **manual** that guides, instructs, directs, and ensures we are doing everything in accordance with how God determined it.

Just like any product comes with a manual to ensure its full and proper use, we too have been given a Manual—God's Word—designed to bring out the very best in us. The Bible isn't just a book of rules; it is a living, breathing guide that reveals our true selves and uncovers the very intent for which we were born. It speaks to our innate design, our hidden abilities, and our untapped potential.

This is where our true identity collides with the One who made us—our Manufacturer. When we align ourselves with His principles, we unlock the life we were always meant to live.

That's why principles are so powerful: they make life predictable. They remove confusion and chaos, and they set the foundation for consistent success. When we live by God's principles, we position ourselves to thrive—not by striving, but by design.

Perhaps all we are really lacking is heeding to the manual: **"He is in the way of life that keepeth instruction: but he that refuseth reproof erreth." (Proverbs 10:17 KJV)**. This verse sets up a powerful contrast between those who accept instruction and those who reject correction.

"Those who follow instruction are on the path that leads to life, but those who reject correction are heading for trouble—and may take others with them." (Paraphrased). But when in our life's role we also attract others and bring them with us.

CHAPTER 5

We are taught that the principles from God's word govern life, making both success and failure predictable. You either heed instructions or reject correction. His philosophy was rooted in the belief that life is designed by God to function according to established laws and principles—just like gravity or seedtime and harvest. When we align ourselves with these principles, we can expect predictable results.

How Principles Make Life Predictable

1. Principles Are Laws That Never Change

    - Just as gravity works the same for everyone, success and failure are governed by principles that apply universally.

    - Example: The principle of diligence—**those who consistently work hard and apply wisdom will reap rewards (Proverbs 22:29).**

2. Success Is the Result of Following Principles

    - Dr. Munroe taught that success is not a matter of luck but of applying the right principles consistently.

    - If you follow principles of discipline, integrity, leadership, and purpose, you will experience predictable success.

    - Example: **A farmer who follows the principles of planting, watering, and harvesting expects a crop—not by chance, but by law (Genesis 8:22).**

3. Failure Is Also Predictable

    - Just as success follows principles, failure is the result of violating them.

- If someone ignores financial principles, they will face financial hardship. If someone neglects relational principles, their relationships will suffer.

- Example: **Ignoring the principle of self-control leads to bad habits and negative consequences (Proverbs 25:28).**

Dr. Munroe also emphasized that our lives are shaped by the principles we live by. If we discover and apply God's principles for life, work, relationships, and leadership, we can predict and create the outcomes we desire—just as surely as a pilot follows the laws of aerodynamics to fly.

Again, **"He is in the way of life that keepeth instruction: but he that refuseth reproof erreth." (Proverbs 10:17 KJV).**

Every manufacturer is obligated to warranty and guarantee their products, so long as the basic principles are adhered to. As an example, when I recently went to an Apple Store after experiencing a problem with my phone, the first thing the representative asked me was if I allowed it to get damaged by water. This is a violation in the manual that carries consequences outside of the warranty. That "Do Not Operate within water" isn't meant to keep you from enjoying your phone, but to secure all its features and benefits. There are a few "Do Nots" in our manual that likewise are meant for us not to miss out on all that we are intended to be. They are designed not to short-circuit our future, not keep us from enjoying life, but to live to the fullest, *"According to his power that is at work within us." (Ephesians 3:20 NIV)*.

The Bible or God's Word is our manual today. Someone said that the Bible stands for Basic Instructions Before Leaving Earth but, you must learn how to read out of it and not into it, getting the principles and understanding from it, and not just the head knowledge. Many of us read with a clouded perspective from

CHAPTER 5

our religions. Thus, deceiving ourselves. If done properly, it can bring out the full God likeness trapped in you!

Success is guaranteed!

> *"You are truly safe when you're covered both horizontally and vertically. That means someone—or a trusted community—must have your back and your front, while also protecting your head (your mind) and your feet (your walk)."—RAH*

This means you should do life alone.

This is why the Wise King Solomon said, **"The purpose in a man's heart is like deep water, but a man of understanding will draw it out" (Proverbs 20:5 ESV).** Understanding destroys frustration. When you understand the meaning of your life, you stop experimenting with it. You no longer live by trial and error, but with clarity and conviction. When you grasp why you are the way you are—how you came to be and emerged as your unique self—you begin to live more effectively. Frustration and disappointment are minimized because your why begins to manage your how. Purpose brings direction, and direction brings peace.

That's why, as I mentioned in a previous chapter, securing and fully understanding our purpose requires the presence of others around us. We need the right community—people who see us, sharpen us, and support our growth.

Napoleon Hill called this the **"Mastermind Group"** principle: a harmonious alliance of two or more minds working actively together toward a definite purpose. He believed that when minds are aligned in unity and clarity, they generate a collective energy that far exceeds the sum of individual efforts.

In other words, you can go fast alone—but you go further, and deeper, with the right people around you. People of understanding, and people who understand you. That kind of community doesn't just accelerate progress—it helps draw out your hidden potential, keeps you accountable to your purpose, and supports you when your strength runs low.

> "...***but a man of understanding will draw it out***" *(Proverbs 20:5 ESV)*

This refers to someone with wisdom, discernment, or insight—whether that's the person themselves, self-discovering, or someone else (a mentor, coach, teacher, or trusted friend). This "man of understanding" can ask the right questions, create the right environment, or give the right guidance to help uncover and draw out what's hidden inside. It turns out to be "**The coordination of knowledge and effort of two or more people, who work toward a definite purpose, in the spirit of harmony." (Napoleon Hill, Think and Grow Rich)**

Apart from self-reflection, having good mentors or a healthy community—people who don't just want to benefit from us but genuinely contribute to our growth—is invaluable. These are wise individuals, capable of drawing out what's hidden within us, like deep waters. They help us recognize and navigate our blind spots.

When a mentor, community, or mastermind group speaks the right words into our lives, they create an environment for growth—just like light, soil, and water do for a seed. That nurturing environment causes the hidden potential within us to emerge and flourish.

That's why I love the quote often used by Dr. Myles Munroe:

> "**The safest place on earth is under authority and in community.**"

CHAPTER 5

Being accountable to a mentor and with people of "common" unity, or a community, are key to purposely unleashing one's full self. A good mastermind group of people who work toward a definite purpose can also be considered men of understanding, to draw out the trapped you, in you.

Even though I often stress the importance of community and accountability for self-discovery and growth, I want to emphasize even more the study of self—to firmly establish one's identity, bring purpose to fruition, and make meaningful progress. After self-discovery, it's crucial to unite in a safe and supportive place. Why? Because iron sharpens iron, and often, a person who thinks they're right can actually be wrong. As Proverbs 14:12 (NIV) warns, **"There is a way that appears to be right, but in the end, it leads to death."**

After discovering yourself, you must remain vigilant against pride and overconfidence.

Do you know how many perspectives we've adjusted through our small groups and fellowships? Numerous. We don't need to lean solely on our own understanding. Instead, we need others who truly understand us to help keep us sharp.

We can never stop learning or consider ourselves to have arrived at a place of knowing it all. There is always more to discover about ourselves. We are complex individuals with deep things inside, waiting to be uncovered and expressed—bringing out our very best to benefit those around us.

A first-century writer and leader warned his contemporaries against pride when he stated, **"So, if you think you're standing firm, be careful that you don't fall!" (1 Corinthians 10:12 NIV).**

In addition, the writer of Hebrews reminded his contemporaries not to fall into the habit of doing life alone or living in isolation. In a letter written to them, he stated:

> **"Let us consider how we can provoke one another unto love and good works—not neglecting to meet together, as is the habit of some, but encouraging one another." (Hebrews 10:24–25, NLT)**

When a person settles into the right place—an environment shaped by a culture of love—they are able to put down roots before growing upward and outward. Just like a tree, growth begins beneath the surface. This kind of foundation cultivates vision, allowing individuals to see clearly how to live and how to carry out their assignment—what Scripture refers to as their "good works."

THE RIGHT ENVIRONMENT CAUSES US TO EMERGE, LIKE LIGHT, RAIN AND SOIL CAUSES A SEED TO GROW

Like-minded people can help bring out the you in you.

While writing this portion of my book in a coffee shop, I noticed a woman next to me writing, editing, and inserting text with deep focus. I leaned over and asked, "Are you writing a book?"

She sighed and said, "Yes."

I followed up with a question that often reveals something deeper: "Who's bringing you out? Who's helping you draw out the information from within? Writing can be terrifying—especially because it brings up so much insecurity, doubt, and fear. We tend to hide behind distractions instead of sitting down and actually doing the writing. So tell me, who's holding you accountable? Who's encouraging you to emerge into your full self and execute your dream?"

CHAPTER 5

She paused and smiled, then responded, "A community of good people—I'm actually texting with them right now while I write."

That moment affirmed my point. It was a right-now confirmation. I love those. Not that you'll need external validation at every step, but coming from a safe place like that—a supportive, purpose-aligned community—makes a huge difference.

I assure you: your impact will be greater when you walk with people who truly have your back in everything you're called to do. That kind of community isn't just helpful—it's suitable for you and for your assignment.

FINDING MEANING OUTSIDE OF YOU

Before we focus on discovering your purpose within, it's important to first help you look outward—beyond yourself. After self-discovery, surrounding yourself with the right people—those who see your potential and push you forward—is invaluable.

But just like an iPhone needs its manufacturer to explain its full function, you need to go to your Creator to fully understand your purpose. Without Him, you risk falling short of what you were truly made for.

God is a God of purpose. You were created with a unique assignment and fully equipped to succeed in it. The end goal isn't a mystery—God reveals it.

Sometimes, what He shows you will feel exciting and a little scary. That's on purpose. It reminds us we can't fulfill our calling alone. God designed your purpose to need support from others in areas where you're not strong. That's how He set it up.

GOING AGAINST YOUR ORIGINAL DESIGN

Finding Your Why in the Mind of the Creator of the Product

> **"We all fell down, and I heard a voice saying to me in Aramaic, 'Saul, Saul, why are you persecuting me? It is useless for you to fight against my will.'" (Acts 26:14, NLT)**

Ultimately, the search for relevance, significance, meaning, and purpose seems to be the main pursuit of us all. We all want to know our why. People who are inquisitive—who take the time to search out the reasons behind things—often attract answers.

As mentioned earlier, Matthew's record of the good news states:

> **"For everyone who asks, receives. Everyone who seeks, finds. And to everyone who knocks, the door will be opened." (Matthew 7:8, NLT)**

It is useless to fight or go in the opposite direction of your true design. Inquisitive people will eventually attract the answers they seek. It's often said that a true student of life is someone who is constantly asking questions—someone who genuinely wants to know.

Dr. Myles Munroe stated, **"The hunger of the student attracts the topic of the teacher."**

I truly believe in the timeless principle:

> **"When the student is ready, the teacher appears." (Unknown)**

When we posture ourselves with readiness, humility, and a genuine desire to grow, life has a way of bringing the right voices, mentors, and lessons into our path—right on time.

CHAPTER 5

Jesus said it best,

"He answered and said to them, 'Because it has been given to you to know the mysteries of the kingdom of heaven, but to them it has not been given.

> *For whoever has, to him more will be given, and he will have abundance; but whoever does not have, even what he has will be taken away from him.'"* (Matthew 13:11–12)

So when He says:

> "Whoever has, to him more will be given…"

He's referring to:

Whoever has:

- **Receptiveness to truth**
- **A desire to understand**
- **Spiritual insight**
- **Faith or a responsive heart**
- **A commitment to pursue the <u>mysteries of the Kingdom</u>**

What is the mystery or secrets of the Kingdom? They are hidden truths about how God works, what He values, and how life is meant to be lived under His rule—truths that require a relationship with Him to fully understand.

The desire to know and understand the nature of something is a crucial part of learning. As I mentioned earlier, this kind of hunger attracts God. He doesn't respond merely on a "need to know" basis—but more powerfully on a "desire to know" basis.

The real question becomes: How badly do you want it?
How much do you really want to know?
How deep is your desire?

Ancient King David captured this beautifully when he wrote:

"Delight yourself in the Lord, and He will give you the desires of your heart." (Psalm 37:4)

Likewise, Napoleon Hill, in his classic book Think and Grow Rich, emphasized:

"Desire is the starting point of all achievement—not a hope, not a wish, but a keen pulsating desire, which transcends everything."

"Your deep desire is your intrinsic wiring—it's the internal blueprint that reveals what you were born to do." (RAH)

True discovery—whether spiritual or practical—begins with a burning desire to understand, to grow, and to align with something greater than ourselves.

I've often found that the prayers God truly answers in my life are the ones tied to the things I deeply desire—the portions I want with all my heart. Therefore, if you're going to come to God, come correct—come with sincerity, clarity, and a genuine hunger for what you're asking.

Praying this way—in alignment with His will—brings responses. As 1 John 5:14–15 (NIV) says, **'This is the confidence we have in approaching God: that if we ask anything according to his will, he hears us. And if we know that he hears us—whatever we ask—we know that we have what we asked of him.'"**

CHAPTER 5

YOUR PURPOSE IN THE CREATOR'S MIND.

Do people truly want to know God—or is it their 'why' they're chasing? The ache to understand our purpose, our reason for being, often burns brighter than the desire to know the One who made us. But what if our search for why is actually designed to lead us to Who? What if, in pursuing meaning, we are being gently drawn to the Maker of meaning? Would we be willing to come to Him—not just for answers, but for relationship? For identity, not just direction?

> **"When a man can't find a deep sense of meaning, he distracts himself with pleasure."**
> **— Viktor E. Frankl**

Because, in the end, there are only two masters pulling at the soul: God or Mammon—our Creator or the means we use to escape Him. And when we cannot find our purpose, when we silence the question of why we're here, we don't just lose direction—we lose ourselves. As Viktor E. Frankl insightfully said, 'When a man can't find a deep sense of meaning, he distracts himself with pleasure.' We trade calling for comfort. Mission for momentary relief. But even pleasure, unchecked, becomes a poor anesthetic for a soul meant to burn with eternal meaning.

Purpose is **"The need that makes a manufacturer produce a specific product." (Dr. Myles Munroe)**

When asking, "What is my purpose?" we should keep this quote by Dr. Myles Munroe in mind:

"Many problems exist in the world we live in. Before you were born, your Creator had you in mind as a solution to some, or at least one of the problems existing during your lifetime. You were meant to solve a NEED through your specific gift and within your niche."

BEYOND THE HUSTLE

Our reason for existence is found in the mind of our Creator. That's why I often say: talking about God doesn't automatically mean we're talking about religion. Many deeply religious people have never discovered this truth. In fact, within religion, many are weighed down by heavy systems and ill-fitting motions—performing rituals but never discovering their reason for being.

Purpose is not found in pressure, performance, or pretense. It's found in alignment. It's about uncovering your gift, identifying your niche, and stepping into the unforced rhythms of grace—the kind Jesus spoke of when He invited us to walk freely and lightly with Him.

That's why the question still echoes so loudly today: **"Burned out on religion? Come to me. Get away with me and you'll recover your life... Learn the unforced rhythms of grace. I won't lay anything heavy or ill-fitting on you. Keep company with me and you'll learn to live freely and lightly" (Matthew 11:28-30 MSG)**.

Jesus recognized the exhausting weight of religion without relationship. He knew that many would feel burdened—not by God, but by systems that had lost connection to the Source. Our true source of purpose is God. But in trying to systematize the sacred, humanity has often reduced the vibrant, life-giving experience of knowing Him into a checklist of rules, rituals, and routines. In doing so, we've turned relationship into religion. And instead of being built up in grace, many of us have been burned out by grind. We traded encounter for performance—intimacy for obligation—and lost sight of the very One we were meant to walk with.

Religion entails **"The worship of a deity through a set of beliefs, expressed through rituals, customs and rites, producing a sectarian distinction and a unique group of people." (Myles Munroe)** People use religion to seek meaning, but their search many times doesn't lead them to the Source

CHAPTER 5

– God. Instead, they make the focus more on the customs or on the sectarian distinction, the means, rather than the end.

ZEAL WITHOUT UNDERSTANDING IS DESTRUCTIVE.

This is why Paul's experience speaks to this context: ***"We all fell down, and I heard a voice saying to me in Aramaic, 'Saul, Saul, why are you persecuting me? It is useless for you to fight against my will" (Acts 26:14 NLT).*** Paul was deeply religious—zealous for what he believed was God's cause. He was fully convinced he was doing God's work. But in reality, he was resisting God's will. He wasn't walking in purpose; he was walking in prideful misunderstanding. In many ways, Paul was burned out on religion without even realizing it—fighting hard for a cause that didn't align with his calling. He was fighting against something, not toward something.

It wasn't until he encountered the living Christ that everything shifted. What he thought was devotion was actually misdirection. And in that divine confrontation, purpose was revealed. Paul discovered that he hadn't been fighting for God, but against Him—and against the very reason he was born.

He stated in another place regarding God and his (Paul's) purpose, ***"… I have made you a light for the Gentiles, that you may bring salvation to the ends of the earth." (Acts 13:47).***

In your zeal are you fighting against the very thing you were built for? ***ZEAL WITHOUT UNDERSTANDING IS DESTRUCTIVE.*** Remember that call and gifts of your God are already imbedded in you.

You can be sincerely arrogant and ignorant. One thing I have learned is that if you are truly sincere and humble in your search, you'll find your way.

The phrase "a contrite heart and broken spirit He will in no wise despise" is from Psalm 51:17. This verse conveys the concept that God never refuses sincere individuals, no matter how distant they may feel.

> *"The sacrifice you desire is a broken spirit. You will not reject a broken and repentant heart, O God." (New Living Translation)*

God values sincerity, humility, and repentance. He welcomes all who come to Him with a genuine desire for forgiveness and renewal. This reminds us that it is far better to humble ourselves willingly than to be knocked off our "beast," as Paul was on the road to Damascus.

SEEKING YOUR PURPOSE FROM THE MIND OF THE CREATOR

> *"Don't let the excitement of youth cause you to forget your Creator. Honor Him in your youth before you get old and say, 'Life is not pleasant anymore.'" (Eclesiastés 12: 1 NLT)*

There are many things in life that can easily distract us from being mindful of our Creator—and from discovering our true purpose in Him. One of the biggest distractions? The excitement of youth. When life feels full of options, ambition, and energy, it's easy to put off reflection and deeper questions. But Scripture reminds us:

> **"Don't let the excitement of youth cause you to forget your Creator... Before you grow old and say, 'Life is not pleasant anymore.'" (Ecclesiastes 12:1, NLT)**

CHAPTER 5

Imagine reaching the end of your life only to realize you've ended up in a place you were never meant to be. Imagine not just losing time—but losing yourself. That's the risk of living distracted. We must remember: the decisions we make today will shape where we land tomorrow.

I've had the opportunity to speak with many multimillionaires in Naples, Florida—through coaching, mentoring, or simple conversation. And a surprising number of them have said to me, "How did I end up here? This was never what I dreamed of when I was younger."

They weren't referring to money—but to meaning. To purpose. To a gnawing sense that somewhere along the way, they exchanged calling for comfort, or destiny for distraction.

One of the most effective things I've done in these conversations is invite people to go back—to revisit the time when they were just 7 to 12 years old. I ask them to recall the dreams that stirred in them during that season of life. At first, many have to pause and sift through layers of memory. But once they find it, the expression on their faces often says it all—surprise, clarity, sometimes even grief.

I first discovered the power of this approach while coaching a well-known architect in Miami, Florida. Our conversations stood out because I did more listening than talking. And in that space of reflection, something became unmistakably clear: many of us have started to become educated out of our dreams by the age of eight.

Somewhere along the way, expectations replaced imagination. Systems taught us what was "practical," and slowly, the wonder of who we were meant to be began to fade. But when we return to those early dreams—not with nostalgia, but with curiosity—we often rediscover the threads of purpose we were always meant to follow.

This one gentleman, an architect, who afterwards ended up being a friend of mine for example, spent his childhood drawing buildings, houses, and even entire communities. His mother, who encouraged him, would tell him, "One day, you'll be a well-known architect." Today, he is responsible for designing many of the iconic buildings that line the oceanfront in Miami.

This revelation was both deeply insightful and profoundly educational for me. It reinforced the importance of reconnecting with our childhood dreams—before the world convinces us to abandon them.

The principle of regressing before progressing holds significant power, as even our wise first century leader Jesus once proclaimed, 'Truly I tell you, unless you change and become like little children, you will never enter the kingdom of heaven' (Matthew 18:3 NIV). The important thing here is to remain childlike in your faith as you journey toward staying in your purpose in life.

> **"People like you and I never grow old... We never cease to stand like curious children before the great mystery into which we were born." —Albert Einstein, in a 1942 letter to his friend Otto Juliusburger**

This beautifully captures his lifelong belief in maintaining childlike wonder.

> **"Our lives are a sum total of the choices we have made." – Wayne Dyer**

Though the excitement of youth touches many areas of a young person's life—impulsive emotions, fluctuating goals, unfiltered desires, and fleeting pleasures—it can also blur the path of purpose.

CHAPTER 5

These intense experiences are not inherently wrong, but without discipline and self-control, they can lead to decisions disconnected from vision and purpose. When we live reactively instead of intentionally, we risk waking up years later with regret—saying what the writer of Ecclesiastes warned:

> "Life is not pleasant anymore."
> (Ecclesiastes 12:1c, NLT)

That's the cost of unexamined youth: growing older in a place you were never meant to be, shaped more by impulse than by intention.

Recall the 65-year-old retired architect from Central Florida mentioned earlier. His story is sobering. For much of his life, he made major decisions based on the expectations and preferences of others—choosing paths that felt "acceptable" rather than authentic. In doing so, he failed to draw out the purpose that was already within him, allowing unauthorized voices to override his original design.

His regret wasn't about success—it was about misalignment. About living a life near purpose, but never in it.

That's why Scripture urges us:

> "Remember your Creator in the days of your youth…" (Ecclesiastes 12:1)

But the truth is, we must remember Him not only in youth, but throughout all of life. Because only the One who created you can consistently point you back to why you were created.

Purposeful and fulfilled living isn't accidental—it's the result of daily alignment with the One who placed purpose within you in the first place.

BEYOND THE HUSTLE

"Destiny isn't written; it's built one choice at a time. The wrong one can tear it all down." – RAH

"Flee youthful lusts!" is also another exhortation from Paul to the young man Timothy. Though this encompasses many different areas in a young person's life, perhaps the strongest and most common is that of sexual desire. This natural drive is not wrong in and of itself, except according to the Bible, our manual, when it's done outside the framework of marriage and practiced as a norm.

"Flee youthful lust". The drive to pursue an orderly life with the assistance of others can lead to a purposeful path, deterring unnecessary distractions. This strong drive is so compelling that even "fleeing" from it can ensure a focused journey. That's why Paul advised young Timothy to **'Now flee from youthful lusts and pursue righteousness, faith, love, and peace, with those who call on the Lord from a pure heart' (2 Timothy 2:22 NASV).**

Let's look at this verse in the context of other youthful lusts that can skew our lives. One can become obsessed with being successful, with gaining riches, or gaining fame. If someone attaches themselves to one of these things, it would be no different from a person living riotously. It is easy to identify a young person having sex with the wrong person and altering their future. However, most of us overlook young people pursuing wealth and fame (greed), college degrees inspired by others (coveting), or hand-me-down dreams (lies). These youthful lusts are just as dangerous to one's purpose.

Why?

Let's talk about the 65-year-old architect once more. He pursued a dream that wasn't his. This pursuit had him forming covenants (agreements) outside of his realm of influence. Was he successful? Yes. Was he fulfilled? Not at all. He was like a smart

CHAPTER 5

phone, used only to make phone calls. He was able to contribute to the lives of those around him but how much more could he have contributed if he'd tapped into his full potential earlier in life?

Not one thing should be above your purpose, not even provision. Because provision doesn't attract purpose, purpose attracts provision.

When you know where you're going, you become intentional about who you surround yourself with—including your life partner. Purpose brings clarity, and clarity empowers wise choices. The people you huddle with—friends, mentors, partners—should be able to help you move toward where you're called to go, not pull you away from it.

Everything and everyone you allow into your life should be suitable for where you're going.
Compatibility isn't just about comfort—it's about calling.
The right relationships don't just feel good—they fit your future.

Ask yourself: Does this person align with my direction? Can they walk with me, grow with me, build with me? Or will they distract, detour, or drain me?
Purpose requires partnerships that propel you forward—not ones that hold you back.

That's why the latter part of the passage says:

> **"...and pursue righteousness, faith, love, and peace, with those who call on the Lord from a pure heart." (2 Timothy 2:22, NASB)**

After Paul tells Timothy to flee youthful lusts, he doesn't leave him aimless. He directs him to replace that pursuit with something greater—something noble. Purpose doesn't thrive in a vacuum. When you let go of the wrong things, you must run toward the right things, and you must run with the right people.

So, what does it mean to surround yourself with those who have a pure heart? A "Pure Heart" in Scripture:

Undivided — A pure heart is whole, not double-minded or half-committed (Psalm 86:11).

Sincere and honest — It's not contaminated by selfish ambition, pride, or hidden motives (James 3:17).

God-centered — It desires what pleases God more than what pleases people or self (Matthew 5:8).

In Practical Terms:

A person with a pure heart is:

    Aligned in motive and mission

    Transparent and humble

    Seeking truth over performance

    More focused on obedience than appearance

So when Paul says "pursue...with those who call on the Lord from a pure heart," he's saying: Surround yourself with people whose hearts are sincerely set on God—people who aren't perfect, but who are pure in pursuit. People who won't tempt you off course, but encourage you to stay on it.

A 70-year-old past mentor of mine once told me,

> **"The two most important decisions you make in life are: first, choosing to pursue God;**

CHAPTER 5

and second, choosing whom you marry. The second, however, has the power to affect the first." — Jose Munoz

Am I saying that getting married will help you find your purpose? Not at all.

Marriage is a covenant—an agreement between two people to live their lives together, to walk through all seasons with love, patience, and commitment. It's not a shortcut to identity or calling. It's a support structure, not a substitute for self-discovery.

When we begin to recognize the purpose God intended for us, we become equipped to marry up—that is, to align with someone who supports, strengthens, and complements that purpose. But here's the principle: you should marry your purpose before you marry a person.

There are cases where the right person can provoke growth, maturity, or even clarity around purpose. But purposeful living should not be dependent on a spouse. If you need someone to "provoke" you into your purpose, consider seeking that encouragement from a healthy community or trusted friendships. A spouse may support, but they should not be the source.

To place that weight entirely on a partner becomes unhealthy. Over time, it creates pressure to provoke, rather than a space to inspire. The journey of discovering your purpose is your personal responsibility, just as your walk with God is personal.

As Scripture says:

> **"... work out your own salvation with fear and trembling. For it is God which worketh in you both to will and to do of his good pleasure." (Philippians 2:12b,13 KJV)**

And again:

> **"Blessed are those whose help is the God of Jacob, whose hope is in the LORD their God." (Psalm 146:5, NIV)**

Your help should first and foremost come from the Lord. Before any person, any partner, or any plan—seek Him. Then, from that place of clarity, alignment, and strength, you'll be better equipped to choose a partner based not just on looks, charm, or chemistry—but on fit.

Because when purpose is of utmost importance, your partner must be someone suitable for it. That's how true complement works—not just two people joining lives, but two purposes moving in harmony.

PURPOSE BEFORE PARTNERSHIP

> God gave man work before He gave him a woman. Before introducing Eve, God gave Adam a specific place (Eden) and a clear assignment—to work and care for the garden (Genesis 2:15). Only after Adam was walking in his purpose did God say, "It is not good for the man to be alone" and create a **helper suitable for him** (Genesis 2:18).

This reveals a divine principle:

> **Purpose comes before partnership.**
>
> The right woman is not just a companion—she is a complement, a co-laborer in purpose.
>
> **"Can two walk together unless they are agreed?" (Amos 3:3)**

CHAPTER 5

In other words:

Discover your purpose before you pursue a partner.

Cultivate your God-given assignment first.

The right person will align with your mission, not distract from it.

God's order is intentional. Work first—then the woman. Not because she is lesser, but because a man rooted in purpose creates a relationship built to thrive. When he leads with clarity, she strengthens that vision—and together, they multiply impact.

Since purpose is discovered both **inside** you and **through** God, it is vital to seek Him first in such a life-altering decision. Yield to:

His Word (your manual),

His Way (alignment with His purpose),

and **His Wisdom** (His perspective).

That's how you secure not just a marriage—but a mission-driven union.

CHAPTER 6

FINDING MEANING IN THE PRODUCT REVIVING THE HIDDEN YOU IN YOU!
(TRIPLE D EVALUATION: YOUR DESIRE, DESIGN, AND DISTINCTION)

DISCOVERING THE PURPOSE ALREADY WITHIN YOU

In this chapter, we're going to dive deeper into your **inherent purpose**—the one that's already been placed inside you. I'll walk you through **three simple ways to study yourself** and begin tuning in to the calling you may or may not even realize is already there.

Purpose is personal, and it's often revealed through what I call **"The Triple Ds":**
Desire, Design, and Distinction.

These three major ingredients are foundational to discovering your God-given identity.

As I often say, **everyone should be a size "Triple D" at the core of their being**—anchored in their **Desire** (how they are wired), aligned with their **Design** (how they were made), and committed to living out their **Distinctiveness** (what sets them apart).

Think of it like this: in any well-made product, each part has a unique function—crafted intentionally by the manufacturer. Every part is different, but none are more important than the others. Uniqueness doesn't mean inequality. It just means **purposeful difference**.
Likewise, you are the way you are on purpose, for a purpose. You've been **fearfully and wonderfully made**—equipped with something this world needs.

THE BEAUTY OF SELF-DISCOVERY IN SPIRITUAL SPACES

I love teaching on self-discovery, especially in spiritual settings. Why? Because in many faith environments, the emphasis is often placed on serving God and helping others—both of which are crucial. But what's often missing is you.

Not a mere duty. Not a general role. You.

I believe that a true understanding of purpose includes a deep love and acceptance of yourself—the you that God intentionally created. After all, the command is to love your neighbor as yourself—which implies you can't truly love others until you've learned how to love and honor yourself.

One of my favorite things to say is:

"Before you can do, you must become."
Because who you are shapes how you serve. Identity precedes impact.

CHAPTER 6

I once read an inscription that has stayed with me:

> "Your life is a gift from God to you. What you become is your gift back to God." —Unknown

Let's explore how to unwrap that gift—you—and begin living from the inside out.

START WITH THE END IN MIND: DESIGNED FOR DOMINION

The **Bible, our manual,** is about **a King, His Kingdom, and His Kids (His children).** That's right—you are part of this grand picture as **His child.** You are just as important in **His divine plan** and the **greater purpose** behind the creation of the earth.

Isaiah 45:18 (paraphrased) reminds us: "Earth was not created to be empty, but to be inhabited with people." That means **us—His children, His ambassadors.**

God did not place us on earth just to wait for the afterlife. He established His Kingdom **through us, His representatives,** to bring His will, His order, and His purpose into reality. We are His **agents, His ambassadors**—tasked with manifesting His will **on earth as it is in heaven** (Matthew 6:10).

It's time to shift our focus from merely anticipating the "**sweet by and by**" to fully embracing our **responsibility in the "sour here and now."** The earth and the world, with its real problems, needs **you—an empowered agent of God's Kingdom, a True World Changer.**

We, through our unique identities, must become specific problem-solvers on earth. By looking attentively into the perfect law of liberty—which is our manual, the Bible—we can discover who we are meant to be and remain steadfast in our unique assignments. We are not to be forgetful hearers but active doers of the Word. Then, as James 1:23-25 affirms, **we will be blessed in what we do.**

As God's ambassadors, we have a divine responsibility to establish His will on earth. The Bible, as the instruction manual—reveals the Creator's full intent and His unchanging purpose. When we find our "why" and embrace it fully, we unlock the fullness of our calling.

Within us resides the greater One (1 John 4:4)—untainted by insecurities, fears, or doubts. Yet, these very things often become obstacles, causing delays and setbacks in fulfilling our assignments and purpose. It is time to rise above them and step boldly into our divine mandate—to influence, impact, and bring transformation as representatives of God's Kingdom on earth. The reason for this book.

By seeking God's Kingdom, we are discovering His true intent for the earth. His intent, purpose, and will (all synonymous) must be our priority if we want to experience true fulfillment and see things work as they were designed to. That is why, when Jesus—the Son of God—taught His disciples to pray, He said:

> **"You should pray like this: Our Father in heaven, help us to honor Your name. May Your Kingdom come; may Your will be done on earth as it is in heaven" (Matthew 6:9-10, paraphrased).**

Heaven is not lacking the rule, reign, and royalty of the King—earth is. That's why you are here—to do your part, make your mark, and advance His Kingdom. This is the privilege God has given us! Let's go and take this thing by force!

> **We're not here to take part; we're here to take over" - Conor McGregor**

CHAPTER 6

God's purpose overrides every plan we may have. That is why we must prioritize the reason for which we were created above everything else. Jesus Himself placed His life assignment above even physical needs. He understood exactly why He was sent to earth, saying:

> "My food," said Jesus, "is to do the will (purpose) of Him who sent Me and to finish His work" (John 4:34, NIV).

When we find and embrace our purpose, we, too, will be able to passionately and enthusiastically complete our assignment. Just as Jesus put His work before meals, we will become so engaged in our calling that the momentum will cause us to even forget to eat or drink—fully immersed in the fulfillment of why we were sent to earth.

When we understand the ultimate objective — to bring the culture of the Kingdom to the ends of the earth — we can work backward from that vision. By aligning ourselves with the Great Commission, we return to our true identity and purpose and then move forward intentionally to fulfill the mission.

Keep the end in mind.
Every king desires to expand his influence into foreign territories—and **God is no different**. As citizens of His Kingdom, we are not just saved to sit—we are **sent to represent**. That means you are called, and already equipped, to extend His influence in a specific, unique area through your gifting.

Sometimes, **having the end in mind**—knowing that you were created to produce fruit, to do good works, and to expand God's rule—helps you get properly equipped for the task.

It aligns your preparation with your purpose.
It keeps your development connected to your destiny.

BEYOND THE HUSTLE

You were made for more than survival—you were made for **impact**.

Again, Let Your Work Speak

Jesus said:

> "In the same way, let your light shine before others, that they may see your good works and glorify your Father in heaven" (Matthew 5:16, ESV).

It is through our work—our God-given assignment—that we influence others. Before we even speak to people about this awesome God, try to first fully embrace our unique calling. When we do, our influence becomes effortless rather than forced. When we discover our life's work, our actions will always speak louder than our words. We won't just talk—we'll operate from a place of substance, where our work itself carries weight and influence.

I understand that this world comes with challenges, obstacles, and setbacks. But the key to overcoming them and solving real problems is discovering your niche—your work. Now we will learn to play our part toward a better world.

This is what I intend to help you do through this book: ignite a hunger within you to seek, discover, and pursue your purpose relentlessly. Your work is tied to your passion—the thing that makes you come alive.

Stay hungry. Stay committed. Keep pressing forward. Step fully into your calling, and you will impact the world as God intended, many times in ways you never dreamed of.

> **"Work is not somewhere you go, but it's a combination of who you are and what you do. You can take this with you to a job setting." - RAH.**

CHAPTER 6

THE TRIPLE D EVALUATION

(Your Desire, Design, and Distinction)

DESIRE: Your Original Wiring

"The starting point of all achievement is desire."
– Napoleon Hill

Interest & Desire are not synonymous. One can come from culture, peer pressure, parents, etc. You can have an interest in something, but not really desire it. Desire is inherent. We need to study it. When it comes to desire, many people are educated out of theirs, like when a young person is educated out of their dreams through the norms in their society or household. These norms can usually turn them into people-pleasers. Society is not designed to enhance your God-given dreams and desires. That's why we call this process "self-discovery." You must discover yourself by going against all unauthorized currents, which include the opinions of others. One way to do this is to tap into your deep desires. Start by asking yourself, "What do I want out of life?" Take time to dream, reflect, ponder and imagine where you'll be most fulfilled in life.

I like to call our deepest desire a pulsating desire or "natural wiring." In other words, you don't have to force what you came into this world to do. You just need to tend to it and mind it like it's your very own business. You came into this world with what you were naturally assigned to do. You give birth to it. You are WIRED for it. Your purpose is as close to you as your deepest desires, constant ideas, persistent thoughts, and reoccurring dreams. Study your desires.

Connecting to your Source who is God, will only bring you right back to His original intent for your life, which is also what you want or desire to do. All we must truly do is align ourselves properly by what King David stated centuries ago, "***Delight yourself***

in the Lord, and He will give you the desires of your heart" ***(Psalm 37:4 ESV),*** Our greatest pleasure comes when we are connected to our Source. The experience just brings out what is naturally in us, without external interferences. It's a combination of Delight + Desire = Destiny.

THE MANUFACTURER (GOD) IS COMMITTED TO YOUR DESIRE.

When we **delight in God** and take responsibility to **work out our own salvation**—as Philippians 2:12 instructs—we're not left to figure it all out alone. The very next verse, **Philippians 2:13**, reminds us that **God Himself empowers us**, giving us both the **desire** and the **ability** to live (act) according to His good purpose.

This means it's not merely about human effort—it's a divine partnership.

God is working in us as we work with Him. This partnership enables us to live in alignment with His will—which is exactly what we were purposed for.

That's why it's so important to **align with your inner, God-given desire**—that deep, pulsating pull in your soul. It's not random. It's how you were wired by your **Manufacturer**. Your desires, when surrendered to Him, often point directly toward your design and destiny.

Here are two versions of this same passage:

> **"For it is God who works in you to will and to act in order to fulfill his good purpose." (NIV)**

> **"For God is working in you, giving you the desire and the power to do what pleases him." (NLT)**

CHAPTER 6

A modern way to say this could be:

"God is imprinting His truth within us, aligning our hearts with His will (what He already intended) and planting His desires deep within our souls."

This reflects the biblical concept found in Jeremiah 31:33 (ESV):

> *"For this is the covenant that I will make with the house of Israel after those days, declares the Lord: I will put my law within them, and I will write it on their hearts. And I will be their God, and they shall be my people."*

This is also why it's so important to raise, train, and encourage children in the way they should go—according to their original wiring, not ours as parents. Our role isn't to project our dreams onto them, but to help them discover who God created them to be.

They should begin from the right starting point—aligned with what excites them, not what satisfies us. Because when a child is nurtured in their natural design, they're more likely to grow into a life of purpose, not pressure.

> **Start children off on the way they should go and even when they are old, they will not turn from it. (Prof 22:6 NIV).**

Identifying God's purpose through the desires of your heart requires aligning your passions, gifts, and convictions with His divine will. Here's a practical approach to discovering your God-given purpose through your desires:

1. Delight Yourself in the Lord

   "Take delight in the Lord, and He will give you the desires of your heart." (Psalm 37:4, NIV)

This verse doesn't mean God grants every wish, but rather that as you seek Him, He shapes your desires to align with His purpose, will or intent. Your deepest, most fulfilling desires often reflect the calling He has placed in you.

2. Identify What Stirs Your Passion

- What excites you?
- What problems in the world do you feel deeply burdened with to solve?
- What makes you come alive when you engage in it?

One of my favorite quotes is **"Don't ask what the world needs. Ask what makes you come alive and go do it. Because what the world needs is people who have come alive." — Howard Thurman**

Your God-given passion is often a clue to your purpose.
I like to call it *the fuel of your intent.* It's that inner fire that keeps you moving—not just for your own fulfillment, but for something greater.

When you pursue the **right desires**—those aligned with how God wired you—they won't just bring you personal joy; they'll also **serve others well** and **bring glory to God**.

> **"Your time is limited, don't waste it living someone else's life. Don't be trapped by dogma — which is living with the results of other people's thinking. Don't let the noise of others' opinions drown out your own inner voice. And most important, have the courage to follow your heart and intuition. They somehow already know what you truly want to become."**
> **- Steve Jobs**

CHAPTER 6

3. Examine Your Inner Strengths and Gifts

   God equips us for our calling. The talents and skills you have aren't random—they are tools for fulfilling your purpose. That is also why when you use them in a regular job setting you work more enthusiastically for that employer. When you are faithful in serving another person's vision, you're being prepared to lead in your own domain. This is why I believe that even in a job setting—whether or not it's your "dream job"—you can still show up with inner enthusiasm and serve wholeheartedly, as unto the Lord.

Because ultimately, you're not just working for people—you're training for purpose.

> "Whatever you do, work at it with all your heart, as working for the Lord, not for human masters." (Colossians 3:23, NIV)
>
> **"We have different gifts, according to the grace given to each of us." (Romans 12 :6, NIV)**

What comes naturally to you? What do others affirm about you? Often, the work you were created to do is connected to the abilities and strengths God has already given you.

Remember that God's gifts and his call are irrevocable. (Romans 11:29 NIV). Irrevocable means it is FINAL. You are not to be changed, reversed or recovered… Therefore, learn to be true to your innate desires and you will not be disappointed. Also, others often recognize it in you.

4. Pay Attention to Open Doors & Opportunities

   God often guides through circumstances. When you move in alignment with His will, you'll notice opportunities that push you toward your purpose. When you become true to yourself in accordance with your innate desires the most unusual things will begin to happen. I refer to these as divine alignments or appointments. They occur more frequently as you draw closer to your delight and desire. As we delight in God, He works in harmony with our desires, bringing about these meaningful connections and opportunities.

That is why the wise King Solomon said, **"A man's gift makes room for him and brings him before great men." (Proverbs 18:16, NASB).*

Another translation would say, "ushers" or "gives access." Also, notices the words, "opens doors" and "opens the way".

> *"A man's gift <u>opens doors</u> for him and **brings him** before great men." (BSB).*
>
> *"....open doors; It **gives access** to important people! (NLT)*
>
> **"A gift opens the way and ushers the giver into the presence of the great." (NIV)**

Look at these words. They denote that our innate gifts are effortless. I like this last one: To "usher" means to guide, lead, or introduce someone or something into a place or situation. It often implies helping someone transition into a new phase, location, or experience.

This is why one of the chief musicians during the time of King (David) stated, **"For promotion cometh neither from the east, nor from the west, nor from the south. But God...." (Psalm 75: 6, 7a..KJV)**

I believe what we are called to do will introduce us to our place or sweet spot in life, even introduce us to ourselves. It also gives us

CHAPTER 6

access and opens the doors to where we are mostly influential. What you are wired for will eventually usher you to your audience, where you'll make the biggest impact. God is committed to you and to this entire process.

Sometimes, God redirects us by closing doors or making us uncomfortable where we are, prompting us to seek what He truly destined us for. I call this "divine discomfort".

5. Seek Confirmation Through Prayer & Wise Counsel

    Pray and ask God to reveal His purpose through your desires.

    Surround yourself with wise mentors or spiritual leaders who can help confirm your calling, by helping you bring it out.

    "Plans fail for lack of counsel, but with many advisers, they succeed." (Proverbs 15:22, NIV)

6. Take Action in Faith

    Many people wait for a loud voice from heaven, but purpose is often revealed as you step out in faith. Start where you are, use what you have, and God will direct your path.

    "Whatever your hand finds to do, do it with all your might." (Ecclesiastes 9:10, NIV)

Sometimes, we must take steps of faith into God's will according to our inherent wiring, rather than waiting around for something to fall into our laps. We can pray while pacing, as the steps of the righteous—those constantly aligning themselves with God's will—are ordered by the Lord, not by chance or coincidence.

> "The LORD makes firm the steps of the one who delights in him" (Psalm 37:23 NIV)

By delighting in the Lord, our desires—if misaligned—are gently transformed and redirected to reflect His purposes and plans for our lives. When our hearts find joy in Him, He shapes what we long for, guiding us toward the path we were truly created to walk. Delight + Desire = Direction.

When your heart's desires are shaped by God, they will align with His will and lead you to your true purpose. Pay attention to your passions, gifts, and open doors, and move forward in faith.

DESIGN: YOUR WAY

Secondly, we must study our design. A plane has wings because it is intended to fly, so do birds. Fish have fins to swim. That's their natural design. A boat is built with an engine behind it and a hull in front of it. Why? It cuts through water to get from one port to another. You never have to teach a fish to swim; they naturally are good at it. They never went to school to learn though they swim in schools. All of these have natural designs to perform or fulfill their purpose. What's your natural design? What are you naturally good at? What comes easy for you and seems to be harder for others? I call this your way. The way you are is lined up with the way you have been designed to serve and change your world. So, with this, you can take into consideration your ethnicity, background, past experiences, and maybe even your height, weight, and overall size. You can also consider your talents, as well as your natural and spiritual gifts. This again is the way you are. The first is your wiring (synonymous to desire). Now, take some quiet time to ponder and study your design.

When a manufacturer creates a new product, he lets the product's intended use govern the design, function, and nature of the product, so that the fulfillment of its purpose is inseparably built into it. This again confirms that your purpose is inherent.

Many of these natural abilities and capabilities can be seen from childhood. That's why the Wise King Solomon stated, **"Train up a child in the way he should go. And, when he is old, he will not depart from it" (Proverbs 22:6 NKJV)**. I cannot stress this passage enough. It has guided me in helping many people throughout my life and service.

The phrase **"the way he should go"** implies that each child comes with their own unique design and desires—a divine wiring and design that's been placed within them from the beginning. It's our responsibility to study them, encourage them, and instruct them according to that design.

We must not become adversaries of our children's natural makeup by directing them down paths that contradict who they truly are. When we do, we risk suffocating their potential—and in some cases, even crippling the very purpose they were born to fulfill.

The word **"should"** in this context carries weight. It speaks to duty, direction, and what is right—not just from a parent's perspective, but from God's original intent. It isn't about enforcing personal preferences; it's about stewarding a child's God-given path with wisdom and grace.

THE NATURAL DESIGN OF A PLANE AND A BOAT

- A Plane is designed with aerodynamics in mind—its wings create lift, allowing it to rise against gravity. The shape of the fuselage minimizes air resistance, and the engines generate thrust to push it forward. Every part of the aircraft works together to help it defy gravity and soar through the skies.

- A Boat is designed with buoyancy in mind—its hull is shaped to displace water in a way that allows it to float. The design ensures stability and movement through the water, with the rudder and sails (or engines) directing its course. Unlike a plane, which must overcome gravity, a boat works with water to stay afloat and navigate.

These designs show that every creation has an intended function. A plane isn't meant to sail, and a boat isn't built to fly. Their design matches their purpose.

As Paul said in Acts 17:28, "For in him we live, and move, and have our being" (KJV), a truth echoed in other translations as "we live and exist in Him" (NLT) or "we live and move and have our being" (NIV). This verse reminds us that our very life, motion, and existence are sustained by God—He is the source of all life and activity. Nothing we do occurs outside His will or knowledge, and our being is rooted in Him. Speaking to the Greeks in Athens, Paul even connected this truth to their own poets, showing that humanity has always recognized its dependence on a higher power.

How This Applies to Us

If human hands carefully design machines to fulfill a purpose, how much more intentional is God in designing us?

THE NATURAL DESIGN OF FISH AND BIRDS

Just as a bird is designed to fly and a fish is designed to swim, we are each created with a natural purpose that aligns with how we are uniquely made.

- A bird doesn't just have wings—it also has lightweight bones and feathers perfectly suited for flight.

CHAPTER 6

It doesn't struggle to soar through the air, because it was *created* for it.

But if you forced that same bird to live underwater, it would struggle and eventually perish—**not because it lacked value, but because it was placed in an environment that violated its design**

- A fish doesn't only have fins, but gills, and a streamlined body, making it perfectly suited to live and move in water. If you forced a fish to live on land, it would suffocate because it wasn't created for that environment.

Likewise, when we recognize and nurture our God-given design—our talents, gifts, and natural inclinations—we thrive. But when we are forced into roles or lifestyles that go against how we were created, we struggle, just like a bird in water or a fish in the air.

This is why again, **Proverbs 22:6** says, **"Train up a child in the way he should go, and when he is old, he will not depart from it."** Every child has a natural direction and guiding them according to their design leads to fulfillment and purpose. Every child comes pre-wired with a unique path. Our role isn't to create that path, but to help uncover it—guiding them in alignment with how they were divinely designed. **Purpose isn't planted by parents—it's discovered through guidance.** When we raise children according to their natural design, not our personal preferences, we prepare them to walk confidently in who they were created to be.

WE SHOULDN'T DISCARD THESE THINGS ABOUT US: (STUDY ALL)

- Height & Weight – Our physical attributes often shape our abilities. Some are naturally built for strength, speed, or endurance, while others have fine motor skills for precision work.

- Personal Gifts & Personality – Some people are natural leaders, others are caregivers, thinkers, or creators. Our personalities aren't random; they guide us toward the roles we are meant to play.

- Natural & Spiritual Gifts – Our talents, whether in music, teaching, problem-solving, or encouraging others, are tools meant to bless the world. Spiritual gifts, like wisdom, discernment, or faith, equip us to fulfill divine purposes.

- Abilities & Talents – Just as a plane must fly and a boat must float; our talents are clues to where we belong. Some are called to speak, build, serve, or innovate.

- Experiences – Even struggles and trials shape us. A stormy sea makes a skilled sailor. Challenges refine us, teaching perseverance and preparing us for our mission.

Your design is not an accident. Every detail—your strengths, weaknesses, passions, and even hardships—is intentionally woven into your life to direct you toward your God-given purpose. Like a plane built to fly or a boat designed to sail, you were created with a divine mission in mind. Seek it, embrace it, and live it.

EN ENCOUNTER IN NAPLES, FLORIDA

One day, while living in Naples, Florida I walked into a law school near my home. As I walked into the admissions office, I noticed a gentleman and his wife picking up materials with information about the school. I asked if it was for them.

The gentleman answered with a smile and confident look on his face, "No sir! This is for my son."

CHAPTER 6

"Where is he?" I asked. "Why isn't he here picking up this information?"

"He's busy doing other stuff and couldn't make it. We are from Washington," he replied, still with that confident grin that extended ear to ear. "I'm a district attorney, my oldest son is too, and my daughter studied law as well. Now I'm picking this stuff up for my youngest."

Now it was my turn. "What is your daughter studying now?"

As I expected, he replied it was in a different field. "She went back to school to study engineering."

"What about the oldest?" I asked.

"He stayed in law," he replied.

"Is he passionate about law?" I asked. His reply was a yes. "However, is it obvious that it really wasn't your daughter's full passion, since she went back to engineering school? Four years of law and then another three in engineering. Obviously, you seem like a strong and influential dad in your household. Is it possible that your influence is causing you to lead your children in what you want them to become, instead of what they want to do?"

I got to tell you, that spilled out of my mouth with such weight and conviction. I couldn't hold back. His wife looked at me as if I had four heads. She was in awe!

I knew I struck a chord and was onto one of those learning curves, so I continued. "We must be careful. The truth is that your son should be here picking up this information on his own. He is of age, right?"

He nodded as his wife continued to look astonished.

BEYOND THE HUSTLE

This university is a well-known Catholic Law School in SWFL, so I found it fitting to quote this passage from the Bible. I explained to him how it was written:

"Train up a child in the way **HE should go** and when he is old, he will not depart from it." (Proverbs 22:6). I added, "We are to encourage them in their desires and in what excites them, not us. In a household, we are better off with a passionate musician than a depressed dentist so to speak or, in this case, a not-too-passionate lawyer."

I also added, "Sir. Try to be careful because we aren't supposed to impose our will on our children, They don't belong to us. You are a steward of them. They are God's to lead in accordance to their unique design and desires. Have you really taken the time to ask him what he wants our of life?"

I sent him on his way, very deflated. I've been doing this to parents ever since I discovered this message about purpose. Some parents have backed off and have seen their children – teens and young adults – excel, to their amazement.

Some have even sent me pictures of their superstar children, dominating in the sports of their own choosing—some with scholarships, trophies, and championship belts—after I advised them to release their children into the sports correlating to their design and desire. The results are amazing.

Three Children from One Household

I remember speaking on this topic in Deerfield Beach, Florida. As I was teaching, three kids walked into the room. I paused my training and asked, "Whose children are these?" and then, "Who are their parents?"

When a couple raised their hands and said, "We are!"—I began casually sizing them up, just by observing their natural design.

CHAPTER 6

One girl was broad-shouldered, not very tall, and carried herself with dominance—like a runner. The other was tall, slim, and had a slightly athletic build, but still carried the grace of a princess. The boy was short and compact, shaped like a textbook safety or cornerback on the defensive side of a football team. Anything outside of that could have put him at risk.

It was a spontaneous moment, and I felt strongly impressed to speak up. In front of everyone, I said:

"Make sure she's in track!" I repeated it with urgency.
"This one—volleyball.
And this young man? Football. Specifically, safety."

Now, I don't go around doing this all the time—but in rare moments like that, when I feel a strong impression, I speak up.

And the results? Incredible. Within months, both parents sent me photos: these same children were now top athletes in their region of Florida—in the very sports I had mentioned. Two of them even received college scholarships because of it.

I truly believe this: **if you take time to study a child—how they walk, how they're built, how they light up—**you'll begin to see patterns.
What makes them come alive often matches their natural design.

Professional NBA Athletics

I remember seeing a picture of Michael Jordan wearing a Chicago White Sox baseball uniform. He was in the dugout, and something about his posture stood out—he didn't look like he was in his element. In that photo, he looked almost out of place... maybe even a little lost.

Later, I learned the story behind the image:

BEYOND THE HUSTLE

Jordan had switched to baseball after becoming a champion in basketball, following the tragic death of his father in a robbery. His father had often talked with him about dual-sport athletes like Bo Jackson and Deion Sanders, and encouraged him that he had the skills to try something new.

So Jordan stepped away from the game that made him legendary and played one season of baseball.
But eventually, he returned to the court—and shortly after, led the Chicago Bulls to another championship.
It took him seven months to regain his competitive edge. That might not sound long, but when you step out of your lane, it takes time to sharpen your skills again and return to your peak performance.

The lesson?
We do ourselves an injustice if we neglect to study, accept, and commit to our full design.
Yes, we might be able to perform in multiple arenas for a time—but truly embracing the lane we were designed for helps us grow, perfect our gift, and move toward our destiny with greater ease and effectiveness.

1 Corinthians 7:20 NKV states, "Let each one remain in the same calling in which he was called." Stay in your lane and you'll win your game.

Be careful about removing your children from a sport they already dominate.
I've seen horror stories—scenarios where a child was thriving in one sport, only for a parent to pull them out and push them into another, one that typically requires years of early training to master.

The result? Discouragement. Frustration. Missed opportunity.

CHAPTER 6

There's a **special kind of discipline** that a child gains from sports—one that the household alone often can't replicate. Commitment, teamwork, perseverance, emotional resilience—these qualities are forged through competition and cooperation on the field or court.

If you're a single parent, lean on this. Let the team environment help shape what you may not be able to reinforce alone at home. It's not a replacement for parenting—it's a complement to it.

There's tremendous value in sports—so much so that **many major corporations hire based on sportsmanship and team experience** even above GPA. Why? Because **character, drive, and coachability** go a long way in the real world.

NOTHING IS WASTED

In addition to our physical attributes such as height, weight, size, and build, as well as our natural talents and positive experiences, it's essential to acknowledge that our negative experiences should not be overlooked. Our trials can transform into triumph of wisdom, and our struggles can inspire a story with a powerful message.

> «In all these things we are more than conquerors» (Romans 8:37)

This verse signifies that believers in Christ—those who remain closely aligned with their Manufacturer—are not merely victorious over life's challenges, but experience a profound and lasting victory through the power of God working in them, for them, and all around them.

Even in the face of hardship, persecution, or suffering, believers are assured of God's unwavering support, enabling them not just to endure adversity—but to triumph over it.

Our past problems perfect us into our purpose, they help design and shape us as both an arrowhead is polished and its staff prepared to hit its bullseye. King David said in his personal struggle and time of challenge, **"The Lord will perfect that which concerns me; Your mercy, O Lord, endures forever; Do not forsake the works of Your hands." (Psalm 138:8).**

Another translation says it this way,

> **"The LORD will fulfill His purpose for me. O LORD, your loving devotion endures forever— do not abandon the works of Your hands." (Psalm 138:8 BSB)**

You are the work of His hands even in tough times. He's devoted to you and to perfecting what He purposed for your life. His purpose at the end shall stand and prevail even in adversity.

David wrote this psalm as a declaration of God's faithfulness in his life. While the exact historical context is not explicitly stated, we can infer that he was going through a season of challenges, uncertainty, or opposition—yet he remained confident that God would complete His purpose in him. You too must believe that whatever season you are in your life, God is devoted to you and in all things, you too are about to overcome because of His purpose prevailing even in our problems.

Several themes in Psalm 138 suggest that David was:

1. Facing Opposition or Trouble – In verse 7, he acknowledges, **"Though I walk in the midst of trouble, You will revive me."** This indicates that David was experiencing distress, possibly from enemies or personal struggles. Revive means to restore or bring back. That's right, your setbacks always contain hidden qualities to comeback! God will make sure you don't miss a beat in your rhythms of grace.

CHAPTER 6

2. Trusting in God's Purpose – The phrase "The Lord will perfect that which concerns me" shows David's faith that God would bring His plans for David to fulfillment, despite any obstacles. You too must nurture your faith through the whole process of your purpose. Remember that "faith comes by hearing the word of God" (Rom 10:17), so stay connected to the manual, the hand guide, to ensure your full success even through trouble.

3. Depending on God's Mercy – He recognizes that God's mercy and devotion to his process is everlasting, meaning that even in his failures or difficulties, he trusts that God will remain faithful to his purpose. Did you mess up in your past? Are you a victim of very deep hurt in your past? Even these will not be wasted.

4. Seeking God's Continued Presence – When he prays, "Do not forsake the works of Your hands," he is asking God to remain with him, to continue shaping his life according to His divine plan.

Possible Contexts in David's Life during this time:

This psalm could have been written during one of several key moments in David's Journey:

1. While fleeing from Saul – When David was on the run, waiting for God to fulfill His promise of making him king, he had to trust that God would "perfect" (complete) what He started even while the person he was submitted to hated him and become his arch enemy.

2. During battles as king – David often faced war, betrayal, and rebellion (even from his own son, Absalom). In such times, he would have needed assurance that God was still in control.

3. In reflection of his life – David may have written this psalm later in life, looking back on God's faithfulness and trusting that God would continue His work in him.

One thing to know is that life is a cycle of tests. Your process of leadership development is lifelong. Just as David trusted God to complete His work despite trials, tribulations, troubles, and test we too can hold onto this promise: God will finish what He started in us (Philippians 1:6). Even when life feels uncertain, when we face failures or hardships, we can rest in the truth that God is still at work, bringing His purpose for us to fulfillment.

One more thing to see in these passages: "Though I walk in the midst of trouble, thou wilt revive me: thou **shalt stretch forth thine hand** against the wrath of mine enemies, and **thy right hand** shall save me. The Lord will perfect that which concerneth me: thy mercy, O Lord, endureth forever: **forsake not the works of thine own hands**." (Psalm 138:7-8 KJV).

We are the works of His hand. You must believe this. Even in trouble, past or present, and of course future because the same God that was with you in the past will be your very present help in times of trouble.

Accept the fact that your deepest past hurts will be used to better the generation you live in now — and the ones that follow. No matter how deep or painful your scars are, He will revive you, make you live again or enable you to emerge once again with LIFE, and revenge is not yours to seek against those who hurt you. God has the final say, and **He will stretch forth His hand against the wrath of your enemies**. Let go and let God! Remember, the purpose of God includes His promise to save you from every situation and never to forsake you, no matter what you have been through. **He will not abandon the work of His hands**. His right hand is stretched out to save you and His left hand to fight for you, and both of His hands (plural) will continually be working in and on you. You are covered in

CHAPTER 6

every situation, because the purpose God placed within you is so important that it will far outlive your pain, your past, and even your temporary pleasures. He will perfect that which concerns you, His purpose.

Purpose will always prevail.

DISTINCTION: YOUR WORK (TRUE WORSHIP)

When you discover YOU, you'll never feel the need to compare yourself with anyone else.
You'll realize there is only one you. Distinction is the contrast that sets similar things—or people—apart. Even with over 8 billion people on the planet, no two are exactly alike. We are each unique by design.

Distinction is a revelation of your authenticity.
I call this our true work—or true worship. It's the expression of our uniqueness, the mannerisms and traits we already possess, used to give meaningful recognition to our Creator.

Remember: we are each uniquely, miraculously, and wonderfully made.

When I speak of worshiping our Creator, I also mean serving others and the world in a way that honors Him. True worship involves becoming who you were created to be—for the benefit of others. It starts with accepting who you areand choosing to use your full self to inspire, encourage, influence, motivate, and ultimately serve the world around you.

Keep in mind the main goal, objective and mission: Make students (disciples) from all nations.

*"**Whatever you did for one of the least of these brothers and sisters of mine, you did unto me" (Matthew 25:40 NIV).***

This powerful truth reveals that worship is not limited to singing songs or attending services—it includes how we treat and serve others. Every person carries a unique gift, and when that gift is sharpened, refined, and developed, it becomes a tool to impact others—especially within your generation. Our calling is twofold: we serve **vertically**, offering our lives and gifts to God, and **horizontally**, by using those same gifts to serve and uplift one another.

WE SERVE BOTH HORIZONTALLY (EACH OTHER) AND VERTICALLY (GOD).

> **"Your worship and your work are deeply intertwined, both serving as expressions of your individuality. True fulfillment comes when your gifts, passions, and purpose align, allowing your work to become an act of true worship—a task rendered unto God for the benefit of others. In this fusion, you step into the fullness of who you were created to be, not only honoring God but also enriching the world around you. "The King will reply, 'Truly I tell you, whatever you did for one of the least of these brothers and sisters of mine, you did for me." (Matthew 25:40 NIV).** After all this is why we were created. *"For we are his workmanship, created in Christ Jesus for good works, which God prepared beforehand, that we should walk in them" (Ephesians 2:10 ESV).*

This workmanship—our unique design and purpose—was prepared beforehand by God for good works (Ephesians 2:10). Walking in these good works means living authentically, aligned with who we were created to be. To walk, work, and worship in harmony forms a threefold cord that cannot be easily broken. This divine rhythm connects our daily steps, our purposeful

CHAPTER 6

labor, and our heartfelt devotion into a life fully lived according to God's intent.

> **When men SEE this they are drawn to the Source. His Light Shed on Your Good Works makes Others want to Connect. (Matt. 5:16 paraphrased)**

Manifesting what's within us is what gives us authenticity.

To be authentic means: 1. to become one's true self. 2. to manifest or express one's true self. 3. to be true to oneself or live in alignment with one's purpose.

Most people are living unauthorized (not them) lives - being someone they were never meant to be.

Don't fail to ask yourself: "Was I created to do this?" (Whether in jobs, activities, or life choices.)

WONDERFULLY MADE AND HIS WONDERFUL WORKS:

> "I praise you because I am fearfully and wonderfully made; your works are wonderful; I know that full well." (Psalm 139:14 NIV)

When is says, "your works are wonderful," it means:

> "Works" refers to everything God has created — including the heavens, the earth, humanity, and specifically you as an individual with a purpose.
>
> "Wonderful" here doesn't just mean "nice" or "pretty"; in Hebrew thought, it carries the sense of something

extraordinary**, **marvelous**, **beyond human ability** or **understanding.

So, when David says, "your works are wonderful," he's acknowledging that God's creation — especially the creation of each human being — is full of awe, purpose, and divine intentionality.

David got a revelation of his authenticity and uniqueness! You can too by being still and studying yourself as God's workmanship. In this context, David is not only admiring the universe but also recognizing himself as one of God's magnificent works. He's expressing deep gratitude and amazement that God made him with care, detail, purpose, and beauty — not by accident or mistake.

In other words:

"His works are wonderful" means everything God creates, including you, is extraordinary, intentional, and worthy of honor and awe. It'll be magnificent if we all got a glimpse or a revelation like this of ourselves.

YOUR TRUE WORK FROM THE BOOK OF ROMANS

Let's consider the counsel of the first-century writer and leader, Paul, to the believers in Rome. He begins by saying:

> *"Therefore, I urge you, brothers and sisters, in view of God's mercy, to offer your bodies as a living sacrifice, holy and pleasing to God— this is your true and proper worship." (Romans 12 :1, NIV)*

CHAPTER 6

This passage provides valuable insight into how we are wired to worship and work. Notice that Paul emphasizes offering ourselves—our entire being—as a living sacrifice. This suggests that worship is not just about songs or rituals but about a life surrendered to God.

The easiest way to begin this process is through quiet time dedicated to self-discovery, which requires sacrifice. The word sacrifice means to put to death or to slaughter. This implies that we must put to death anything that hinders our true worship (our authentic self)—such as pride, fear, and slothfulness (including procrastination).

THE HIDDEN TREASURE IN THE DIRT

Imagine a farmer walking across his field when his plow strikes something hard. Curious, he stops and digs a little. Beneath the dirt, he discovers the corner of an old, buried chest. The chest is not shining or beautiful at first — it's covered in layers of hardened mud, dust, and years of decay. It takes hours, even days, of careful digging, scraping, and cleaning just to reveal what's inside. But when the dirt is finally removed, he finds treasures more valuable than he ever imagined — gold, jewels, priceless artifacts.

The treasure was always there.

It didn't lose its value because of the dirt.

But the layers had to be removed to see its true worth.

Even so," **But we have this treasure in earthen vessels, that the excellence of the power may be of God and not of us." (2Cor 4:7).**

In the same way, life's experiences, wounds, failures, and wrong beliefs often bury the true version of ourselves — the version God originally designed. Returning to our true, authentic self in Christ takes patience, surrender, and a willingness to let God, the Master Potter, gently remove what doesn't belong. Only then does our true worth shine through, just as it was meant to from the beginning.

Isn't it interesting how much effort it takes just to return to our true, authentic self—the person God created us to be? To discover this, we must intentionally set aside time for reflection, growth, and alignment with God's purpose.

How do we do this? Let's continue reading Paul's advice to the believers in Rome.

"Do not conform to the pattern of this world but be transformed by the renewing of your mind. Then you will be able to test and approve what God's will is – his good, pleasing and perfect will" (Romans 12 :2 NIV). This journey of self-discovery requires reeducating (reprogramming) ourselves or as Paul states, "Renewing our minds."

The prefix "re-" in English generally conveys the meanings "again" or "back." In the case of the word "renew," the prefix aligns with the meaning "again." The term "renew" originates from the Middle English renewen, which combines "re-" (meaning "again") with "newen" (meaning "to make new"). Thus, "renew" essentially means **"to make new again."** Thus, a born-again experience.

"Do not conform to the pattern of this world but be transformed by the renewing of your mind."

Also, the term "renewing" is derived from the Greek word anakainōsis, which signifies a process of making new again or renewal. In this context, "renewing" does not imply returning to a previous state but rather undergoing a continuous transformation

CHAPTER 6

toward a new, divinely inspired way of thinking. This transformation involves aligning one's thoughts and attitudes with God's will, moving away from worldly influences.

Therefore, in Romans 12:2, "renewing" emphasizes an ongoing process of spiritual growth and transformation, leading believers toward a mindset that reflects God's purposes, rather than reverting to a former state.

The biblical phrase "if any man be in Christ" is from 2 Corinthians 5:17, stating that if someone is united with Christ, they are a new creation, with the old things having passed away and all things becoming new.

The word renew entails **going back to the original intent for which we were created**.

Remember that God is a God of Purpose. He didn't revamp his original purpose for earth and mankind upon sending His Son Jesus to us. No. He came to restore what He originally had intended. Man lost dominion and Christ came to restore dominion. The finished work on the cross was to give us back what we lost.

> **"Then Jesus came to them and said, "All authority in heaven and on earth has been given to me. Therefore, go and make disciples of all nations, baptizing them in the name of the Father and of the Son and of the Holy Spirit, and teaching them to obey everything I have commanded you. And surely, I am with you always, to the very end of the age." (Matthew 28: 18-20)**

And now we have the mind of Christ, our true identity and mandate: "…for,**"Who has known the mind of the Lord**

**so as to instruct him?" But we have the mind of Christ."
(1Cor 2:16 NIV)**

What God has started, He will complete until the very day of Christ. However, we must intentionally find time to return to the center of the Potter's wheel, where His power can make us brand new—smashing thoughts and strongholds (mindsets) that are already present, and starting afresh. Returning to the distinct person we were created to be—before the world's systems and society educated us out of it—requires that we refuse to conform to them. We are not to accept or be shaped by the unauthorized opinions of others.

Only then can we experience, through self-discovery, who we truly are—or were intended to be—in accordance with the intent (or will) of the Maker, who created us for good works before the foundation of the world. That person is the one we must tap into. It requires courage and the willingness to stand against both internal fears and external peer pressure. Taking a stand and fixing our faces like flint—determined to make this possible—will ensure that we are neither confounded nor ashamed. It is possible to get it right in the face of so much adversity. It's you against the world.

The phrase "greater is he that is in you, than he that is in the world" from **1 John 4:4** (KJV), emphasizes that the power of God residing in believers is greater than the power of the world and its evil influences. You got this but must do your part to come apart and renew your minds.

"As a man thinks in his heart so is he." This very important saying **"as a man thinks in his heart, so is he" (Proverbs 23:7)** means that a person's character and actions are a reflection of their inner thoughts and intentions. It emphasizes the importance of inner values and beliefs over outward appearances. In essence, a person's true nature is revealed through

CHAPTER 6

their thoughts, feelings, and motives, not just their behavior. So, we must start from the inside out by positioning ourselves.

I remember clearly in 2010 when I parted ways with the fitness industry, where I had spent the last seven years. What a time that was. I truly enjoyed every day of that season in my life. I had found my niche after returning from my missionary experience (1995–1998) in Trinidad and Tobago — another extraordinary 3½ years filled with learning, development, and deep, life-shaping experiences. It was after this season that I transitioned into the fitness world.

But now that chapter was complete. I parted ways with a company I had worked for for 7 years. I desperately wanted to know what the next phase had in store for me. Sensing the importance of this transition, I chose to retreat into a private setting to find myself and to seek clarity for my new assignment. I have always believed in properly graduating from every phase of life, making it my goal to never leave a season of education prematurely.

Determined, I drove 3½ hours to my friend's condo in Central Florida, setting my heart like flint — fully resolved that I would not leave confused, confounded, or ashamed. I anchored myself in the truth of **Isaiah 50:7**, which says, **"For the Lord God will help Me; therefore, shall I not be confounded: therefore, have I set My face like a flint, and I know that I shall not be ashamed."** To "set your face like flint" means to be unwavering and resolute in your purpose, even in the face of uncertainty and adversity, just as the Servant of the Lord had done in that passage.

There is always a divine partnership: God has His part — He is devoted — and we have ours — we must be determined. We must sacrifice time, get away from distractions, and become resolute, almost demanding to know His will, which is always good, pleasing, and perfect for our next season of life.

In this spirit, I made a personal vow: I would not eat until I received a revelation or a "download" from heaven regarding my next steps. To my amazement, within just 30 minutes, answers began to flow. I saw passage after passage, especially from the book of Romans.

Throughout my missionary years in Trinidad and Tobago, Guyana, and Jamaica, I had been diligent in studying the scriptures and theology. No matter where I lived, I made it a discipline to memorize Scripture. Yet it wasn't until this pivotal moment — when I received the revelation of my purpose and assignment for the next phase of my life — that the Scriptures I had long quoted came alive in a fresh, powerful way. They aligned with the vision God was showing me for the rest of my journey. It was breathtaking.

One particular verse that stood out was **Romans 8:28:**

> *"And we know that in all things God works for the good of those who love Him, who have been called according to His purpose."*

The downloads I received made perfect sense. Everything I had walked through — the training, the transitions, the passions — was being woven together by God for my good and His greater purpose. My identity, assignment, and future became undeniably clear. It was a moment I will never forget.

This was now a combination of both the scripture and its application. The principal thing in life is not just the knowledge, but the application - wisdom. Because knowledge doesn't fulfill, it only puffs up if not combined with understanding and then applied.

No wonder King Solomon said, *"Wisdom is the principal thing; Therefore, get wisdom. And in all your getting, get understanding." (Proverbs 4:7 NKJV)*

CHAPTER 6

The Apostle Paul stated in **1 Corinthians 8:1:**

"Knowledge puffs up, but love edifies."

While knowledge can be empowering, its true value emerges only when it is understood and applied effectively. As Francis Bacon is often quoted, "Knowledge itself is power." However, knowledge becomes truly powerful when it is comprehended and utilized appropriately. When applied effectively, knowledge not only empowers the individual but can also be shared and multiplied, benefiting others and leading to collective growth.

True effectiveness is when knowledge is tied to the true purpose of a thing.

At that time, I even got my purpose or mission statement: *"Firing People up to Pinpoint and Pursue Their Purpose."*

I believe that a mission or purpose statement that one makes up for themselves personally can help them state the course for their life assignment. If you get one write it down and take it seriously.

> **"Growth attracts the right guide. Mentors don't create your purpose—they recognize and affirm what God already deposited in you."**

FROM BEYOND HALFTIME TO FULL ASSIGNMENT: LIVING WITH INTENTIONAL PURPOSE IN YOUR SECOND WAVE

So much transpired during that revelatory moment. I wrote earlier that I saw two numbers, but I wasn't sure how to organize them. At first, it seemed impossible to place the higher number before the lower one. The numbers I saw were 8 and 9. I initially planned to leave them in that order, but something didn't sit right with me. I felt uneasy—like I was trying to force a round peg into a square hole.

It just didn't fit.

Shortly afterward, I had a lunch meeting with my mentor at the time, along with another individual—the founder of a very successful ministry (organization) in Estero, Florida. It was truly a divine connection. I vividly remember him handing me a book written by his friend, Bob Buford, titled Beyond Halftime. The timing couldn't have been more perfect. I was 41 years old at the time.

Forty is halftime—a point of reflection and realignment. Forty-one marked the beginning of my second half, a time to try and get it right.

Our conversation was absolutely edifying. Somewhere in the middle of it, I shared my experience in Central Florida and the numbers 9 and 8—or 8 and 9—that I had seen. He briefly clarified that the correct order wasn't the second one I mentioned, but the first: 9 and 8.

He explained that 98% of humanity doesn't know their purpose. In that moment, I felt a deep confirmation. A wave of peace came over me, affirming that he was right on target—and that I would never have to question that experience again. It was crystal clear.

Our conversation about the book and my personal revelation was deeply impactful, especially because I was 41 years old at the time. I recognized it as the beginning of a significant second wave of life—a season focused on meaning, purpose, and giving back.

CHAPTER 6

In his book Halftime: Moving from **Success** to **Significance**, Bob Buford introduces the concept of "halftime" as a pivotal transition period in midlife. This phase serves as an opportunity for individuals to pause, reflect on their achievements during the first half of life, and intentionally plan for a more meaningful and purpose-driven second half.

Buford emphasizes that while the first half of life often centers on attaining success—measured through career advancement, financial gain, and personal accomplishments—the second half should focus on significance. This shift involves seeking deeper fulfillment by aligning one's efforts with personal values, passions, and a desire to contribute positively to others and society.

Not from this book, but a while after I got my vision statement. It was a long one, but went hand in hand with who I was and I embraced it: "Helping Competent Leaders Discover Themselves, Their Value, and Fulfill Their Personal Purpose, In Order For Them to Go Back into Their Sphere of Influence and Impact It With The Right Message in the Right Method."

While Halftime introduces the idea of this transition, Beyond Halftime, his other book, serves as a companion guide, offering deeper insights.

In Beyond Halftime Buford emphasizes the importance of self-reflection and listening to one's inner voice to navigate this phase effectively. He encourages readers to slow down and truly engage with their heart's desires and life's rhythms, suggesting that such intentional reflection is crucial for discovering and pursuing a meaningful legacy.

- The role of silence and prayer in personal growth.

- Strategies for giving that yield meaningful results.

By addressing these areas, Buford aims to guide individuals toward a fulfilling and impactful second half of life, moving beyond mere success to a life of lasting significance.

"From Drift to Destiny: Lessons Sparked by *Outwitting the Devil* and the Pursuit of a Purposeful Life"

Later, I was introduced to an experience from a book written by another gentleman called "Outwitting the Devil".

In Napoleon Hill's Outwitting the Devil, he presents a fictional dialogue where the 'Devil' asserts control over 98% of people, labeling them as 'drifters'—individuals who lack definitive purpose and direction in life. Conversely, the remaining 2% are described as 'non-drifters' who have discovered their definite purpose and actively pursue it with determination and focus. Hill emphasizes that overcoming fear and procrastination is essential for transitioning from drifting to purposeful living.

I couldn't believe it when I listened to this book while exercising in Fort Lauderdale. It confirmed 100% everything I've seen in my experience in 2010. Even the verbiage in the book aligned with my revelation. There I have it! I'm sure of my message, my identity, my purpose, and my vision in life after halftime.

Did you know that Napoleon Hill wrote Outwitting the Devil in 1938, but due to its controversial content, the manuscript remained unpublished for several decades. It was eventually released to the public in June 2011, with annotations by Sharon Lechter. I listened to it on 3/20/20.

"A mentor is not always someone you meet; it can be someone whose book you read or whose life you study." (Roberto Hernandez)

CHAPTER 6

CONTINUING FROM THE BOOK OF ROMANS: (PART 2)

Paul goes on to say even more, *"For by the grace given me I say to every one of you: Do not think of yourself more highly than you ought, but rather think of yourself with sober judgment, in accordance with the faith God has distributed to each of you" (Romans12:4 NIV).* We are naturally powerful beings with potential, capabilities, and an amazing intellect, we are to slaughter even our own pride by not thinking too highly of ourselves. Remember, we slaughter Fear, Self-Doubt, Slothfulness, and Pride. Four things that will rob us of our Authenticity.

We aren't better but different, remember that. It is through humility that we emerge to our unique and authentic true selves. Sober judgment means not to be too full of self.

King Solomon said, *"Let someone else praise you, and not your own mouth; an outsider, and not your own lips" (Proverbs 27:2 NIV).* He's warning us if this distraction.

When we praise ourselves, we can easily fall into pride and *"Pride goes before destruction, a haughty spirit before a fall" (Proverbs 16:18 NIV).* We are only as potent as the Source with which we are connected. Lacking confidence or being overconfident causes us to miss our mark. We must recognize who our Creator is to be confident with what has been instilled in us. That's why Christ Himself said, *"If you remain in me and I in you, you will bear much fruit; apart from me you can do nothing" (John 15:5 NIV).* Pride needs to be slaughtered continually. We find our way to true worship (service) through openness or brokenness. If we are open to these truths (principles), we won't have the need to be broken.

Ultimately, the way we are wired to worship—serving both God and others—becomes the full expression of our self-emergence.

Our purpose is revealed through serving with both our natural and spiritual gifts, as well as through the authentic expression of our unique individuality.

The phrase "fearfully and wonderfully made" from Psalm 139:14 reminds us that we were created in a unique and awe-inspiring way. It affirms that each of us was intentionally designed with distinctiveness and a specific purpose in mind.

I mention natural gifts alongside spiritual ones because we were born with certain abilities—we came into this world already equipped. Once we discover these gifts, we can begin to flow in them naturally. Life becomes easier when we operate in alignment with how we were designed. It feels like second nature.

But discovery is only the beginning. After identifying our gifts, the next step is to develop and refine them. This process of growth prepares us to serve others with excellence.

As Proverbs 18:16 says, "A man's gift makes room for him and brings him before great men." Once our gifts are sharpened, they will usher us—guide us, bring us, and steer us—into the very spaces and among the people we are called to serve.

We all have different functions and if we are to flow in our unique purpose, we'll have to learn how it is done. I go back to the words Jesus spoke, which are best described in the message translation of **Matthew 11:28-30**. I stated it before and it will do us well to read it again, ***"Walk with me and work with me – watch how I do it. Learn the unforced rhythms of grace. I won't lay anything heavy or ill-fitting on you. Keep company with me and you'll learn to live freely and lightly."***

CHAPTER 7

TAPPING INTO YOUR GIFT

"Try not to become a man of success but rather try to become a man of value." – Albert Einstein

Finding your gift is key if you're going to be influential and passionately inspire others toward a noble end. Dr. Myles Munroe taught that when you discover your gift, you're ready to lead—and that it is only through your gift that you can lead smoothly and effectively. This is so true.

Too often, we focus on what the market offers or what appears promising externally. But the real breakthrough doesn't come from what's around you—it comes from what's within you. My advice: don't look outside of yourself for direction. Look within. That's where your gift resides—and that's where true influence begins.

You came into this world already carrying greatness. The journey is to discover what that greatness is.

Greatness means living a life of **significance**, recognizing your **importance**, and embracing your **value**. It's not about fame or status—it's about knowing who you are, why you're here, and how your presence makes a difference.

Remember, ***"God's gifts and his call can never be withdrawn" (Romans 11:29, NLT).*** They are already within you. You've been fully equipped for your assignment.

So seek—and you shall find. But don't seek outwardly. **Look within.** That's where your calling lives. That's where purpose begins.

Your value is the treasure hidden within you. It resides at the core of your being, and it's through this inner wealth that you serve your world and your generation.

I love how Paul described it more than 2,000 years ago: ***"We now have this light shining in our hearts, but we ourselves are like fragile clay jars containing this great treasure. This makes it clear that our great power is from God, not from ourselves" (2 Corinthians 2:7 NLT).***

God makes no mistakes—nor does He change His mind about your calling or your gift. His purpose for you is fixed and intentional.

I love how Paul expresses this same truth in another translation: **"God never changes his mind when he gives gifts or when he calls someone"** (Romans 11:29, GW). No matter where you are in life, His calling still stands—and His gifts are still active within you, waiting to be fully awakened.

He placed it where it is easy for you to find it. Therefore, if you want to be happy, be fulfilled and live-in alignment with your calling, **"Do not strive to be a man of success,"** like **Albert Einstein** said, **"but instead strive to find your value."**

Your gift is your value—but it is also your function. As Scripture reminds us, **"Each person should remain in the calling to which they were called"** (1 Corinthians 7:20).

CHAPTER 7

Just like the members of our physical body are given to us as gifts, each of us has been given spiritual and functional gifts to fulfill our unique role. The books of Romans and 1 Corinthians both teach that these diverse functions are distributed among the members of the body—as gifts, each according to their grace and purpose.

STORY OF A YOUNG MAN SLEEPING IN HIS VAN

A few years ago, I felt a clear prompting to travel from Naples, FL to Orlando. Deep down, I knew it was God nudging me to go—but I wrestled with the idea. I had three very justifiable reasons not to make the trip:

I didn't really know why I was going.

My tires were worn out and needed replacing.

Gas was expensive at the time—about $60 just to fill the tank.

It was a 3½-hour drive, and I did everything I could to avoid it. I convinced myself the timing wasn't right. But then something unexpected happened—my car suddenly stopped on the road, right in the middle of heavy rain.

Naturally, I did what most people would do in a moment like that: I examined myself and began to apologize to God. Deep inside, I already knew the truth—the prompting had come from Him, and I had ignored it. In that quiet, sobering moment, I told God I would leave first thing in the morning—at 6 a.m.

To my amazement, as soon as I finished praying and looked up at my rearview mirror, I saw the roadside attendant standing near my gas tank with a gallon of gas. In that moment, I knew exactly what the problem had been. Overwhelmed with relief and gratitude, I began to weep, recognizing God's hand in such a simple yet profound provision.

BEYOND THE HUSTLE

When I finally reached Orlando, my first stop was a nearby Starbucks. I sat down at a table and began a phone conversation with an associate. We started talking about vision and the importance of discovering our gifts. While I was speaking, I noticed a young man nearby listening intently to every word.

After I hung up, he respectfully approached me and asked if he could have a few minutes of my time. "I live in my van," he said.

In the past, I might have responded with pity—but this time, something different rose in me. I said, "Wow! Almost every millionaire has slept in their car at least once." Then I asked, "How old are you?" He replied, "Nineteen." I looked at him and said, "You're well on your way."

We talked about school, his aspirations, and what he was doing with his life. He then asked if I'd like to see his van. Inside were blankets, a pillow, and a surprising amount of video and camera equipment. I asked him where he ate and showered, and he explained that a kind woman allowed him to park in her yard and use a shower located in a backyard shed.

With his basic needs covered, we continued our conversation about purpose. He shared that listening to my phone call had confirmed everything he'd been feeling inside. I asked, "What is the right path?" He replied with conviction, "My friends and family keep telling me to sell my equipment and get a place to live—but this is my gift. I can't sell my gift. I'd rather sleep in my van and sacrifice comfort than give up what I need to serve the world."

We talked more about his vision, and it was so vivid, I knew school would be necessary to help bring it to fruition. I asked how things were going in that area. He said, "There's one class I just can't pass. I've tried several times, but I keep failing. I guess I'm just not good at that one type of math."

CHAPTER 7

I looked him in the eyes and asked, "What time does the admissions office open at your school?" He said, "9 a.m." I told him, "Be there at 8:30. Sit near the door and tell them, 'I need a tutor, and I can't leave until one is assigned to me.'" I gave him my number and said, "Call me right after. God will open the door for you. This is your time and season."

To my surprise, he called just 30 minutes later while I was on my way to my next stop.

He said, "You won't believe what just happened. Right after we spoke, the owner and CEO of Full Sail University, Gary Jones, walked into the same Starbucks and greeted me—by name! He remembered me from a school event two years ago where we connected over our mutual love for The Chronicles of Narnia."

He continued, "I told him everything I just told you, and to my amazement, he said exactly what you said: 'Meet me at the admissions office at 8:30 a.m., and I'll assign a special tutor to help you.'"

After graduation only months after, Radner Amil stepped fully into his calling—directing films in Puerto Rico. When he sent me pictures and videos of himself working on set, walking in his purpose, I was in awe.

All I could do was praise and thank God. I've shared his story everywhere I go.

Here's what I've learned: God is more committed to your purpose than you are.
All He asks is that you believe—and move forward in faith.

START BY BEING A LEADER IN ONE THING

"The meaning of life is to find your gift. The purpose of life is to give it away." – Pablo Picasso

DEFINITION OF "GIFT" IN ENGLISH:

A gift is something freely given—without strings, expectation, or repayment. Whether it's a physical item, a kind act, or a skill, the principle is the same:

> "...Freely you have received; freely give." (Matthew 10:8)

We all came into this world carrying a unique gift—one that's divinely woven into our calling. It's not random. It's intentional.

The Greek Meaning of "Gift":

In the New Testament, the word gift traces back to the Greek word charis (χάρις), meaning grace—unearned favor.

From charis comes charisma (χάρισμα):

A grace-gift—a divine empowerment given by the Holy Spirit (see 1 Corinthians 12, Romans 12).

These aren't just talents. They are spirit-breathed assignments—meant to build others, serve the Body of Christ, and fulfill your God-given purpose.

> "Your gift is not your own. It's God's grace on your life—given freely, not for your benefit alone, but to serve your generation with something only you carry."

> **"If you can't find your calling, tap into your gift -like an arrowhead, it'll point you straight to it." - RAH**

CHAPTER 7

The gifts and calling of God are without repentance—meaning, God doesn't change His mind about what He's called you to do or what He's already equipped you with (Romans 11:29).

If God has called you, that calling is still active—even if you've ignored it or left it dormant. Just because you haven't stepped into it doesn't mean it disappeared. It may simply need to be stirred up again.

Paul told Timothy to **"fan into flame the gift of God" (2 Timothy 1:6).** Why? Because gifts don't grow cold on their own—they cool when we stop fueling them. The gift is still there, but it needs fire.

The good news? Fire is available. One of Christ's primary assignments was to **"baptize you with the Holy Ghost and fire" (Matthew 3:11)**. Fire represents life, passion, and power—the spiritual fuel to reignite your calling.

Often, you don't need something new—you just need fresh fire to do what you were born to do.

Bored people chase novelty and end up toiling.

Fired-up people stay in their lane—and transform it. Keep in mind that "Boredom breeds busyness, not breakthrough." (RAH).

Bored people can fall into the habit of chasing the next new thing, hoping it will spark something inside. But in the end, they're just toiling. Purpose driven people don't need something new—they just need a fresh fire.

> **"I'm writing to encourage you to fan into a flame and rekindle the fire of the spiritual gift God imparted to you when I laid my hands upon you. For God will never give you the spirit of fear, but the Holy Spirit who gives you mighty power, love, and self-control." (2 Timothy 1:6-8 TPT).**

Tapping into our gift requires us to **narrow things down**. The tendency is to want to do everything—we overload our lives, even our kids' schedules, with multiple activities, sports, and commitments, running all over town.

It's fine to explore and try different things—**especially in seasons of discovery**—but when it comes to purpose, we must learn to **simplify and focus**.

Purpose thrives in clarity, not chaos.
You've got to find your **niche** and stay in your lane.

If not, it becomes easy to slip into the trap of being a **jack of all trades but master of none**. We end up moving through life **experimenting**, but never truly **experiencing** what it means to go deep, grow skillful, and get things done with excellence.

MASTER ONE THING: HOW FOCUS FUELS VISION AND MULTIPLIES IMPACT

If you're in real estate, it's tempting to want every slice of the pie—wholesale, property management, residential sales, commercial, and more. While there's nothing wrong with exposure to different streams, true success comes when you focus on one thing and master it.

I worked for a company that eventually did all of the above—and more. But the visionary behind it, Derek Hovey, founder of Stonebridge Real Estate Group, didn't start that way. He made his first million by focusing exclusively on wholesale properties, working for another company before launching his own. He honed his craft, mastered that niche, and built momentum.

Four years later, he launched a One-Stop Shop, strategically appointing skilled individuals to oversee each department. His motto?

CHAPTER 7

"We've created a system that will make available all the services needed to invest in the Florida Real Estate Market in One Place."

That vision gave rise to multiple departments—wholesale, residential sales, property management, construction, inspections, title, and even marketing. But it all started with mastering just one thing.

When you commit to mastery, it becomes easier to partner with others and expand your vision. Derek once tried sharing his ideas with a former employer, but they couldn't see what he saw. The environment didn't nurture his vision. So he left—and started building.

Afterwards, he did more than he ever imagined, exceeding what he envisioned yesterday.
That's how vision works: it grows in the right environment. It accelerates when it's anchored in your niche. And once it gains momentum, the sky truly is the limit.

"Your Gift Is the Key to Your Niche—And the Foundation of Your Leadership."

Tyler Perry once shared in a YouTube video about his journey, offering a powerful piece of advice: **Do ONE THING.** Focus on that one dream you've held onto all along. From that single focus, other opportunities will naturally branch out—just like a tree.

Think of the tree trunk growing strong and tall as it reaches for sunlight and moisture. That trunk represents your core dream or vision. As it grows, branches sprout—new opportunities and successes emerge from that one foundation.

Tyler's one thing was directing a single play. That was his niche and starting point. Today, he's not only an acclaimed actor and director but also a motivational speaker, author, and producer.

BEYOND THE HUSTLE

All these "branches" grew from that one solid trunk: a clear vision aligned with his niche.

Once homeless, Tyler Perry now leads one of the largest movie studios in the United States. Imagine what nurturing your niche can accomplish.

Opportunities surround us constantly, but what truly matters is where we focus our attention. Focus creates momentum and strength, which fuel persistence, passion, and perseverance.

When you are centered in your gift and purpose, work never feels like just a job—even if it is one. Your niche is where your natural strengths and passions meet—a place where you thrive effortlessly and make the greatest impact.

Here's a clear definition for the word "niche":

Niche (noun)

1. A specialized segment of the market for a particular kind of product, service, or interest.

2. A role, position, or area where someone or something fits naturally or is particularly effective.

3. (Biology) The specific environment or role an organism occupies within an ecosystem.

In simpler terms:

A niche is your unique space—the specific area where you thrive, serve best, or stand out.

> **"There is one quality which one must possess to win, and that is definiteness of purpose, the**

CHAPTER 7

> **knowledge of what one wants, and a burning desire to possess it." – Napoleon Hill**

When we have a definite purpose, we, without a shadow of doubt, can put all our eggs in one basket under this concept. Acquiring knowledge to build on this one undeniable concentration.

This type of focus entails concentration, which is the key that opens the door to fulfillment and true success.

> **"The first law of success… is concentration to bend all the energies to one point, and to go directly to that point, looking neither to the right nor to the left." – William Matthews**

You will never reach or experience your full potential in your work until your priorities become habitual. You must discover what inspires and excites you. You must pour yourself into something you undoubtedly believe in.

GIFT, LEADERSHIP, AND SUCCESS.

Gift is your inherent ability. It is what ultimately brings you true success. When you discover your gift, you won't have to ever toil. The Wise King Solomon said, "***A man's gift makes room for him, and brings him before great men" (Proverbs 18:16 KJV).*** The words, "Makes room for him" denotes, "Procures him free access to great men," or other sources toward success. In Hebrew it means, "Enlarges him." In other words, your gift "frees you from the straits and oppressions; and brings you before great men – procures you favor and free conversation with them" (Benson's Commentary). Another translation, (NIV) states it this way, "A gift opens the way and ushers the giver into the presence of the great."

Discovering one's purpose has more to do with releasing and deploying yourself. It's being prepared to serve your gift at every opportunity. In season and out of it. Most people wait until they have a title, get a promotion, or a degree to fulfill their purpose. You should always better your gift for easier access. Because only your gift, not your title or anything else can take you where grace can.

> **"TRUE LEADERSHIP IS THE CAPACITY TO INFLUENCE OTHERS THROUGH THE DISCOVERY, DEVELOPMENT, AND DEPLOYMENT OF YOUR GOD-GIVEN GIFT FOR THE BENEFIT OF OTHERS."**
>
> **— FROM ME, BUT INSPIRED BY DR. MYLES MUNROE**

True leadership doesn't begin with a title or position, but with a person discovering their gift—something they were born with—and then using that gift to serve and solve problems for others. According to Dr. Munroe, you don't seek leadership; you become it by becoming a person of value through your gift.

Leadership is the result of purpose.
When the purpose of a thing is known, it produces audacity and confidence toward its assignment. **True leadership is not rooted in manipulation, fear, or intimidation—it is the ability to influence through inspiration.** And that inspiration comes from a deep conviction, anchored in a clear vision that flows from knowing your purpose—your why.

To lead means to govern, to exercise authority, and to take dominion—whether over your own life or as you inspire others to move willingly. **Your area of gifting is the true source of your leadership.** It doesn't require toil or striving, because it flows from your God-given design—not from something outside of you. It's not something you chase—it's something you uncover.

CHAPTER 7

Our responsibility is to **develop and refine** our gifts. As we do, those gifts will **usher us into the presence of greatness**, open doors, and lead us into divine opportunities prepared just for us.

When you discover your gift, you unlock the leader within.

Success is **"the accomplishment of an aim or purpose."** That's right—it doesn't mean having lots of money, though that is often a byproduct. True success is accomplishing what you've focused your attention and energy on. You can only be truly successful when you've discovered your purpose.

Most of us have the wrong concept of success, which is why we hustle while chasing it. Remember, **"Being successful in the wrong assignment equals failure."** If you accomplish something you were never given stewardship over, you've done nothing of true value.

I believe that's why **Albert Einstein** said, **"Try not to become a man of success, but rather try to become a man of value."**

HOW TO BECOME A PERSON OF VALUE (F.O.C.U.S)

To become a person of value, we must become significant. Significance means "sufficiently great or important enough to be worthy of attention." In essence, significance places you in high demand. And let's be honest—we all desire that on some level. Anyone who says otherwise may not be fully honest with themselves—or may be operating under a form of false humility.

But here's the Kingdom truth: In God's system, greatness and humility are not at odds—they work hand in hand.

When the disciples sought positions of honor and prominence, Jesus didn't rebuke their desire for greatness—but He redefined it. He taught a countercultural principle:

> **"Whoever wants to become great among you must be your servant, and whoever wants to be first must be your slave—just as the Son of Man did not come to be served, but to serve…" (Matthew 20:26–28, NIV)**

Jesus also made it clear in Matthew 18:3–4 that unless we become like little children—humble, dependent, and trusting—we cannot enter the Kingdom of heaven.

In essence, true greatness in the Kingdom of God is marked by humility, servanthood, and childlike faith.

True significance isn't found in rising above others—it's found in lifting others higher.

HOW THIS RELATES TO US TODAY

Many of us long to be called upon when a specific need arises—to be significant and to make an impact in our generation. That desire is not wrong—it's a sign of purpose awakening within us, a reflection of a need we were uniquely created and equipped to fulfill.

The desire to be great is God-given.
But Jesus reminds us of a kingdom principle: before we can rise, we must bow. Before we can lead, we must learn to serve.

In the Kingdom of God, elevation always follows humility.
Ministry and influence are not about platforms, positions, or power. They are about surrender. They are about washing feet

CHAPTER 7

when no one's watching—not just holding microphones when everyone is.

If we truly want to serve our generation in this hour, we must adopt the posture of children—teachable, trusting, and humble. And we must embrace the heart of servants—willing to give more than we take, and to build others rather than build only ourselves.

As Dr. Myles Munroe often taught, true leadership flows from purpose, and purpose flows from gifting. But gifting is never for self-glorification—it's for the benefit of others.

> **"Whoever wants to be great among you must be your servant." (Matthew 20:26)**

So if you want to be great—good.
But remember: greatness in God's Kingdom always begins with a towel, not a title.

In the Kingdom of God, greatness is not measured by how many people serve you, but by how many people you serve.

You were born to serve your gift to the world—and it is far better to serve than to be served.

> "The greatest among you will be your servant." — Matthew 23:11 (NIV)

When Jesus spoke about becoming a servant—or even a slave—He wasn't speaking about humiliation. He was revealing the secret to influence. A servant is someone who discovers what they were created to do and commits their life to doing it so well, with such consistency and excellence, that they become indispensable. They are, in a sense, **"owned" by their gift**.

That's why Paul could say, "I am a slave to Christ" (Romans 1:1). He was mastered by his purpose.

Desire is proof of purpose.
That inner longing to be significant, to make an impact, to be called upon—that's not pride; it's design. It's the whisper of your assignment calling out to you. But here's the catch: in the world, people chase greatness through dominance. In the Kingdom, **you achieve greatness through service.**

You become so faithful in serving your gift—so consistent in delivering value—that **leadership becomes inevitable.**

Leadership, then, is not a pursuit—it's a byproduct.
You don't have to fight to be seen. You just keep showing up to serve. And eventually, what you carry becomes too powerful to be ignored.

So yes—the desire to be great is God-given.
But it must be purified in the fire of servanthood. Everyone wants to be remembered. Everyone wants to be the first name called. But here's the real question:

What are you willing to give… so that others can live?
That's the true measure of Kingdom greatness.

Therefore, "Whoever wants to become **great** among you must be your servant, and whoever wants to be **first** must be your slave…" (Matthew 20:26–28, NIV)

In order to achieve that, we need to F.O.C.U.S.– Focus on a Concentration Until Successful. Find your niche and make it grow.

When we become specialists in a specific area, we increase our significance in that area. As an example, many general practitioners go back to school to specialize in one thing, like neurology. They believe that getting a specialty in one area makes them more significant and puts them in higher demand. Note the word "demand"—called upon. That's right, many of them

CHAPTER 7

go back to school to relearn. They become specialists through concentration. This is true focus.

To fulfill our purpose effectively, we must be single-minded. Single-mindedness is not a bad thing—neither is narrow-mindedness in this context. To be narrow-minded simply means that one has found not just their niche, but their micro-niche. Concentration on one thing, as stated before, protects us from being the jack of all trades and never mastering anything well. Narrow- or single-mindedness keeps us from wavering in the pursuit of our goals. Finding and focusing on our micro-niche helps us say no more effectively to competing alternatives.

> **"The most successful people have always been those of concentration, who have struck their blows in one place, until they have accomplished their purpose. They are of one specific idea, one steady aim, a single and concentrated purpose." – John Mason**

When we take the time to focus, find our own lane, and drive there, we can become an authority in that area. We become the person who comes to others' minds when they need something specific. That one area is our focus. We were never intended to do it all, but rather to be an important (significant) ingredient in life's whole dynamic.

BACK TO MY WHOLESALE DAYS

I remember a conversation I had with that same visionary of Stonebridge Real Estate Group, —Derek. At a time when I was seriously considering walking away from wholesale real estate, he stopped me in my tracks and simply said, "Think it over."

He told me I was one of the best he'd seen in the business. Very encouraging and definitely not meaning to put myself in a peddle stool, but sometimes someone on the outside must remind us of what we naturally do well. Not because I was the loudest in the room or had all the flashy deals—but because I operated with a kind of ease, instinct, and excellence that couldn't be taught. He saw it.

And that's the thing about gifting—when something comes naturally, when it flows from you effortlessly, it's easy to underestimate its power. It's easy to get restless and look for the next thing. We tend to want to always do, instead of becoming.

I thought about shifting into residential real estate, and I even tried it for a while. But the truth is—it drained me. What gave others energy left me exhausted. The joy, the fire, the spark I had in wholesale just wasn't there. That was the moment I realized: sometimes the key isn't leaving your lane—it's learning how to grow within it.

See, wholesale real estate is the trunk of my tree. It's where my roots run deep. But even from one trunk, many branches can grow. Creativity, innovation, leadership, education, mentorship, partnerships—there are countless ways to evolve without abandoning the soil that nourished you.

What I needed wasn't a new field—I needed a fresh perspective. Maybe I didn't need to jump ship but instead build a bigger one right where I stood.

So now, I don't see wholesale as limiting—I see it as a foundation. A launching pad. A lane I'm not only called to stay in but called to expand. Does this resonate with an area that you are to take by force?

CHAPTER 7

THE WRONG TYPE OF PRIDE

This is why First Century Writer Paul stated, *"Just as a body, though one, has many parts, but all its many parts forms one body... Even so the body is not made up of one part but of many" (1 Corinthians 12:12a,14 NIV).* Every part has a function, and that function benefits the entire organism but only if it stays contently in its own authoritative role – your gift and niche is that role.

Staying under the wrong authority can bring with it a form of pride. The wrong kind of pride can easily infiltrate our hearts and get the best of us. This, ultimately, is one of humanity's greatest downfalls. As I mentioned before, the wise King Solomon stated, **"Pride goes before destruction, a haughty spirit before a fall" (Proverbs 16:18 NIV).**

Sooner or later, what is misaligned will collapse—not because God is cruel, but because He is committed to truth. Many fall not from a lack of desire, but from being in the wrong lane, pursuing a function they weren't graced for. When you move outside of God's will, you are forced to rely on your own strength—and what begins in the flesh must be sustained in the flesh.

And that's not just tiring—it's depleting. Spiritually draining. Soul-wearing.

But there is a better way.

When you align with God's design and surrender to His direction, the burden is light, and the yoke is easy. Your strength is renewed, and your labor becomes worship, not weariness.

Let this be the lesson: Stay in your grace lane. It won't just bless you—it will preserve you.

Remember **Romans 12:3**? It states, "***Do not think of yourself more highly than you ought, but rather think of yourself with sober judgment, in accordance with the faith God has distributed to each of you (NIV)***" Your gifting is your inherent value already placed in you by God, your Source. Staying in your area of gifting makes living easy and our service to our generation lighter and effective. I'm going to repeat Jesus's words once more, because I really need you to get this, ***"...Walk with me and work with me – watch how I do it. Learn the unforced rhythms of grace. I won't lay anything heavy or ill-fitting on you. Keep company with me and you'll learn to live freely and lightly" (Matthew 11:28-30b MSG).***

A man usually thinks of himself more highly than he ought when he steps outside of himself or operates in an unauthorized lane. Why? Because to stay afloat, he must constantly strive to prove himself to feel relevant. But when you're in your area of concentration—operating in your God-given gift—there's no need for pride, because all you're doing is being yourself. When you truly tap into your innate gifting, there's no need to strain or boast; grace carries you.

The Wise King stated, ***"Like clouds and wind without rain is one who boasts of gifts never given" (Proverbs 25:14 NIV).***

"FOCUS YOUR GIFT, SERVE THE WORLD, AND GIVE BACK WITH PURPOSE."

"What a man can be, he must be." – A quote from **Maslow's Hierarchy of Needs.**

This quote forms the basis of the perceived need for self-actualization. This level of need refers to a person's full potential and the realization of that potential. Maslow describes this level as the desire to accomplish everything that one can and to become the most that one can be. He also states that individuals

CHAPTER 7

may perceive or focus on this need very specifically. As an example, one individual may have the strong desire to become an ideal parent. In another the desire may be expressed athletically. As for others, it may be expressed in paintings, pictures, or inventions. Maslow believed that to understand this level of need, the person must not only achieve the previous needs but master them.

In his later years, Maslow explored a further dimension of needs, while criticizing his own vision of self-actualization. The self only finds its actualization in giving itself to some higher goal outside oneself, in altruism and spirituality. That new need was "Self-Transcendence." In other words, when we find our true self, we then conclude that we were all born to leave an impact and legacy. Remember that the word "gift" is a thing given willingly to someone without payment. I believe that this is the principle of the verse that states, ***"Freely you have received; freely give" (Matthew 10:8 NIV).***

The Lord was commissioning His disciples to give from the most valuable treasure they had received directly from Him—the Kingdom of Heaven. You came into this world with God's deposit already within you. The gift you possess was placed inside you from the beginning. These special abilities and capabilities were given so that you could freely offer them in service to others.

The phrase **"It is more blessed to give than to receive"** is found in the New Testament in **Acts 20:35**. Here's the full verse:

> **"In everything I did, I showed you that by this kind of hard work we must help the weak, remembering the words the Lord Jesus himself said: 'It is more blessed to give than to receive.'" (Acts 20:35, NIV)**

Interestingly, these words of Jesus are not found in the four Gospels, yet Paul attributes them directly to Him during his farewell speech to the Ephesian elders. This indicates that the saying was well known among early believers, even if it was never formally written down in Gospel accounts.

Paul went on to make it clear that no one could accuse him of taking more than he gave. As a servant of Christ, he gave himself fully to his calling—pouring out his life not for personal gain, but to serve and strengthen others.

Therefore, our journey doesn't end with simply becoming our full selves. The goal is to become our full selves **for the benefit of others**.

A YOUNG GIRL AT A COFFEE SHOP

As I mentioned earlier in the book, I learned that my primary calling in life is to provoke people to pinpoint and pursue their purpose. I remember working from my laptop at a local Starbucks in Pembroke Pines, Florida, when I struck up a conversation with a 17-year-old girl who was doing her homework.

I asked her what she was studying.

"Nursing," she replied.

Then I asked, "Is this really what you're passionate about?"

Without hesitation—like so many students navigating college under pressure—she said, "No! I actually love education. I always pictured myself teaching children."

So I asked the obvious next question, "Then why are you studying nursing?"

She launched into an explanation filled with all-too-familiar reasons: her parents' influence, her grandma being in nursing,

CHAPTER 7

the promise of higher pay, job security, etc. It's amazing how often we let these external factors dictate what we'll spend four years—or more—studying, even when our hearts are pulling us in another direction.

In that moment, I shared a scenario that came to mind:

"Okay, young lady, hear me out. Let's say you graduate with a nursing degree. After college, you meet the man of your dreams—he's successful, has a great job, and provides well for you and your family. You have children and end up staying home to care for them. Now think about this: you just spent four years preparing for a career you never really wanted, and you may never even use that degree.

Now flip the script. Imagine you follow your passion instead. You pursue education. You become a teacher—someone who is genuinely excited to walk into the classroom every day. Somewhere in your future classroom, a seven-year-old child is sitting at her desk. She's watching you, learning from you. Her home might feel like a living hell—but because you followed your gift, you're becoming a light in her darkness. The only sense of peace and joy she experiences in this season of her young life is when she walks into your classroom. She begins to believe in herself because you believe in her. That same child grows up and makes a profound impact—and you played a pivotal role in shaping her path.

Do you see how honoring your purpose creates a ripple effect that can bless generations?

That's how following your heart makes the next hundred years better. Passion creates provision. Don't let the lure of a slightly bigger paycheck steer you off course. You weren't made to settle—you were made to serve through what you love."

To me, that was just a casual conversation—something I do often, talking purpose with strangers wherever I go.

But a week later, I returned to that same Starbucks to work again—and to my surprise, the same young woman approached me, beaming with excitement.

"Hey! Remember me?"

At first, I didn't, but she reminded me of our conversation.

She said, "The next day, I went straight to the admissions office and changed my major. I told them I couldn't waste any more time. I needed to follow what's in my heart. I'm switching to education."

She continued, "Even though my parents were pressuring me to stick with nursing, I knew I had to listen to that voice inside. After making the switch, it felt like a massive weight had been lifted off my shoulders."

I smiled and said, "I'm proud of you. You won't regret it. Remember the scenarios I gave you—the husband, the family, the child in the classroom. Maybe not all of it plays out exactly that way, but the point is: we don't need to know the full picture. We're meant to enjoy the journey—and impact lives along the way."

"The steps of a good man are ordered by the LORD: and he delights in his way" (Psalm 37:21 NKJV). Notice it says "steps" – moment by moment.

I believe with all my heart that if I had a way to contact her today, I would have more pages to write about. The ripple effect of following one's passion and purpose goes beyond the pages of this book.

To confirm my point, it is said regarding Jesus:

CHAPTER 7

> **"Jesus did many other things as well. If every one of them were written down, I suppose that even the whole world would not have room for the books that would be written." – John 21:25 (NIV)**

It is said, "Greater things shall you do"—a promise spoken by Jesus Himself. If that is true, then imagine the ripple effect we are meant to create in our generation and the generations to come—not by striving, but simply through our obedience.

Every act of obedience becomes a seed. Every surrendered "yes" carries the potential to shift lives, transform atmospheres, and echo through time. Jesus started the movement—but through us, it continues, expands, and multiplies.

Legacy is not built on grand gestures alone, but on consistent obedience to God's voice—day by day, moment by moment. These lines top with following your heart's desire, where his laws are written and embedded.

He says in **John 14:12, "Very truly I tell you, whoever believes in me will do the works I have been doing, and they will do even greater things than these,"** then we must consider the magnitude of this promise.

This was the moment I realized that work isn't just something we do—it's the fusion of who we are and what we're called to do. We don't simply "go to work." We discover our work—our life's assignment—and then, if necessary, bring it into a job setting. That's where fulfillment lives. It's not just about compensation; it's about purpose.

That's when I fully embraced the title my mentor gave me: Purpose Man. And rightfully so. I'm possessed by this topic. I provoke people to pinpoint and pursue their purpose. I'm passionate about helping others find their true work and commit to walking it out.

I don't just do this in a formal job setting—I do it over tea, coffee, lunch, or dinner. It's who I am. It's in my nature. Throughout this book, I'll share how I discovered this purpose within myself. After that discovery, I connected with mentors who guided me through the philosophy of self-discovery.

Never forget this: you cannot impart what you do not possess. You must become before you can do. You work on yourself first—refining and developing your gift—so that, when you step into your assignment, you're empowered to help others discover who they are and fulfill their purpose through their gift.

One of the questions to answer toward self-discovery is, "What Do I Want to Do for Humanity?"

CLUES TO YOUR GIFT

One of the easiest ways to identify your gift is to notice what comes naturally to you—and what you love doing most. Your gift is fun; you could do it all day without growing tired. It flows from your deepest desires and ignites your passion. When you're engaged in it, you may even forget to eat or drink because you're completely consumed by it. You'd gladly do it for free, not because it lacks value, but because it fulfills you on the inside long before it ever rewards you on the outside.

CHAPTER 8

DISCOVERING YOUR WORK BEYOND YOUR JOB

> "Your work is a combination of who you are and what you do. Work is not a place you go to; your job is. You can take your work to a job setting." – Robert Hernandez

"Work isn't something you clock into—it's something you carry. It's the unique blend of who you are and what you're called to do. Your job may change, but your work shows up wherever you go." - Roberto Hernandez

Your job is just one setting for your work to be expressed in, but your purpose goes wherever you do.

> "Let your light so shine before men, that they may see your good works, and glorify your Father which is in heaven." — Matthew 5:16 (KJV)

The key and intent aren't living to be seen but living to be significant. But it is in your significance that you will be seen.

This passage aligns beautifully with our unique divine work—not just actions, but purpose-filled expression that reflects the Creator.

Your work is more than a task—it's a reflection.

It's the combination of who you are and what you carry. When you walk in your divine assignment, when your gift flows effortlessly, when your impact is undeniable—that's not ego, that's evidence.

YOU ARE GOD'S HANDIWORK.

Ephesians 2:10 says it plainly. You were crafted by the Creator, shaped on purpose, for purpose. So, when people see your light, when they witness your excellence, your authenticity, your brilliance—it draws attention not to you, but through you. Imagine the true damage you can do to the enemy's territories when you possess all of this when you arrive.

You don't shine for applause. You shine to reveal the Artist.

Your work is worship. It's how heaven shows up in boardrooms, classrooms, studios, and street corners. The glory doesn't stop with you—it points back to Him. Thus... **"that they may see your good works and glorify your Father which is in heaven."**

So don't dim your light. Don't shrink your gift.

Let it shine.

Because every time someone is impacted by your work, they've just had an encounter with His workmanship.

I chose the word work intentionally—because it's deeper than a job title or a paycheck. Work speaks to assignment. It speaks to identity. It speaks to purpose. One of the questions that has

CHAPTER 8

helped me in my own journey of self-discovery is this: **What gets me angry?** And it is a question that throughout this exercise you will answer for yourself. For as long as I can remember, one thing that's always stirred something in me is watching people settle for jobs they clearly hate—serving in spaces they have no passion for. Have you ever been served in a business setting by someone who despises what they do? You can feel it. The energy is low, the excellence is missing, and the experience suffers. That kind of disengagement in everyday life has always bothered me—not just because it's uncomfortable to witness, but because it signals something deeper: a generation disconnected from purpose. I couldn't just sit back and accept that. I knew I had to become part of the solution.

This is where my foundation and Mission came for "firing people up (or provoking them) to pinpoint and pursue their purpose."

In my early years as a believer, I began to notice something that troubled me: people stepping into roles within the church that didn't reflect their true calling. Some would sing—not to shift the atmosphere or usher us into the presence of God—but in a way that drew attention to their own pain. They weren't operating from their area of grace. Their intentions may have been sincere, but sincerity alone doesn't equal placement.

Others pursued leadership platforms when perhaps their real assignment was to serve faithfully behind the scenes—like driving the church van so others could attend service. But instead of driving the bus, they unknowingly drove the church into confusion. The truth is: when we misunderstand our purpose, we misuse our position. And when that happens, we risk missing what God is doing in the moment—and doing a disservice to the people we're meant to serve.

I recall one particular moment when a young woman stepped up to sing. Her eyes were closed, emotions heavy, and she struggled through the song until, overwhelmed, she dropped the microphone and left in tears. It wasn't because she didn't love God—it was because she wasn't in the right place for her gift to flourish. Misalignment will always create frustration. It doesn't mean someone lacks value—it simply means they haven't yet discovered where they're most effective.

Many times, people are searching for affirmation and identity through performance. But when we pursue platforms for validation, we often sacrifice authenticity. The church isn't a place to prove ourselves—it's a place to become who God designed us to be.

That's why leadership in the church must be more than organizing ministries—it must be about stewarding people's purpose. As leaders, mentors, and visionaries, we're called to do more than assign tasks—we're called to help people find the lane where they can thrive. I've always struggled when I see leaders using people as means to an end, building personal visions without regard for the gifts entrusted to them.

People are not placeholders—they are God's workmanship. They are meant to be placed in environments where their gifts can grow, develop, and make a real impact. True spiritual leadership is not about control—it's about cultivation. It's not about using people—it's about unlocking them.

POSITIONING PEOPLE FOR PURPOSE THROUGH GIFT DISCOVERY

Ephesians 4 reminds us that the purpose of the fivefold ministry—apostles, prophets, evangelists, pastors, and teachers—is to equip others for works of service, so that the body is built up in strength and maturity. Being out of your function affects other people, the body as a whole. It's not about spotlight or status—it's about stewardship.

CHAPTER 8

When people are nurtured into their true callings, we don't just avoid failure—we grow something powerful. A unified, healthy, purpose-driven body. An environment where people don't run from their calling but rise in it.

"EACH PERSON SHOULD DO THEIR OWN WORK!"

Let us read **Ephesians 4:11-16** in the NIV to gather some key points:

So Christ himself gave the apostles, the prophets, the evangelists, the pastors and teachers, [12] to equip his people for works of service, so that the body of Christ may be built up [13] until we all reach unity in the faith and in the knowledge of the Son of God and become mature, attaining to the whole measure of the fullness of Christ. [14] Then we will no longer be infants, tossed back and forth by the waves, and blown here and there by every wind of teaching and by the cunning and craftiness of people in their deceitful scheming. [15] Instead, speaking the truth in love, we will grow to become in every respect the mature body of him who is the head, that is, Christ. [16] From him the whole body, joined and held together by every supporting ligament, grows and builds itself up in love, as each part does its work.

The key phrase "**as each part does its work**" holds weight. Here we find a thoughtfully crafted reflection drawn from Ephesians 4:11–16 that highlights the purpose of true leadership in the function of the fivefold ministry with an emphasis on equipping, imparting knowledge, inducing work, maturity, and alignment in the body:

When we take a close look at Ephesians 4:11–16, the heart of the passage is revealed in the final words: "**as each part does its work.**"

That single word—work—isn't just about effort. It's about purpose, position, and function.

Christ Himself gave the fivefold ministry—apostles, prophets, evangelists, pastors, and teachers—not for status or control, but for equipping. Their assignment is to guide, mature, perfect, and position every member of the body, so each one can step fully into their own God-given work.

Since true leadership involves developing other leaders—and a leader without purpose is illegitimate—we are called to ignite and inspire others **to identify and pursue their purpose.**

The goal?

to equip his people for works of service

That the body grows—not just in size, but in unity, stability, and spiritual maturity.

That we are no longer infants—no longer tossed by trends, confusion, or every new wave of teaching, but grounded in truth, anchored in love, and strong in function—secure in our individual work.

When every part is nurtured, aligned, and activated, the body becomes a living, thriving, whole organism—not built on a few, but built up by all.

The strength of the body is found in the alignment of its members—and the power is released when **each part does its work**.

There's a crucial truth to grasp in this chapter: your work and your job are not the same thing. Some people discover their work. Others only ever find a job. And a few learn how to balance both—for a season.

CHAPTER 8

So, what's the difference?
Your work is your life's assignment. It's your gift, your purpose—what you were uniquely born to do. Your job is your profession, your skill or trade. It's how you earn a living while you're discovering or developing your true work.

Your work, in other words, is what you were born to do. It's who you are. Your job is what you are paid to do—and for the most part, you'll continue doing a job until you discover your true work. But you can also use your job for what it is: "a phase of education at a company's expense" (Roberto Hernandez).

When you approach your job with a servant's heart, rather than resenting or wasting the opportunity, you'll often find yourself developing skills, building habits, and gaining insights that will ultimately serve your greater purpose. If you're careful and diligent, your work will eventually outgrow your job—and at that point, you won't call it a job anymore. You won't even say you're 'going to work.'

You'll be showing up to be *you*—the living, breathing expression of God's handiwork.

Your Job Is Where You Get an Income.

Your Work Is Where You Make an Impact.

The word for **"work"** in Greek is érgon (from ergō, "to work, accomplish"). Érgon refers to a **deed or action that fulfills an intent, inner desire or intention**—a purposeful act driven from within. In this light, we could say that érgon doesn't just mean doing something—it means **becoming**. Your true life's work is when **the "you" in you becomes visible—manifest** in the world around you.

(NAS Exhaustive Concordance of the Bible with Hebrew-Aramaic and Greek Dictionaries, © 1981, 1998 by The Lockman Foundation. All rights reserved.)

Even in English, "work" is defined as **a deed that carries out an inner desire, intention, or purpose**. When someone is walking in their true life's work, they're not just doing a job—they've **become** who they were always meant to be. They are fully aligned with what has been within them all along.

You can be in YOUR life's work. And here's the beauty of it: **no one can take it away from you.**

Why?
Because **you can be fired from a job, but you can never be fired from yourself.**
You can retire from a job, but **you can't retire from your true identity.**

In fact, I've seen it time and again—some people only discover their creativity, passion, and calling **after** they lose a job. That loss becomes the doorway to their purpose.
They didn't just find another position—they found **themselves**. They stepped into their **life's work**.

This is why I stress a lot on this verse:" Start *children off on the way they should go, and even when they are old, they will not turn from it" (Proverbs 22:6 NIV).*

When we're young, there are things that naturally interest us—and often, we pursue them freely, without hesitation. Sometimes that exploration happens because our parents open their checkbooks and enroll us in a sport or activity we're drawn to. Other times, it's because a teacher or mentor notices our interest and steps in to nurture it.

CHAPTER 8

These small moments—simple acts of support—can significantly shape where we flourish later in life. It's often that simple. This doesn't mean every childhood interest becomes a career, but those early experiences can lay the foundation for our future platform. If it sparks their interest—not yours as the parent—go with it. You might be tapping into that child's natural wiring. Most times you are.

As we grow older, however, we often get educated out of ourselves. We step into a world that prioritizes survival over self-awareness—making ends meet and paying the bills tends to overshadow the unique callings that began to surface in our younger years.

Many people end up in careers or paths they were never designed for—not because they lacked potential, but because they unknowingly entered unauthorized lanes. That's why we all need to return to childlikeness—not in immaturity, but in curiosity, honesty, and authenticity.

We must rediscover ourselves to recover our true design.

> "*And said, Verily I say unto you, except ye be converted, and become as little children, ye shall not enter into the kingdom of heaven*" *(Matthew. 18:3 KJV).*

Children who are educated and trained to be themselves will remain true to who they are all the way to the finish. Here is another Translation of Proverbs 22:6 (KJV): "Train up a child in the way he should go: and when he is old, he will not depart from it." That verse isn't just about good behavior—it's about cultivating the path that aligns with their natural design. **Train!**

When a child is trained and nurtured in their gift, they'll grow into their life's work—and never retire from it. That's when a parent can truly rest, knowing they've done their part.

BEYOND THE HUSTLE

Our purpose—our life assignment, our true work—is the source of all fulfillment. Imagine reaching the end of your life and feeling the deep regret of never having done what you knew you were born to do. That sense of incompletion is avoidable—but only if we live with intention.

Jesus, the greatest leader who ever lived, modeled this perfectly. Near the end of His life, He confidently said to the Father: **"I have glorified You down here on the earth by completing the work that You gave Me to do" (John 17:4 AMP).**

That kind of boldness doesn't come from wishful thinking—it comes from clarity of purpose and obedience to your assignment. Knowing and completing your work gives you the audacity to finish strong and the confidence to say, "I did what I came here to do."

The apostle Paul declared, *"For I am already being poured out like a drink offering, and the time for my departure is near. I have fought the good fight, I have finished the race, I have kept the faith." (2 2 Timothy 4:6–7 (NIV)*

Paul didn't just live with purpose—he *finished* with purpose. Near the end of his life, he described himself as being "poured out like a drink offering." In other words, he had emptied himself—his time, his energy, his gifts—for the very purpose for which he was born. He held nothing back.

That's the power of discovering your life's true work: you don't just make an impact while you're alive—you leave this world empty of regret and full of legacy. Paul lived and died poured out. He didn't go to the grave full—he went empty, because he gave everything he was assigned to give.

When we discover our true life assignment—our real work—we don't just become productive, we become whole. Fulfillment flows from living what God placed in us before birth. Many stay

CHAPTER 8

frustrated because they mistake a job for their purpose. But your true work isn't a title or paycheck—it's the real you, waiting to be revealed.

May we all live in such a way. Purposefully. Boldly. Poured out.

A question toward self-discovery is, "What Is the Most Important Thing I Could Do with My Life?

Another one is, "What Would I Rather Be Doing?" and yet another, "What must I do?"

We'll go over steps in the following chapters on how to tap into yourself and uncover your reason for existence. But for now, let me remind you of what we've already discussed: **your work is inherent—it's already inside you!**

Isn't it interesting that we often have to be retrained and re-educated just to be ourselves again? We live in a world filled with so many lies about identity that it can feel like swimming against the current. Peer pressure—from society, media, even our own families—can bury the truth of who we were created to be. And it doesn't stop there. We're bombarded by external expectations and internal doubts, all painting distorted pictures of what success is supposed to look like.

Discovering who you really are requires courage. It means overcoming both outside influence and the false ideas we've adopted about ourselves. That's why it's called *self-discovery*. You must want it as desperately as air—and become bold and relentless in your pursuit of it.

But remember this truth: all who truly seek will truly find.

THE MIND VS. THE WORLD

**"Man can alter his life by altering his thinking."
– William James**

The world does not know the real you—the you that your true work will reveal. That means it's not qualified to point you in the right direction or introduce you to yourself. The world is not authorized to define you. Not your peers, friends, or even your family can do this with accuracy. Neither the education system, government, media, workplace, nor religion has the authority to uncover your identity.

That's why it's called self-discovery. It's your personal responsibility to find your work and your purpose.

And it starts with the mind.

> "As a man thinks in his heart, so is he" (Proverbs 23:7, NKJV).

This profound truth reveals that how a person thinks in their heart—their inner subconscious mind—ultimately shapes who they become. The heart, in this context, is more than emotion. It's the place where thoughts, beliefs, and desires are stored. It's also the place where true reprogramming begins.

What we believe about ourselves, our potential, and our future takes root in the heart—and those beliefs shape our identity, our actions, and our destiny.

That's why your thoughts matter.

When you renew your mind with truth and purpose, you begin to renew your life. When you shift your internal narrative to align with who you were truly designed to be, you activate change from the inside out.

CHAPTER 8

Paul, a first-century leader, wrote this in his letter to the Romans:

> **"Do not conform to the pattern of this world, but be transformed by the renewing of your mind. Then you will be able to test and approve what God's will is—his good, pleasing and perfect will" (Romans 12:2, NIV).**

That "will" is your purpose.

Your purpose cannot be fully experienced until your mind is renewed. Transformation doesn't come from mimicking the world—it comes from thinking differently and choosing to be true to who you really are.

There are three primary enemies of purpose—and the world is one of them.

1 John 2:15 (KJV):

> **"Love not the world, neither the things that are in the world. If any man loves the world, the love of the Father is not in him."**

James 4:4 (KJV):

> **"Ye adulterers and adulteresses, know ye not that the friendship of the world is enmity with God? whosoever therefore will be a friend of the world is the enemy of God."**

These scriptures point to a crucial truth: when we become consumed with the world—its systems, materialism, pride, and fleeting pleasures—we develop a divided heart, distancing ourselves from God's love and from the clarity of our life's purpose. We cannot flirt with the world and think we'll discover and live our our God-given purpose.

The other two enemies of purpose are:

The flesh (our carnal desires), and

The devil (the accuser and deceiver).

Imagine all the pressure—both internal and external—coming against the real you.
That alone proves something: you must be a serious threat to the lies of this world when you begin the journey of self-discovery.

Your **true identity** is rooted in your **Creator**.
What God intended when He formed you—His will and purpose for your life—can only be realized through an intentional separation from the systems, values, and noise of this world.

This separation is the first step toward self-discovery.
When Paul wrote, *"Do not conform to the pattern of this world"* (Romans 12:2), he was saying: **Don't blindly submit to the world's systems, values, or expectations**—especially if they conflict with God's will and your internal conviction. If you do, you'll slowly drift from your original design.

Separation from the external noise quiets the internal noise.
And *both* must be silenced if you're ever going to discover your true self.

> **"The less clearly we see the reality of the world – the more our minds are befuddled by falsehood, misperceptions, and illusions – the less able we will be to determine correct courses of action and make wise decisions."**
> **– M. Scott Peck**

Peck is saying that **truth is a prerequisite for wisdom**. If you want to live well, you must first see clearly. That starts with

CHAPTER 8

confronting illusions and seeking truth—about life, purpose, identity, and reality itself. You can't live right if you don't see right.

Imagine and think about this for a while. We have been befuddled from all sides – internally and externally. In other words, unable to think clearly but, especially from a world that has been independent of God's true standards and principles for living. Which is our true inheritance as well. We honestly must be valiant to experience our true selves. Not being conformed to the huge world where we live and reprogramming (renewing) our minds completely. We need constant moments of stillness for tapping into our true selves and what God intended for our lives. Stop to think and reprogram, just like a vehicle yields into various gas stations, to stay fueled.

To gain the right perspective, make wise decisions, and take the correct course of action, we must constantly work on our minds and quiet the noise that clouds our thinking. As Ralph Waldo Emerson once said,

> **"Sow a thought and you reap an action; sow an act and you reap a habit; sow a habit and you reap a character; sow a character and you reap a destiny."**

Our thoughts are seeds—and our destiny is the harvest. That's why inner clarity is so crucial.

Remember what Jesus said in Matthew 11:28–30 (The Message Translation)?

> **"Get away with me and you'll recover your life. I'll show you how to take a real rest. Walk with me and work with me—watch how I do it. Learn the unforced rhythms of grace. I won't lay anything heavy or ill-fitting on you. Keep**

company with me and you'll learn to live freely and lightly."

When we align with Him, we begin to live from a place of peace—not pressure. That's how we reprogram our minds and renew our perspective. That's how we begin to live with wisdom.

THE POWER OF A JOB

"Your job is a phase of education—at the company's expense." — RAH (RAH)

Long ago, a man named Nehemiah held a prestigious position as a cupbearer to the king. Though it was an honorable role, it wasn't his life's work—or what we might call his "dream job." While he faithfully served the king, Nehemiah carried a vision deep within him: to rebuild the walls of Jerusalem for the protection and restoration of his people.

That vision never left him. It stirred quietly in the background of his day-to-day responsibilities. Even while working his nine-to-five, Nehemiah stayed connected to his greater purpose. And in time, his faithfulness positioned him for favor. When the moment came, he received the king's blessing—and the resources—to pursue and fulfill his life's true assignment.

This is why we must choose jobs with intention and humility. We often don't know exactly why we've been placed in a certain position, or what we're meant to extract from it. That job—even if it feels beneath your gifting—could be the very place where you gain training, develop discipline, learn critical people skills, or make the connections that will launch you into your purpose.

Don't despise small beginnings. The job you're in now might just be the soil where your dream is taking root.

CHAPTER 8

It says, *"When Nehemiah learned about the condition of his home province being in great trouble, the wall of Jerusalem being broken down and its gates burned with fire. He sat and wept. For days he wept and mourned. Then he fasted and prayed" (Nehemiah 1:4).* He was identifying with his work, while at his job. Your life assignment will burden you down, until you take action. That's why the self-discovery question of importance, "What must I do?" should not be taken lightly.

It doesn't matter how much someone earns—because it's entirely possible to be successful in the wrong assignment. If your current position isn't equipping you, developing you, or preparing you for your next phase—your true platform—then you may be investing energy outside of your real success.

When you've found your life's work, your purpose, there's a divine assurance that whatever you need to move forward will come. Resources, favor, and clarity will align for the task ahead. As Scripture reminds us, *"All things will work in your favor— not only when you love God, but when you are walking in alignment with His purpose for your life." (Romans 8:28, paraphrased)*

And yet, just like in Nehemiah's case, sometimes the very job you're in contains the resources, relationships, or training needed for your life's work. Nehemiah received everything he needed from the king—permission, favor, protection, and materials—to fulfill his divine assignment.

"And the king granted me what I asked, for the gracious hand of my God was upon me" (Nehemiah 2:8, ESV). The job was a bridge, not the destination.

So don't think too highly of yourself in a job setting. That role may be temporary, but it can still be strategic. Approach it with humility, excellence, and vision—because God can use your current assignment to prepare and resource your real one.

Now here is the correct translation and you should read it aloud and program it into your subconscious: ***"All things work together for good—not just for those who love God, but for those who are called according to His purpose"* (Romans 8:28, NIV).**

MY FITNESS INDUSTRY JOB

After returning from my missionary work in Trinidad & Tobago, I re-entered corporate America, securing a position in the fitness industry. Armed with insights from my missionary experiences, I approached this role with a mission-centric mindset. To my surprise, I was promoted to manager sooner than anticipated. In my first week, I outperformed all other counselors combined in sales. This momentum led colleagues to frequently ask, "Are you the new GM?" indicating their recognition of my emerging leadership.

Initially hesitant about this opportunity—especially after a less successful attempt in South Florida months earlier—I sought signs for clarity. Accepting the role led to seven years of impactful service, where I discovered my niche in sales. The recommended readings from my superiors bridged my biblical knowledge with practical application, enabling me to teach principles effectively without overt scriptural references.

During membership sign-ups, I often found myself offering counsel to couples, drawing from Dr. Myles Munroe's "Single, Married, Separated, and Life After Divorced" book and other resources. This mirrored my missionary efforts in Trinidad, where I had guided couples away from divorce. At the gym, I facilitated connections leading to marriages, assisted newcomers—among the approximately 97–100 new daily residents moving to Orlando between 2004 and 2006 —in finding business opportunities, and directed individuals to local places of worship. This period was marked by vibrant growth and meaningful

CHAPTER 8

interactions, underscoring the profound impact of integrating mission-driven principles into everyday professional settings.

This ties the idea of purpose, alignment with one's calling, and the certainty that everything necessary for success will come when you're in the right place at the right time.

Paul stressed this truth when he said, "***Each person should remain in the situation they were in when God called them. Were you a slave (employee) when you were called? Don't let it trouble you. But, if you can gain your freedom, do so" (1 Corinthians 7:20,21 NIV).*** He's stressing the importance of prioritizing your "calling," but being open to advancement, entrepreneurship, or stepping into greater freedom—just not at the cost of abandoning your true work or losing sight of your divine calling.

Being trained in a field or profession is always a valuable platform, because proper training equips a person to serve more effectively and with excellence in their gift—ultimately allowing them to make a greater impact. What does this tell us? It means you'll be able to do what you were born to do on a greater scale.

This may be why Peter wrote, **"Servants, be subject to your masters with all respect, not only to the good and gentle <u>but also to the unjust</u>" (1 Peter 2:18 ESV)**. Why? Because even unjust treatment can become a tool for character-building—and it cannot stop you from fulfilling your purposeful assignment, even in a job setting. What doesn't break you can build you. In fact, those very challenges often refine you for greater influence.

YOU CAN'T QUIT YOU

"The value of life is not in its duration, but in its donation. You are not important because of

how long you live; you are important because of how effective you live." – Dr. Myles Munroe

Your job can be taken from you if you get fired, but your work can never be taken from you. You can't fire yourself from your work. In fact, even your disappointments and discouragements become training ground and fuel for your work. That's if you stay in a "Can-Do Mentality." Rock Bottom has a way of catapulting a person to their true self and life's work. I've seen it in so many people. **"We can do all things through Christ who strengthens us" (Philippians 4:13).** Most of us find our work in crisis, as it is an incubator to creativity and innovation. Troubles, temptations, trials, and tribulations try our faith and help produce the patience needed to become mature and character-proven in our work, life assignment, to the point where we ultimately lack anything. *(Read James 1:2-4).*

THE BUSINESS OF BECOMING: HOW PAIN PRODUCES PURPOSE

One day in New Jersey, I reconnected with a good friend of mine named Luis Cruz. He had lost his furniture company and had to start over with a job delivering appliances. His back was giving out on him, but he kept pressing forward. After customers repeatedly asked if he'd take their old appliances off their hands, he came up with a business idea: he charged them to remove the old units and then sold them through Craigslist and other online platforms. Everybody was happy. Instead of seeing it as a burden, he saw it as a ladder.

Before he knew it, this road got him out of debt and into a new, thriving business—one that eventually allowed him to build his dream home and sustain his family.

The one thing I noticed about Luis was his resilience and attitude, which caused him to rise and thrive. I was deeply inspired

CHAPTER 8

by how he became creative in the midst of his circumstances. Attitude always alters our abilities. The right ones.

I was so moved by his story that I intentionally asked if I could invite a relative of mine to his house for Christmas dinner. Luis had invited me, so I asked if I could bring along this relative of mine, who was going through something similar. The connection turned into exactly what I had envisioned. As Luis shared his story, it sparked a transformation in my brother—another life changed, and one I knew I'd have to include in my next book.

The ripple effects of finding your work beyond your job—simply by assuming the right attitude—are endless. This, I can assure you.

You can look forward to reading my relative's full story in my upcoming book.

ROCK BOTTOM: THE CATAPULT TO SELF-DISCOVERY.

When you learn your life lessons well, you don't just make an income—your story begins to make the biggest impact. This platform prepared Luis for an even greater opportunity. Today, he is the owner of a successful demolition company that helps other families sustain themselves. I witnessed this entire process of progress. When you treat every phase of a job with the right attitude—as an educational and character-building experience—you will be rewarded.

The ripple effect his journey continues to have on others' lives is absolutely amazing.

Your dedication to your life's calling not only shapes your own path but also profoundly impacts countless others—including those you have yet to meet. By embracing your purpose and its process with unwavering commitment, you become a source of inspiration and blessing, extending far beyond your immediate reach.

This is what my friend Luis's life teaches us.

Prioritize creating a meaningful impact while earning an income. While financial stability is important, the true measure of success lies in the positive difference you make in others' lives. By focusing on impact, you not only contribute to the greater good but also discover deeper fulfillment and purpose in your work.

Remember: leave this life finished, not merely rich.
Prioritize impact over income.

BEYOND SUCCESS: LIVING FOR LEGACY, NOT JUST A LIVING

Paul showed this reality in his own life when he said:

> **"For I am already being poured out like a drink offering, and the time for my departure is near. I have fought the good fight, I have finished the race, I have kept the faith. Now there is in store for me the crown of righteousness, which the Lord, the righteous Judge, will award to me on that day—and not only to me, but also to all who have longed for his appearing" (2 Timothy 4:6–8, NIV).**

Paul had no plans to retire. How could he? He was pouring everything into his life's work.

Imagine doing what you love—living so purposefully that not another minute is wasted, fully committed to what you are meant to do for the rest of your life. That's how exciting your life assignment can be! It fuels you. It pushes you forward. Not even death

CHAPTER 8

can stand in the way, because it's not the duration of your life that matters—it's your donation. Not how long you live, but how effectively you live.

You can leave this world having said, like the greatest leader of all time, "It is finished." Jesus was only 33 years old when He died. The Bible says:

> **"After this, Jesus, knowing that all things were now accomplished... He said, 'It is finished!' And bowing His head, He gave up His spirit" (John 19:28a, 30b, NKJV).**

What was finished?
His life? No.
His legacy? Not at all.

What was finished was His assignment—His work. The ripple effect of His life continues to this day. Love Him or hate Him, His name remains the most powerful and recognized name in all the world—because He completed His purpose.

> **"Therefore God exalted him to the highest place and gave him the name that is above every name"(Philippians 2:9, NIV).**

You too can be remembered. Your name—your reputation—can live on through the work you do. Your impact can live through the lives of those you inspire.

Jesus said:

> **"I have brought you glory on earth by finishing the work you gave me to do" (John 17:4, NIV).**

Your job is temporary; your work is permanent.

And something permanent is meant to last—unchanged, enduring beyond your years.

As Romans reminds us:

> "For God's gifts and His call can never be withdrawn" (Romans 11:29, NLT).

WHY JOBS?

Maybe you're reading through this chapter, and you've felt that jobs should be thrown out altogether. Hold on, let's not get ahead of ourselves especially in a society where entrepreneurship is credited higher than a job. Jobs are just as important for mankind. Jobs allow us to stay busy and not be idle. They also help us develop skills. The importance of a job is that it allows us to exercise potential, hidden capabilities.

Sometimes, you may not realize the potential and gifts you possess until you step out and pursue something meaningful. For example, a teenager working at a fast-food restaurant may not be aware of their natural hospitality skills until the manager recognizes it. It doesn't matter where they are placed in the restaurant – be it behind the counter, at the counter, on the floor, or in the bathroom – their hospitable nature shines through. The manager acknowledges this quality and rewards them, perhaps making them the employee of the month. While the teenager may not think much of it, the truth is that this job reveals and nurturing their gift of hospitality. Not everyone has this grace, so it's important to be faithful in whatever job or role you find yourself in. Promotion follows afterwards, and you are placed in a department of that company that allows you not just to shine but bring more value to that establishment. This is when we serve wholeheartedly **"Not with eye service, as men pleasers; but as the servants of Christ, doing the will of God from the heart" (Ephesians 6:6 KJV).**

CHAPTER 8

AUTHORITY BEFORE AMBITION: THE HIDDEN KEY TO UNLOCKING YOUR PLATFORM

I have known of a young lady who dreamed of building her interior design business into a sustainable living, but for years she struggled to get off the ground. When I spoke with her, I told her this: **"Find someone who is already walking in that business and work for them."** If you seek, you will find a mentor, a leader, someone you resonate with—often that person is ready to pass the baton, perhaps preparing for retirement or a new season, but they desperately need someone to receive their knowledge and wisdom.

Your own platform is already waiting for you, but you cannot jump ahead and start running before you have been given the authority to lead. You may have the power—the skills, the talent, and the ability—but you lack the authority, the permission, and the access that comes from submission to someone who holds that authority. This is a principle many miss: **You must submit to an existing authority to be catapulted into your own platform.**

As Myles Munroe taught me, **"Leadership is influence that is transferred, not taken."** You cannot just claim a platform; you must be entrusted with it. Authority flows through relationship and submission—not rebellion or impatience. When you humbly serve under a mentor, you are being prepared and authorized to step into your own leadership, fully equipped.

Very few people understand this, but it's the key to unlocking your full potential. If you try to bypass this process, you risk delay, failure, or burnout. But if you embrace it, your time will come, and your platform will rise with power and purpose.

SERVING BEFORE LEADING: HOW FAITHFULNESS UNLOCKS YOUR CALLING

Your gift has a way of ushering you into your assignment. Your faithfulness to a job—working for someone else—is your education and empowerment at that company's expense. Potential is the privileged ability to carry out your life's work. Be faithful in your present job, no matter how long it takes you to get out and onto your own platform, because as Jesus said, *"If you have not been trustworthy with someone else's property, who will give you property of your own?"* (Luke 16:12 NIV). If you are faithful in the little, you are faithful in the big. Be a faithful servant to someone else before you can master what is your own.

YOU DO NOT KNOW (IT'S OKAY NOT TO KNOW EVERYTHING)

There are some things you aren't supposed to know the end results about. Why? Because if you did, you would try to expedite the process to reach your destination faster. We live in a microwave society: we want to get rich quick, gain power fast, find health with just one pill. You get it, right? We don't appreciate the process of development.

In some cases, the process is more important than the purpose itself because it builds the character necessary to sustain the purpose. The journey is as important as the destination because of what you'll learn along the way.

No wonder the wise King Solomon said in the English Standard Version (ESV):

> *"**As you do not know the way the spirit comes to the bones in the womb of a woman with child**, so you **do not know the work of God** who makes everything. In the morning sow your seed, and at*

*evening withhold not your hand, **for you do not know which will prosper**, this or that, or whether both alike will be good." (Ecclesiastes 11:5,6)*

Don't jump the gun prematurely. This is why you should not rush to leave a job to get into your own work or entrepreneurship. These jobs can contain the skills and capabilities you need for the next phase of your work and influence.

You don't know what God may be doing behind the scenes in every phase you are called to go through, including every job you have or have had.

These verses emphasize the unpredictability of life and the importance of diligence and faith in God's work. It could be that the Lord will grant you success in both your 9-to-5 and your own assignment. Maybe your 9-to-5 is meant to fund your life assignment. Note, "… **for you do not know which will prosper**, this or that, **or whether both alike will be good**."

For Nehemiah, this process provided everything he needed for his life's work—the very burden that weighed heavily on his heart while he was on the job.

NEHEMIAH'S TRANSITION: FROM CUPBEARER TO BUILDER OF THE WALL

Nehemiah held the honorable role of **cupbearer to King Artaxerxes** (Nehemiah 1:11)—a position of deep trust, influence, and proximity to power. But his ultimate calling went far beyond serving the king. It was to rebuild the broken walls of Jerusalem and restore the dignity and protection of his people. That divine burden didn't come to him once he stepped into leadership—it *found him while he was still working his job*.

Myles Munroe often said, *"The place where you are right now is training for where you are going. Your job is not your work—it's your classroom."* Nehemiah's job in the palace wasn't wasted time; it was preparation. **His role gave him access to royalty, training in diplomacy, and exposure to administrative systems**—skills he would later need as a city rebuilder and spiritual reformer.

> **"In the month of Kislev… I questioned them about the Jewish remnant that had survived the exile, and also about Jerusalem… When I heard these things, I sat down and wept."** — *Nehemiah 1:1-4*

Nehemiah felt the *burden of building* long before he ever touched a stone. He carried a deep emotional weight that revealed his calling. *Your calling is often tied to the problem that bothers you the most. Purpose is discovered not only through passion, but also through burden.*

But notice—Nehemiah didn't just jump into action.

He **prayed first.**

> **"Then I prayed to the God of heaven, and I answered the king…"** — *Nehemiah 2:4-5*

Myles Munroe's powerful definition of prayer still echoes in my mind:

"Prayer is man giving God the legal right and permission to interfere in earth's affairs. It is a heavenly license for earthly intervention."

Why is this important? Because, as we read in Ecclesiastes 11:5–6, "As you **do not know** the path of the wind, or how the body is formed in a mother's womb, **so you cannot understand**

CHAPTER 8

the work of God, the Maker of all things." Prayer gives us access to participate in that unseen work—right from our current situation.

Nehemiah understood this. Before requesting resources, before rallying people, before building anything—he *petitioned heaven*. His success wasn't built solely on strategy—it was born in the secret place.

> **"O Lord, let Your ear be attentive to the prayer of Your servant... Give Your servant success today by granting him favor in the presence of this man."** — *Nehemiah 1:11*

The king granted his request, gave him letters of endorsement, military escort, and building materials. Why? Because Nehemiah had divine backing.

FAVOR FOLLOWED HIS FAITHFULNESS.

And even once he transitioned into leadership, Nehemiah continued to rely on prayer and discernment. He faced resistance, mockery, and sabotage—yet remained grounded because he never stopped seeking God's guidance.

> **"We prayed to our God and posted a guard day and night to meet this threat."** — *Nehemiah 4:9*

Nehemiah didn't just work hard; he worked *with heaven's license*. That's what made the difference.

KEY TAKEAWAYS:

- **Don't despise your current role.** It may be your preparation ground.

- **Burden precedes assignment.** Pay attention to what breaks your heart.

- **Don't skip the process.** Nehemiah didn't abandon his post until he had God's timing and favor.

- **Pray at every stage.** As Myles Munroe taught, prayer invites God's intervention into human affairs.

- **Be faithful where you are.** Your platform is often birthed out of your service to someone else's vision (see Luke 16:12).

NEHEMIAH'S FAVOR-FILLED TRANSITION

From Cupbearer to Contractor—"When Prayer Opens Doors Kings Can't Close"

When the favor of God is upon you because of faithfulness: When the moment came to speak to the king, he didn't just ask for permission—he asked for provision.

> **"If it pleases the king... send me to the city in Judah where my ancestors are buried so that I can rebuild it."**(Nehemiah 2:5, NIV)

He then boldly requested safe passage, official letters, and even timber for construction—and the king granted him everything.

> **I also said to him, "If it pleases the king, may I have letters to the governors of Trans-Euphrates, so that they will provide me safe conduct until I arrive in Judah? And may I have a letter to Asaph, keeper of the royal park, so he will give me timber to make beams for the gates of the citadel by the temple and for the**

CHAPTER 8

**city wall and for the residence I will occupy?"
And because the gracious hand of my God
was on me, the king granted my requests.**
(Nehemiah 2:7–8 NIV).

Nehemiah's story reminds us that transition is not rebellion when it's rooted in revelation, submission, and divine timing. He didn't leave his post prematurely. He prayed, planned, and then presented—and God's favor did the rest.

MYLES MUNROE TAUGHT US THAT THIS LEADERSHIP (YOUR LIFE ASSIGNMENT) IS BIRTHED FROM THREE SOURCES:

1. **Intentional Training:** Munroe believed that leadership is not a position or title but a skill that can be developed through intentional training and continuous learning. He encouraged individuals to invest in their personal and professional development through education, mentorship, and practical experience. By intentionally seeking out opportunities to grow and improve their leadership skills, individuals can become more effective and influential leaders. Submit to mentors.

2. **Crisis:** Munroe taught that crisis can be a catalyst for leadership development. He believed that facing challenges and adversity can help individuals discover their true leadership potential and strengths. Crisis situations provide opportunities for individuals to demonstrate resilience, problem-solving skills, and courage, which are essential qualities of effective leaders. By navigating through crises with grace and wisdom, individuals can grow and mature as leaders. When you loose your job, you might be at the verge to find your work.

3. **Self-Discovery:** Munroe also emphasized the importance of self-discovery in leadership development. He encouraged individuals to take the time to reflect on their values, beliefs, strengths, and weaknesses to gain a deeper understanding of themselves. By knowing who they are and what they stand for, individuals can lead with authenticity, integrity, and purpose. Self-discovery allows leaders to align their actions with their values and make decisions that are in line with their true selves. I love when people tell me they feel lost. That humility is the starting point of self-discovery (Matthew 5:3).

By engaging in intentional training, embracing crisis as a learning opportunity, and engaging in self-discovery, individuals can develop the skills, resilience, and authenticity needed to become effective and impactful leaders in their personal and professional lives.

THE THREE PILLARS OF PURPOSE-DRIVEN LEADERSHIP

1. **Purpose:** True leadership stems from understanding and embracing one's purpose in life. When individuals are connected to their purpose, they are able to lead with passion, conviction, and direction. Munroe believed that every person has a unique purpose and calling, and when they align themselves with it, they become natural leaders who inspire and influence others.

2. **Potential:** True leadership is born from recognizing and maximizing one's potential. He believed that everyone is born with innate gifts, talents, and abilities that, when developed and harnessed, can lead to great leadership impact. By investing in personal growth and development, individuals can unlock their full potential and become effective leaders in their spheres of influence.

CHAPTER 8

3. **Passion:** Lastly, Munroe highlighted the importance of passion in birthing leadership. He taught that true leaders are driven by a deep passion for their work and a genuine desire to make a difference in the world. Passion fuels perseverance, resilience, and creativity, enabling individuals to overcome obstacles and inspire others to follow their lead.

By understanding and embracing your purpose, maximizing your potential, and leading with passion, you can birth true leadership that positively impacts your community and the world around you.

Myles Munroe also emphasized the importance of intentional training, crisis, and self-discovery in developing effective leadership: These are the cradles to your leadership role.

AN EXPERIENCE WITH A FUTURE POLITICIAN

I remember attending a wedding in South Jersey years ago. I sat at a table with some very interesting individuals. Amongst them was one individual who looked through my website from beneath the tablecloth. He did this for 20 minutes after I gave him business card. He showed some arrogance and pride while I conversed with other people, trying to disrespectfully butt into my conversation with others, without saying "excuse me". I purposefully ignored him. At one point when he interrupted me one more time with a question, I responded, "When you really want to know you can ask me this question again. Perhaps on another occasion. In the meanwhile, I am busy with these precious folks. You know how to find me."

30 minutes later I found him in the bathroom. The bathroom was large and very fancy. He stopped me and apologized saying, "I read through your website "purposeman.com" I wanted to first of all say sorry. I'm lost!" He continued. "I have mentors who would fly into town right now if I needed them in their own private jets.

BEYOND THE HUSTLE

They would come at my request and at my demand, so to speak. I guess I'm spoiled and this is what contributes to my arrogance. Again, sorry for disrespecting at that dinner table."

At this time, he started crying. He added, "I read your website while you were talking and answering all those other people's questions. I really wanted to be part of it since I overheard some of the things you were mentioning to them. I felt I lost the opportunity. Anyway, I'm lost. Can you help me?"

I was impressed by his humility. People were coming and going from that large fancy bathroom. I noticed how they stared at us but respectfully let us continue to chat. Something was special about this individual, but I didn't know him. They did. This wasn't my hometown, and I only knew the parents of the bride, the bride and the husband, together with a few other folks who were close to them.

At this point I asked him, "What kind of work are you doing now?" I also asked him, "what did you study and graduate from? His present job was in government and his major at Rutgers University was a master's in political science. At that moment I told him, "You are in your purpose. Just learn to always stay humble. You will be the next leader in this city. I happen to know this city was once in the "Associated Press" as one of worst cities with the most crime in the United States. According to The Associated Press in 2004 to be exact. He was able to identify the burden he had to help this city with its challenges at one time. That's why he studied Political Science and was closely aligned with his assignment, working in a particular department in government. But he let pride destroy his vision, and his haughty attitude caused him to fall from his place of grace. Now you understand why I constantly mention pride throughout this book—it's important to always walk in awareness.

Months later he contacted me joyfully to tell me he was running for commissioner in Camden, New Jersey. I told him, "That

CHAPTER 8

was only the beginning." A few months afterwards, he won and became elected. His tears kept on flowing during our initial conversation because of the genuine burden he carried for that particular assignment. I've been doing this for a while and after asking a few other equations I was able to help him "pinpoint and Identify" his life work. Do you see how what you studied and presently work in can provide the equipping, tools, and empowerment to take you to where you are supposed go as it relates to your work? The hindrance that caused a blind spot for him was just pride and haughtiness. "Pride always goes before destruction and haughtiness before a fall." (Prov 16:18). You already have grace, but God will always give more grace to the humble, while the haughty He looks from afar off.

> **"But he gives more grace. Therefore, it says, 'God opposes the proud but gives grace to the humble.'" (James 4:6 ESV).**

Arrogance and pride will keep you from your life work. This passage highlights the importance of humility and God's response to the haughty. **Proverbs 3:34** also states, **"Toward the scorners he is scornful, but to the humble he gives favor." (ESV)**

God shows favor, grace, and support to those who are humble and lowly in heart, while opposing and resisting those who are proud and haughty. Maintaining a positive attitude is crucial for staying aligned with your calling and recognizing the significance of your life's work. Why is this important? Because when you approach your work with humility, starting from a position of humility and looking up to the higher purpose, you acknowledge the value of your calling. Conversely, when you operate from a place of pride and arrogance, looking down on others, you risk taking your work for granted or viewing it with contempt.

Humility is a virtue that is consistently emphasized in scripture, and those who humble themselves before God are promised His grace and favor. In times when you may feel stagnant or uninspired, humility allows you to remain open to receiving a "second wind" to rejuvenate your passion and purpose. Grace and favor serve as an extra boost to propel you forward, but they cannot coexist with pride, which hinders your ability to fully embrace the blessings and opportunities that come your way.

BE-ATTITUDES, NOT DO-ATTITUDES

The Beatitudes, presented by Jesus in Matthew 5:3–12, serve as a foundational guide for aligning our inner posture with the values of the Kingdom of Heaven. I call them Be-Attitudes, not Do-Attitudes—because they are less about outward performance and more about inward transformation. These teachings of Jesus offer a blueprint for living a life of depth, purpose, and spiritual fulfillment. They reveal who we are meant to be before we focus on what we are called to do.

The Beatitudes: Attitudes for Purposeful Living

Each Beatitude begins with "Blessed are," highlighting virtues that lead to divine favor and a meaningful life—not just in personal growth, but also in preparing us for purposeful impact: You are blessed to be a blessing.

1. **Poor in Spirit** – Recognizing our spiritual neediness opens us to the Kingdom of Heaven. Dependence on God is the first step toward true leadership.

2. **Those Who Mourn** – Acknowledging sorrow leads to divine comfort. Compassion is born in the heart that has known pain. What pains you about this world?

3. **The Meek** - To embrace humility, to control one's strength and passions rather than being controlled by them. Humility allows us to inherit the earth because it grants the strength to lead without pride or arrogance.

4. **Those Who Hunger and Thirst for Righteousness** – A deep desire for justice and righteousness results in fulfillment. A passionate pursuit of what's right fuels lasting purpose.
   What injustices would you like to see restored in the world?

5. **The Merciful** – Showing mercy ensures we receive mercy in return. Mercy strengthens relational influence and trust. It's hard to do anything lasting without it.

6. **The Pure in Heart** – Maintaining purity grants us the vision to see God. Clarity of heart brings clarity of direction—without prejudice.

7. **The Peacemakers** – Promoting peace identifies us as God's children. Peace-builders carry the authority of Heaven into conflict. When peace leads, we'll always see clearly what God wants.

8. **Those Persecuted for Righteousness** – Enduring persecution for doing right aligns us with the Kingdom of Heaven. Endurance under pressure proves the strength of your calling.

These teachings challenge conventional views of success and happiness, emphasizing internal transformation over external achievements. By embodying these attitudes, individuals align themselves with God's purpose, finding true fulfillment and resilience in their spiritual journey.

STUDENTS: BROKE, BUT NOT POOR: THE MINDSET THAT BUILDS LEGACY

While in college or university preparing for your life's assignment, it's important not to prioritize material things over the pursuit of wisdom. I'm of the belief that a good student often learns best in conditions that aren't always favorable. Those very constraints have a way of sharpening the mind and shaping character.

There's a difference between being broke and living in poverty. Broke is a temporary financial condition—it can be overcome. Poverty, however, is a deeply ingrained mindset, a state of internal lack that often lingers far longer than it should. Being broke, especially as a student, can be likened to a "retreat"—a necessary withdrawal before a greater advance. That perspective may be counter-cultural, but it's powerful. It reminds us that discomfort is not always a curse—it can be preparation.

This season can actually be one of your greatest gifts: a time for growth, clarity, and character formation. It positions you to value the right things in life—not status, stuff, or comfort—but substance.

As Proverbs reminds us:

> **"Wisdom is the principal thing; therefore get wisdom: and with all thy getting get understanding." — Proverbs 4:7, KJV**

Choose wisdom over wealth. If you gain wisdom in the midst of tight seasons, you'll have the foundation to steward abundance when it comes. Wisdom doesn't just help you make a living—it helps you make a life.

Here are some principles and pointers that highlight why being "broke" during your student years can actually be more effective and meaningful than you might think:

1. HUNGER SHARPENS FOCUS

When you don't have excess resources, you're forced to focus on what truly matters. You cut out distractions, prioritize your

CHAPTER 8

studies, and make intentional decisions. Hunger—both literal and metaphorical—keeps your senses sharp and your purpose clear.

> "Necessity breeds innovation. Luxury breeds complacency."

2. IT BUILDS DISCIPLINE AND DELAYED GRATIFICATION

Being broke teaches you how to say "no" to temporary pleasures for the sake of long-term gain. That's a muscle most people never develop because they always have what they want. But students who go without learn how to control their appetites, rather than be controlled by them.

3. YOU DISCOVER THE VALUE OF SMALL THINGS

When you don't have much, every book, every meal, every opportunity becomes a treasure. You learn to appreciate and steward the little you have. That kind of gratitude builds humility, contentment, and resilience.

4. IT FUELS CREATIVITY AND RESOURCEFULNESS

When resources are tight, creativity kicks in. You find ways to get books cheaper, borrow materials, share tools, hustle ethically, and connect with people who can help. Creativity thrives under pressure—scarcity becomes the catalyst for innovation.

5. IT EXPOSES WHO YOU REALLY ARE

Money can mask character. But when you're broke, your true self is revealed. Do you quit when it's hard? Do you grow bitter—or better? That "broke season" often purifies motives and exposes the grit that comfort might keep hidden.

6. YOU LEARN TO RELY ON GOD (AND YOUR HIGHER PURPOSE)

Without the means to do it all yourself, you're forced to lean on God. That dependence builds spiritual maturity, trust, and clarity of vision that abundance rarely cultivates. When you're in need, you start praying and walking by faith.

7. IT KEEPS YOU IN STUDENT MODE

Too much money too soon can make you feel like you've already "arrived." But when you're broke, you stay humble, teachable, and hungry to grow. You remain in learning mode—and that's exactly where lasting transformation happens.

8. YOU BUILD RELATIONSHIPS OVER RESOURCES

When you don't have much, you lean on people, not possessions. Some of the deepest and most loyal friendships are forged during seasons of lack. And later in life, you'll realize those human connections are worth far more than material wealth.

I've seen, heard, and even lived stories where vehicles with over 150,000 miles lasted throughout someone's entire college journey. We didn't just walk by faith—we drove by faith. We depended on God for every small resource we needed, and the

CHAPTER 8

experiences were unforgettable—like that of a missionary on a divine assignment, where every need was met at just the right moment. After all, **"The sacrifices of God are a broken spirit; a broken and contrite heart, O God, you will not despise"** (Psalm 51:17).

> Leadership is ultimately about influencing others. As I say, "If you make a sale, you will earn a commission. If you build relationships, you will earn a fortune!" — RAH

Being broke is not a permanent state—it's often a temporary classroom where life teaches its most valuable lessons. In certain seasons, especially as a student or visionary in the early stages of purpose, scarcity can be a divine setup for stewardship. When you have little, distractions are few, and your focus sharpens. God sometimes allows lean seasons not to punish us, but to prepare us—to teach us how to live effectively in every cycle and season of life.

Let me be clear: I am not condoning lack. I'm emphasizing wisdom. The goal is not to remain in insufficiency but to let wisdom refine your priorities, strengthen your character, and align your perspective. When abundance comes—and it will—you'll be mature enough to manage it. Wealth without wisdom becomes waste, but wisdom will always attract wealth in due season.

> "How much better to get wisdom than gold, to get insight rather than silver!" (Proverbs 16:16, NIV)

> "By wisdom a house is built, and through understanding it is established; through knowledge its rooms are filled with rare and beautiful treasures." (Proverbs 24:3–4, NIV)

True wisdom eventually produces durable wealth—not just in finances, but in favor, influence, and understanding. When we choose wisdom over wealth, we invite the kind of prosperity that endures.

Proper stewardship, then, begins with managing more than just money—it starts with managing you.

You are God's most valuable investment. Discovering who you are, why you exist, and how you're designed to function is the highest form of stewardship. Because if you can't manage yourself, you can't manage what God entrusts to you.

That's why this next section is so critical. It's time to pause, reflect, and take inventory of your life. The process of self-discovery is not self-centered—it's Kingdom-centered. It allows you to locate where you are so you can properly manage where you're going.

CHAPTER 9

14 QUESTION - STEPS TOWARD SELF-DISCOVERY

A GUIDED JOURNEY TO YOUR GOD-GIVEN IDENTITY

I encourage you to take some time to evaluate your life purpose and write your vision. Below I have included numerous questions to ask yourself in this self-discovery process. For some, it may take a while as you sit and dig deep to answer these questions. The result will be well worth it. I myself did this together with other assignments and it has helped immensely.

When we understand what our Creator naturally deposited in us, who we are, what we can do, and why we exist, we have no problem tapping into our full self - The You in You! Remember, it is all about opening that prison door so that the real you can be let out like King Solomon said, ***"The purpose in a man's heart is like deep water, but a man of understanding will draw it out" (Proverbs. 20:5 ESV).*** May you get a better understanding of yourself and be let out to serve in your gift and leadership role.

Have fun discovering yourself!

KEY #1: WHAT IS MY DEEPEST DESIRE?

Not what I have a general or passing "interest" in, but rather a deep yearning or aspiration to do. Here is another way to answer it. What is the thing I want most out of life? Your deep desire has to do with your original writing. There is a purpose as to why you desire something so much.

KEY #2: WHAT AM I TRULY PASSIONATE ABOUT?

What do I really care about? What gifts and abilities do I especially enjoy using? What is the thing I simply must do? What energizes me? What makes me forget to eat or sleep? Passion is the fuel to your purpose.

> **"If you have a strong purpose in life, you don't have to be pushed. Your passion will drive you there." — Roy T. Bennett**

Study what makes you come alive and have no regrets.

KEY #3: WHAT MAKES ME ANGRY?

Not destructive anger, which is selfishly motivated, but constructive anger that is based on compassion for others and a desire for people to be treated right; anger that is grieved by injustices and that leads to positive action to remedy problems. Remember me saying that we are problem solvers?

In the world there are troubles, *but "be of good cheer," said the Great Shepard, "I have overcome the world" (John 16:33 NIV).* In his assignment when Jesus saw the crowds, *"he had compassion on them, because they were harassed and helpless, like sheep without a shepherd" (Matthew 9:36 NIV).* His compassion caused him to move into his leadership role. He

CHAPTER 9

became the world's Chief Shepard and was well qualified. His compassion and assignment entailed *"doing good and healing all that were oppressed" (Acts 10:38b NIV).*

I believe that compassion is "compressed passion" that is delivered to hurting humans. Compassion is when we start to feel their pain and causes discomfort. It almost obligates us to act. What makes you hurt for others? Be of good cheer, or encouraged, because our greatest example of leadership showed us how it is done by being moved with his compassion. Let what angers you lead you. Anger does not have to be destructive, but constructive when channeled appropriately.

What do I wish I could change about the world? What are the things I consider unjust, inadequate, or inferior in quality?

KEY #4: WHAT IDEAS ARE PERSISTENT IN MY HEART AND THOUGHTS?

What recurring dreams do I have in my life? What ideas never leave me? What ideas, inventions, or innovations keep coming back to me? What is my vision for my life or others' lives? If it is in your mind, it may be something to occupy yourself in. You may have to mind your business. If you are having the right thoughts that aren't limited to personal ambition, but a far greater vision entailing your generation, chances are they are right. *"The thoughts of the righteous are right" (Proverbs 12:5a KJV).* Trust in your thoughts because it is God's greatest way of communicating with you.

KEY #5: WHAT DO I CONSTANTLY IMAGINE MYSELF DOING?

What do I dream about becoming? What gifts or skills would I use and develop to become this? What is my vision for my life or others' lives? Remember that the imagination is key because it helps paint a picture thoroughly that sometimes is greater than your present reality. Imagining is when you allow yourself to regurgitate your dreams. When you see it in your heart, imagine it in your mind, believe it, you can achieve it.

"Now to him who is able to do immeasurably more than all we ask or imagine, according to his power that is at work within us" (Ephesians 3:20 NIV). God doesn't give you the gift of imagination to frustrate you, but to pull you out of mediocrity. "Using your imagination," stated Dr. Munroe, is like taking a tour of your dream, checking out every detail of it, and then telling God, "Let's go there!'"

> **"Whatever you vividly imagine, ardently desire, sincerely believe, and enthusiastically act upon... must inevitably come to pass!"** – Paul J. Meyer

KEY #6: WHAT DO I WANT TO DO FOR HUMANITY?

What kind of impact would I like to have on my community? What do I want to pass along to the next generation? What would I like to be remembered for? What problem would I like to solve? What need would I fill?

Remember that is the most important question in the whole dynamic. Why? Because if you are to be a true world-changer you need a vision that involves the world. Remember that ambition is usually what you want to get out of this world. Vision is what you see yourself depositing into it. We are most significant when we deposit into this world through serving others. Think of how you can change or impact the world through your gift.

CHAPTER 9

KEY #7: WHAT WOULD BRING ME THE GREATEST FULFILLMENT?

What three endeavors or achievements have given me the greatest satisfaction and fulfillment in life so far, and why? What motivates and gratifies me the most, and how can I incorporate it into my life as my vocation or life focus? What activities, projects, courses, jobs, and hobbies have brought me the most fulfillment? Think about these things and jot them down on a piece of paper. Perhaps immediately, or later, they will begin to make sense to you in the grand picture of your vision.

KEY #8: WHAT WOULD I DO FOR NO MONEY OR OTHER COMPENSATION?

What activities am I currently receiving satisfaction from that I'm not being paid for? What am I so dedicated to that I would continue to do it even if I stopped receiving money for it? What would I do for no compensation? What would I spend most of my time doing for free?

For many people their hobbies became their gratifying assignment. The Apostle Paul said something that really caught my attention.

> *"For though I preach the gospel, I have nothing to glory of: for necessity is laid upon me; yea, woe is unto me, if I preach not the gospel! For if I do this willingly, I have a reward; but if against my will, I have been entrusted with stewardship. What is my reward then? Verily that, when I preach the gospel, I may make the gospel of Christ without charge, that I abuse not my power in the gospel" (1 Corinthians 9:16-18 KJV).*

This is something Paul just had to do regardless. Look at these statements: "I have nothing to glory about" or "be boastful about," "for necessity is laid upon me" or "an obligation is laid upon him," I am entrusted with stewardship" or "a trust committed to him," "make the gospel without or offer it free of charge," and "That I abuse not my power." This had become his life assignment whether paid or not.

KEY #9: WHAT WOULD I RATHER BE DOING?

What do I wish I were doing when I am doing other things? What makes me feel most at home when I am doing it? It's your sweet spot.

KEY #10: WHAT WOULD I DO IF I KNEW I COULD NOT FAIL?

What endeavor, enterprise, creative work, project, or plan would I engage in if it were risk-free? If money were no object? If I didn't worry that I had the wrong background, the wrong looks, the wrong job experiences, or the wrong anything else?

KEY #11: WHAT IS THE MOST IMPORTANT THING I COULD DO WITH MY LIFE?

Above all other things, what is the most significant thing I could do with my life? What do I want to happen in my life? How do I want to live my life based on my values and beliefs?

CHAPTER 9

KEY #12: WHAT ENDEAVOR OR ACTIVITY WOULD BEST CONNECT ME TO MY CREATOR?

What draws me closest to God? Scripture **reminds us, "He is the vine; you are the branches. If you remain in him and he in you, you will bear much fruit; apart from him you can do nothing" (John 15:5 NIV). Key #12: What endeavor or activity would best connect me to my Creator? Drawing close to God requires steadfastness—refusing to compromise the values He has instilled in you. It demands that you remain authentic to yourself, for true connection flows from being fully aligned with both your divine purpose and your God-given identity.**

KEY # 13: WHAT COMES EASY FOR ME AND HARDER FOR OTHERS?

Have you ever found a task that takes little effort for you to complete? What about something that you've observed others trying to attempt and thought, "It's not as hard as you're making it." You could, for example, have two boys born in the same house. Brothers that are total opposites. One can pick up every instrument and play it without sheet music. The other can't hold a tune. One can pick up any sports ball and dominate the field. One couldn't catch something to save his life. Trust me, there are those things that come easy to us but are harder for others. Just like there are some things that are harder for us, yet they come easy to others. What are those in your life?

KEY # 14: WHAT DO PEOPLE USUALLY SAY I AM GOOD AT?

This is probably one of the easiest ways to begin identifying your gift—simply by listening to others.

Comments like:

> "Wow, you make that look so easy."

> "If I ever have a problem with this, I know you're the one to call."

These compliments, performance reviews, or even school report cards often reveal things others see clearly in you—things you might overlook in yourself. Sometimes, the people around us can recognize our gift before we do. Be sure to open your ears. Pay attention to what they notice in you.

"What Is My Gift?" Checklist:

Ask yourself the following:

1. Do I enjoy this so much that time flies when I do it?
2. Does this align with my deepest desires or passions?
3. Have I ever gotten so involved in it that I forgot to sleep or eat?
4. Would I do this even if no one paid me?
5. Can I visualize this bringing real value—and one day earning income—as I continue to develop and perfect it?

If you answered "yes" to most or all of the above, you're likely looking at your gift. It might not be fully refined yet, but it's already present, and it's already powerful.

(Many of these questions excepted from In Charge by Dr. Myles Munroe, others are formed by Roberto Hernandez)

CHAPTER 10

VISION: HOW YOU WILL ACCOMPLISH YOUR PURPOSE

"Sow your seed in the morning, and at evening let your hands not be idle, for you do not know which will succeed, whether this or that, or whether both will do equally well" (Ecclesiastes 11:6 NIV).

WORKING YOUR JOB UNTIL YOU FIND YOUR GIFT

Ultimately, you need to ask yourself in every scenario you face in life, *"Is this where I envisioned myself?"* If you are not where you have envisioned yourself, then where you are currently is only temporary. Are you at a "temporary" job? Then serve there well and acquire as much education as you can. As mentioned earlier, your jobs should elevate you closer to where you envision yourself.

When people don't know their life's work or purpose and have no clear vision for their lives, most wake up to a job they hate, going to a work setting with people they dislike, getting paid less than what they are worth, and dying too young from frustration—simply because they don't know why they exist. They fail to see the purpose of their temporary job and have no vision to look beyond what they currently see.

When you walk in God's vision for your life, even trials become stepping stones—tools He uses to guide you toward your divine purpose. How much more, then, a temporary job? Even that can be a training ground, a platform, or a passageway toward your calling.

The first-century writer and leader Paul wrote in 1 Corinthians 7:21–23:

> **"21 Were you a bondservant when called? Do not be concerned about it. (But if you can gain your freedom, avail yourself of the opportunity.) 22 For he who was called in the Lord as a bondservant is a freedman of the Lord. Likewise, he who was free when called is a bondservant of Christ. 23 You were bought with a price; do not become bondservants of men"** (ESV).

What does a bondservant mean in today's society?

In biblical times, a bondservant was often someone who willingly served a master under a contract or agreement. They committed to serve for a specific period (or indefinitely), exchanging labor for support and protection.

In today's world, the concept can relate to individuals who feel bound to a job or employer due to financial obligations, lack of opportunities, or contractual agreements. This can sometimes create a sense of limited freedom or dependence on their employer for stability and livelihood.

CHAPTER 10

This passage encourages individuals to focus on their spiritual identity and relationship with God, rather than becoming overly concerned with societal status or external labels. True freedom and lasting fulfillment are found in being united with Christ—where our purpose is sealed. He not only redeems us from sin, or missing the mark, but also liberates us from the limitations and pressures of the world. In Him, we discover our true worth, purpose, and identity.

Always remember your Creator and what you were created for, especially in temporary situations. My friend, I guarantee you—you will make it through any scenario once you are led by a vision greater than yourself. Ultimately, we are called to live from the inside out, guided by internal vision.

> *"Even if your current situation appears successful, if it doesn't align with your true self and vision, you may end up living an unfulfilled life."* – Roberto A Hernandez

VISION WITHOUT ACTION IS LIFELESS

One of my favorite quotes says it best:

> "Don't ask what the world needs. Ask what makes you come alive and go do it. Because what the world needs is people who have come alive." – *Howard Thurman*

Howard Thurman, a pivotal figure in the Civil Rights Movement, emphasized the importance of individuals aligning their lives with personal vision and passion. He believed that when people engage in what brings them true joy and fulfillment, they are empowered to impact the world in meaningful ways. His teachings remind us that true influence begins with authenticity—pursuing what makes you come alive—not simply conforming to external demands. Vision is not just about dreaming; it requires acting. Because vision without action is lifeless.

Many people assume that starting a business automatically means they're living in their purpose. But owning a business is not the ultimate measure of success. **Discovering and operating in your life's work is.** Countless people have built businesses in areas they are not passionate about—perhaps meeting a need in the world, but one that doesn't match what makes them come alive. Their enterprise might serve others, but it doesn't align with the private vision they once saw before serving publicly.

Remember this: You can never truly impart what you do not possess. Yes, you may earn a great income, live in your dream house, and drive an expensive car—but if you haven't discovered your true self, you're not truly successful. You're not in your life's work. You're not living according to your personal vision. Maybe you've settled due to fear of the unknown. But deep down, you know that real fulfillment comes from aligning with your passion and purpose—what makes you come alive.

One of my favorite quotes by the late Dr. Myles Munroe puts it this way:

> **"Being successful in the wrong assignment equals failure."**

That statement alone has caused many business leaders to pause and reevaluate. I've spoken in rooms filled with highly successful people—industry leaders, CEOs, influencers—and yet, many of them were not truly operating at their highest level. Why? Because they had disconnected from their personal vision. But I've also witnessed the incredible transformation that happens when they're reintroduced to it. Suddenly, they begin to tap

CHAPTER 10

into something much deeper, producing far more than they ever imagined possible.

STORY OF A PASTOR'S ASSISTANT IN ORLANDO

After one of my speaking engagements titled *"How to Thrive in Crisis"*—delivered shortly after the 2008 recession—a man approached me privately. He was the assistant pastor of one of the largest churches in Central Florida. In his office, he confessed something surprising: he was an entrepreneur at heart and wasn't sure how he had ended up co-pastoring for so many years.

Originally, he had stepped in temporarily to fill a need in his local church. But temporary turned into permanent. Meanwhile, his heart and mind constantly dreamed of launching businesses. He shared visionary ideas—brilliant, timely, and filled with innovation. As he spoke, the energy in the room shifted. His eyes welled with tears. He was *coming alive again*, simply by revisiting his buried vision.

The ideas he shared were so remarkable I briefly considered acting on them myself—but they weren't mine. I laughed it off and told him something I've told many people since:

> **"If you stay in that comfort zone any longer, you're robbing the world of the wealth inside of you. Worse, you're occupying a space meant for someone else."**

When we align ourselves with our personal vision, we bless the entire organization or ecosystem we're a part of. But when we're out of place, we disrupt the flow. It's like putting someone without a true calling in the pulpit or in front of a congregation—when perhaps they were meant to drive the church bus. Instead, they end up driving the church out of wack. Misalignment affects more than just you; it throws the entire system out of balance, creating confusion, frustration, and spiritual stagnation.

When you *return to your vision*, not only do you revive yourself—you activate those around you. As Howard Thurman said:

> **"What the world needs is people who have come alive."**

Coming alive starts with identifying what stirs your heart and compels your soul. That process may require risk and courage, but once you take that leap of faith, everything begins to align. Your audience (the world needs you to be you)—your purpose—has been waiting for your full manifestation all along. And with that manifestation comes **provision**.

> "God provides where He guides. Where He leads, He meets the need. And when you do His will, He pays the bill."

Romans 8:28 tells us,

> "All things work together for good to those who love God and are called according to His purpose."

But many are like this assistant pastor—**unauthorized in their current assignment**. They're operating from fear, comfort, or doubt, rather than faith. Some remain stuck because of financial security, others because of uncertainty. I followed up with that man over the years. He's still in the same role—and not a happy man.

THE RESTLESS HEART OF MISALIGNMENT

Solomon captured this tension in *Ecclesiastes 3:11 (NLT)*:

CHAPTER 10

> "God has made everything beautiful for its own time. He has planted eternity in the human heart…"

This reveals a deep truth: every human heart longs for more. We were designed for divine purpose—planted with eternity. But when we don't live in alignment with that purpose, we feel a deep inner restlessness.

> **"Hope deferred makes the heart sick, but when the desire comes, it is a tree of life."** — *Proverbs 13:12*

People often ask how to start. I tell them plainly:
Faith is not the absence of fear—it's moving forward in spite of it.
We don't need to see the full picture on how to proceed. God rarely reveals everything at once.

> "A man's heart plans his way, but the Lord directs his steps." — *Proverbs 16:9*

As Dr. Myles Munroe often taught, this means we must trust divine guidance, even when the next step is unclear.

Too many people, in search of comfort, trespass into places they were never meant to be—jobs that fit their fears, not their calling. I'm not advocating recklessness. We shouldn't leave our job prematurely. But we **can't afford to get stuck** either. When you recognize your purpose, you must begin to **see beyond what your natural eyes can see**. Vision is spiritual sight—insight into your future assignment.

THE FAITH WALK TOWARD PURPOSE

Acting by faith means moving even when the path is unclear. It means trusting your God-given vision, taking bold steps, and showing up daily for your assignment. Don't jump without a plan, but don't stay paralyzed either. Take **measured, consistent action.**

> "In the multitude of counselors there is safety." — *Proverbs 11:14*

Talk to wise mentors. Don't isolate yourself during transition seasons.

> "Don't rush the process. There are lessons in your current season that prepare you for the next." — *Roberto A. Hernandez*

Even in roles we don't necessarily enjoy, we can still serve with excellence. A job may be temporary, but work—your life's assignment—is eternal. Both can uncover hidden gifts and activate untapped potential. When approached with purpose, even a temporary job can become training ground for the next level of your destiny.

> "Don't rush the process. Good things take time. Great things take patience." — *Unknown*

> "To everything there is a season…" — *Ecclesiastes 3:1*

Stay until your current assignment matures you. But know that jobs are replaceable. **Work is not.** Your life's work is your **calling**, your job is just your career.

> "In all labor there is profit, but mere talk leads only to poverty." — *Proverbs 14:23*

> "There is nothing better than to enjoy food and drink and to find satisfaction in work. These pleasures are from the hand of God." — *Ecclesiastes 2:24*

CHAPTER 10

Whether you're flipping burgers or managing a company, do it with excellence:

> *"Whatever you do, do it heartily, as to the Lord..."*
> — *Colossians 3:23–24*

NEHEMIAH: FROM JOB TO PURPOSE

Nehemiah transitioned wisely. He left his post under the king with honor, permission, and purpose. We should do the same.

> "Small daily improvements are the key to staggering long-term results." — *Robin Sharma*
>
> "Write the vision and make it plain..." — *Habakkuk 2:2*

Your job is not your end—it's a means. Use your 9 to 5 to sow seeds for your life's true work. Be willing to invest in your vision before expecting others to buy into it. Don't let idle comfort keep you from taking daily steps toward your destiny.

Vision gives structure to your purpose. **Purpose is your "why." Vision is your "how."** Vision is the house your life's work lives in.

When you have a vision, even a temporary job becomes meaningful. You work smarter, lead better, and contribute more.

Here's why vision-driven employees stand out:

1. **Purpose fuels performance** – They bring energy and intention.

2. **They extract value while giving it** – They grow through every experience.

3. **They take ownership** – They're not just earning a check, they're fulfilling a mission.

   "When you know your purpose, you bring value wherever you go—even if you're just passing through." — *Dr. Myles Munroe*

FINDING YOUR PLACE IN THE RACE

In life, **finding your place** is the only way to truly run your race. You're either living **in your purpose** or moving **toward your vision**—and both are essential.

Purpose is your *original intent*, the reason you were created. **Vision** is a *glimpse of that purpose in motion*—a snapshot of a preferred future. It may seem overwhelming at times, but it should also stir excitement deep within your soul. It's not meant to intimidate you; it's meant to inspire you.

When you discover your life's work—your true assignment—you'll no longer feel the need to compare yourself with others. You won't chase applause or bend to please people. **You'll be free.**

Free to become.
Free to create.
Free to lead.
Free to serve with authenticity.

Because when you know your place, you can run your race—with clarity, with confidence, and with conviction.

CHAPTER 10

YOU DO YOU, YOU BE YOU

This is what the first-century writer Paul tried to communicate to his students when he wrote,

> **"…But each one must examine his own work, and then he will have reason for boasting in regard to himself alone, and not in regard to another. For each one will bear his own load."**
> (Galatians 6:4–5 NASB)

As mentioned before, only people who are outside of their authorized work enter the danger of becoming prideful; others simply take pride. When we are in our own work and have examined it well, we can boast or take pride in our accomplishments with confidence. Why is this? Because people in their life work are just being themselves. Therefore, why become prideful (arrogantly)?

Prideful people are often competitive and usually operating in something they are not called to be in or called to do. They are outside of themselves. People who are cooperative are typically celebrating each other's good works and accomplishments. You can be confident in your vision.

When a skillful eagle flies high in the sky, he is just doing what he was naturally born to do. Flight is in his DNA. Though majestic and skillful at capturing prey in the sky and on the ground, he's just being himself—an eagle.

If a fish could talk and tried to accomplish the goal of soaring like an eagle, it could easily look down at the other fish below the sea and say, *"Look at me! Check out what I'm doing! You can't soar like me?"* Pride easily creeps into people outside of their calling.

Humility is the by-product of being in your life work, your purpose, and carrying out your vision. Here, one is simply minding their own business.

Humility comes from the Latin word *humus*, which means earth or ground. So, when someone is "humble," they are "grounded" or "low to the ground" in spirit—not prideful or lifted up. People who are in their spot are down-to-earth. **Confidently humble.** Confidence and Arrogance aren't synonymous.

MANAGING PEOPLE INTO THEIR NICHE

> *"It's not the people you fire who make your life miserable. It's the people you don't."* — **Dick Grote**

DISCIPLINE WITHOUT PUNISHMENT: THE PROVEN STRATEGY THAT TURNS PROBLEM EMPLOYEES INTO SUPERIOR PERFORMERS

I never had to fire someone from employment. If employees weren't performing well for an extended period of time, I would ask them questions about their vision, dreams, desires, gifts, and the direction they were looking to go in. I would find out what was in them. You'd be surprised how many people just settle—taking up space without adding value to their job or to the company they are presently with.

I would ask questions like:

- "What are you doing here?"

- "What brought you here in the first place?"

- "What are your goals?"

- "Where do you see yourself in the next few years?"

CHAPTER 10

- "Why aren't you in something that could at least enhance your dream and refine your gifts?"

I would present alternatives and even went as far as making phone calls to help ensure they were placed in an area aligned with their niche —someplace that coincides with their vision.

I would have them do most of the work, because it's important for people to figure things out on their own. Nonetheless, there were many I did assist who needed the extra push. After all, that's what I do: **Provoke People to Pinpoint and Pursue Their Purpose.**

I helped them by managing them out—into their passion or into a role that served as a learning phase or a stepping stone toward their life's true work. I guided them toward their purpose by helping them articulate their own vision—or at least move closer to it, where they could begin to refine their skills.

Many later thanked me. When you help someone discover their gift and passion, you empower them to step into their life's work. By helping them **capture a personal vision**, you point them toward the path where their true success lies—because it's their gift that will ultimately make room for them and lead them to fulfillment.

I like the word **"assignment"** because it creates urgency and makes work more personal. It is a divine or personal mandate that gives life direction, meaning, and impact. We must find our work—it's our life assignment.

In the spirit of my mentor Dr. Myles Munroe, **life assignment** would be defined like this:

> *"Your life assignment is the reason you were born—the unique work you were sent to Earth to*

complete. It's tied to your gifts, passions, and the problems you were created to solve."

By walking through these steps with these employees, I was strengthening their vision. Vision is a glimpse into your purpose—it reveals the direction and expression of why you were created.

Or, a little more poetically:

"Vision is the snapshot of your purpose—it allows you to see in part what you're destined to fulfill in whole."

I would help employees visualize how they will accomplish their purpose. Though sometimes it may begin in blurry segments, other times—or later—it becomes more vivid. **We walk by faith, not by sight.**

THE ROOTS OF VISION

The Greek word often associated with *vision* in a biblical or philosophical sense is:

- **Horasis** (ὅρασις) – meaning sight, appearance, or vision (from the root **horaó** – ὁράω – "to see, to perceive, to discern")

However, the idea of *vision* meaning "coming into view" is best captured in the Latin language. Here's why:

1. LATIN ORIGIN – WHERE THE WORD COMES FROM

- **Original Word:** *visiō* – meaning a sight, appearance

CHAPTER 10

- **Root Verb:** *vidēre* – meaning to see

This is where we get English words like *vision*, *video*, and *visible*.

Vision literally means "the act of seeing" or "what comes into sight."

2. THE CONCEPT OF "COMING INTO VIEW"

The meaning of vision as "coming into view" is about something appearing, manifesting, or being revealed to sight.

But in a biblical and purpose-driven sense, vision isn't just about optical sight—it's **spiritual perception**, an **inner seeing** of what's possible or destined.

> *"The only thing worse than being blind is having sight but no vision."* — Helen Keller

This is the powerful quote by Helen Keller, who was both blind and deaf, yet became an iconic author and advocate.
This means that physical sight is one thing, but *vision*—knowing your purpose, seeing beyond your current reality—is far more powerful.

She also once said:

> **"Although the world is full of suffering, it is also full of the overcoming of it."**

Vision will make you into a problem-solving machine with no setbacks whatsoever—no matter what physical impediments you may have. You aren't looking at them. That is the **POWER of VISION**.

> **"I can see, and that is why I can be happy, in what you call the dark, but which to me is golden." - Unknown**

True vision isn't about what your eyes can see—it's about what your heart perceives and your purpose pursues.

Sight gives you facts, but **vision gives you direction**.

We can help others draw out what they have inside of them by focusing not just on **out-sight**, but **insight**.

Talk to people about their **personal vision** *before* you mention the corporation's overall vision. Just to see if they fit—and so everyone's time is valued and not wasted.

To help individuals tap into their inner potential, it's important to focus on their personal vision *before* introducing the organization's overarching goals.
By first gaining insight into their unique aspirations and values, we can better assess alignment and ensure that everyone's time is respected and used effectively.

This approach prioritizes understanding individuals' inner motivations and strengths (choosing **insight** over **out-sight**), allowing for a more purposeful and productive collaboration that benefits both the individual and the organization.

> **"The purposes of a person's heart are deep waters, but one who has insight draws them out."** *(Proverbs 20:5, NIV)*

We can help them **revisit their vision** and come to their own conclusions about where they should be in this present phase of life.

CHAPTER 10

This verse beautifully illustrates how purpose and wisdom reside deep within us—like a hidden well—and it takes insight, often through reflection, counsel, or divine guidance, to draw them out.

I want to always be a man of **INSIGHT**, helping men and women look within, reminding them of who they truly are—and going from there.

When a person isn't sure where to go in life but still comes to you for a job, you can **sell them on a skill** that can develop them until they figure it out on their own.

I've spoken with many young people about the psychology and life lessons they can learn through **sales**—especially before they embark on their careers.

I would ask them to give me at least **two years**, while we both work on helping them discover their true vision.
But if they excitedly found something better or within their niche, I'd simply ask for **two weeks' notice**.
We would shake on it, and I was never disappointed—because people don't care how much you know **until they know how much you care**.

Sales is deeply rooted in psychology.
In fact, some of the most valuable life and leadership lessons are learned in sales because it trains people in areas like:

1. EMOTIONAL INTELLIGENCE

- Reading people

- Managing your emotions during rejection and setbacks

- Building rapport and trust

2. PERSUASION AND INFLUENCE

- Understanding how people make decisions
- Applying principles like reciprocity, scarcity, and social proof *(based on Robert Cialdini's 6 Principles of Influence)*

3. RESILIENCE AND GROWTH MINDSET

- Handling "no" and learning not to take it personally (without losing confidence)
- Developing grit and persistence

4. ACTIVE LISTENING & COMMUNICATION

- Learning to hear what's not being said - tuning into tone, silence, and intention
- Asking powerful questions that unlock deeper needs

5. CONFIDENCE & SELF-AWARENESS

- Sales helps you understand yourself better—your strengths, fears, and your ability to lead conversations

We could say something like this:

Sales is one of the greatest teachers of practical psychology.
It's where theory meets real people—and real emotions.
For young people, it's more than just learning to sell a product;
It's learning how to read people, bounce back from rejection, and influence with integrity.
These are **life skills**, not just **sales skills**.

CHAPTER 10

I CAN SEE CLEARLY NOW

Vision is so important to our purpose. It gives us discipline and perseverance.

Whether we realize it or not, we are either living in our purpose or visualizing where we want to be. Vision is just as important as purpose. As visionaries we believe in our visions more than in our present situations. That's what fuels us to keep on going. If God gave you a vision, an internal picture of a preferred future, He intends for you to believe in it for "**without faith it is impossible to please God" (Hebrews 11:6 NIV).**

Faith in one's vision is what keeps us alive until we've carried out our purpose. **"Now faith is the confidence in what we hope for and the assurance about what we do not see. This is what the ancients were commended for" (Hebrews 11:1, 2 NIV).** Another translation states the latter part of verse one this way, **"being the proof of things (we) do not see and the conviction of their reality (faith perceiving as real fact what is not revealed to the senses" (AMP).** In other words, we "see" it, but it hasn't yet become a reality. Which reminds me, fearless visionaries believe in their visions more than in their present realities. Vision is the purpose in pictures! Believe in the pictures more than the present.

> *"The chasm between dreaming and achieving is discipline." - Trista Sue*

WHAT WE MEAN WHEN WE SAY, "INVEST IN A DISCIPLINE"

To invest in a discipline means to make a deliberate and sustained commitment to a specific field of study, skill, or area of expertise. It involves devoting your time, energy, money, and mental effort—not just to pass through it, but to understand it, master it, and ultimately contribute to it.

This kind of investment becomes far easier—and more powerful—when guided by a clear vision. Vision gives your discipline direction. Without vision, discipline feels like drudgery; with vision, discipline becomes devotion. You're not just grinding—you're growing toward something that matters.

When your educational or professional discipline is aligned with your vision, it becomes more than training—it becomes preparation for your life's work.

"Where there is not vision, the people perish." (Proverbs 29:18 KJV) Another translation states, **"they run wild" (NLT)** and yet another states, **"people are uncontrolled" (NCV)**, and lastly, **"the people cast off restraint" (NRSV)**. In other words, where there is true vision discipline is inevitable. Where there is not, people do whatever and even run wildly, in circles.

People have a reason to live disciplined lives when they have a picture of a preferred future that's vivid and real. An athlete trains, eats, and practices because of a picture that he sees of a trophy. Vision keeps us in line until the full manifestation of our purpose is accomplished or becomes a reality. For instance, I saw the ending of a finished product while writing this book. After that picture (which was so clear), I positioned myself in inspirational settings to complete it.

Discipline serves as self-imposed boundaries that propel us toward our goals. As our vision evolves, we continually strive for growth, embracing a new way of life rather than temporary habits. This is how we slaughter procrastination. As **2 Corinthians 5:7 (NIV) states, 'For we live by faith, not by sight.'"**

Faith in one's vision also empowers us to persevere through tribulations, tests, and trials. These are inevitable, because

CHAPTER 10

life is full of testing. Our faith is only as strong as the test it endures. Therefore, don't despise where you are right now—you could simply be going through a test.

Joseph, a character from the Old Testament, is one of the best examples of this. He was a dreamer. He believed in his dreams and in his vision so strongly that he openly spoke about them to his brothers. He saw himself as someone highly influential—so much so that his brothers would one day bow before him.

In the end, that vision became reality:

> **"Joseph was the ruler of the land. He was the one who sold grain to all the people of the land. And Joseph's brothers came and bowed to the ground in front of him" (Genesis 42:6, NLT).**

These relatives were too familiar with him and thought they knew him well. His brothers became jealous and envious, eventually throwing him into a pit. Afterwards, they sold him into slavery and told their father that a wild animal had killed him. This serves as a fair warning: don't be too quick to share your vision with just anyone—especially with those who are overly familiar with you or who think they have you figured out.

> *"Joseph had a dream and when he told his brothers, they hated him even more" (Genesis 37:5).*
>
> *"When he told his father and his brothers, his father criticized him by asking, "What's this dream you had? Will your mother and I and your brothers come and bow down in front of you?" So, his brothers were jealous of him, but his father kept thinking about these things" (Genesis 37:10, 11 GWT).*

He made it to a strange land far away from his jealous brothers, but the test did not stop there. He was later falsely accused of trying to make a pass on his boss's wife and was cast into prison. ***"So, he took Joseph and threw him into the prison where the king's prisoners were held, and there he remained" (Genesis 39:20 NIV).***

In these two places of testing the scriptures record that God was with him. ***"But the LORD was with Joseph, and showed him mercy, and gave him favour in the sight of the keeper of the prison" (Genesis 39:21 NKJV).***

THE POWER OF VISION: JOSEPH'S EXAMPLE

In the pit and in prison, Joseph did not lose sight of his picture. His **vision kept him alive**.

Eventually, he ended up in the palace, where he would fulfill his purpose. It's easy for us, reading from the outside, to see how each step in Joseph's journey strategically moved him closer to the dream he once had. Being falsely accused and thrown in jail wasn't a setback—it was a setup. It positioned him around the right people. Those people gave him access to Pharaoh, and that audience— that experience—placed him in a position of power and influence, where he could see himself stepping into the very role he had been prepared for all along.

Joseph's life is an **excellent example of faith in one's vision**, preserved through persecution. He believed in what God showed him, even when his circumstances contradicted it.

GOD PERFECTS WHAT HE STARTS

God is a **God of purpose**. He deposited His original intent—His purpose—**in you**.

CHAPTER 10

There are very few interruptions or detours that can extinguish what He started **when you believe in your vision**.

Psalm 138:7–8 (NKJV) says:

"Though I walk in the midst of trouble, You will revive me;
You will stretch out Your hand against the wrath of my enemies,
And Your right hand will save me.
The Lord will perfect that which concerns me;
Your mercy, O Lord, endures forever;
Do not forsake the works of Your hands."

Another translation renders verse 8 this way:

"The LORD will fulfill his **purpose** for me. LORD, your faithful love endures forever; do not abandon the work of your hands." (Psalm 138:8 CSB)

The word "perfect" here means to **complete, fulfill,** or **bring to maturity**.
This means that no matter what we face, **God is working behind the scenes** to ensure that His vision and purpose for our lives will come to full completion.

God's mercy endures forever—this simply means practically that **He doesn't give up on what He started**, even when we feel shaken. Hang in there!

VISION ANCHORS YOU

Despite our own plans, even our detours, God's **purpose prevails**.

That's why **no plan we create can override our purpose** when our vision is:

- **Set** in our spirit

- **Believed** in our heart
- **Acted upon** by faith

Proverbs 19:21 (AMP) reminds us:

> "Many plans are in a man's mind, but it is the Lord's purpose for him that will stand."

Vision is birthed from **strong conviction** rooted in purpose. This is why people who carry vision often appear **possessed by their assignment**—they are driven by divine design.

Those **recurring thoughts, ideas, and dreams you can't shake**? They're not random. They are **God-breathed**, inflating your spirit with the specific assignment heaven assigned to your name.

VISION FUELS IMAGINATION

Visions make you **daydream**.

Joseph daydreamed and saw himself doing his work on a throne, even while he was tending his father's sheep as a young shepherd. Vision gave him the ability to **see beyond the present**, and so he endured every trial knowing something greater was ahead.

What do you constantly imagine yourself doing?

Take that seriously—it might just be your divine assignment in disguise.

PURPOSE AND VISION: THE WHY AND THE HOW

- **Purpose** is your **why**.

CHAPTER 10

- **Vision** is your **how**.

So, ask yourself:
How will I accomplish my life's vision?

That question is where your purpose gains traction. It's where your gift meets discipline, and your destiny begins to unfold.

THE ART OF SAYING "NO"

Saying "no" can feel negative—especially in a culture that celebrates being a "yes" person as helpful and agreeable. But when it comes to your vision, learning to say no is essential. If you don't master this early, distractions will pull you away from what truly matters, causing you to waste precious time—which really means wasting your life. You might even expend your energy helping others build their visions while neglecting your own. Protecting your vision requires learning this art as soon as you have a clear vision.

THE ART OF SAYING "NO".....

1. **Vision Demands Focus**
   "The greatest enemy of progress is distraction." When your vision is clear, not everything deserves your time or attention. Saying "no" isn't rejection—it's redirection.

2. **Purpose Filters Your Choices**
   Purpose acts as a filter. When you know who you are and why you exist, you gain confidence to say "no" to opportunities, relationships, and demands that don't align with your purpose.

3. **Every "Yes" is a "No" to Something Else**

Dr. Munroe emphasized that time and energy are limited. Saying "yes" to every request dilutes your ability to fulfill your vision. Leaders must prioritize what matters most.

4. **The Power of Discipline**
   Discipline is saying "no" even to good things in order to pursue the best things—those aligned with your God-given vision. This discipline is the hallmark of visionaries.

5. **Guard Your Vision Against Vision-Drainers**
   People who don't understand your vision may try to pull you in different directions. Dr. Munroe taught that you must lovingly but firmly say "no" to influences that side-track your destiny.

When your vision is clear, everything in your life should support it. Your vision becomes the standard by which you measure every choice—what you read, watch, how you spend your free time, and even the people you surround yourself with. If something doesn't feed your vision, it's a distraction. Vision gives your life focus; without it, you risk drifting through life doing a lot—but achieving very little that truly matters. Always seek what is **RIGHT**, not merely **GOOD**, for your vision.

YOU MUST CONCEPTUALIZE YOUR VISION

Because God has placed your purpose inside of you, you are the sole guardian of your vision—responsible for nurturing it and bringing it to fruition. Just as a father protects his child, you must safeguard your vision. Having a clear vision is essential for fulfilling your leadership role on earth, reflecting your unique purpose.

To unveil your purpose and vision, consider asking yourself these questions:

- What have I always wanted to do?

- What is my heart's deepest desire?

- What thoughts, ideas, plans, and dreams have remained consistent within me?

- What specifically can I do to fulfill my plans and dreams?

When you begin to see your vision clearly, you will be able to fulfill your life's purpose and become the leader you were created to be. This vision must be very clear because you need a specific target to work toward; otherwise, you risk not accomplishing your purpose.

Note: A vision is not the same as a purpose statement, nor is it the same as a goal or an objective.

- A **statement of purpose** gives a general description of your overall calling in life. It is philosophical and abstract.

- A **vision statement** is concrete and practical. It has specific emphasis and definable boundaries.

- A statement of purpose can have many aspects and applications, whereas a vision statement is precise and focused.

- Only when you develop a precise statement of intention can you create the goals and objectives that will enable you to fulfill your vision.

Here are examples illustrating the difference between purpose and vision:

- **Purpose Statement:** My purpose is to improve the quality of education for inner-city children.

Vision Statement: My vision is to fund and create two magnet schools for grades 9–12 in [city, state].

- **Purpose Statement:** My purpose is to improve the quality of education for inner-city children.
  Vision Statement: My vision is to earn a master's degree in education, become a reading specialist, and help teachers develop student-specific programs to help elementary children overcome reading disabilities.

- **Purpose Statement:** My purpose is to improve the quality of education for inner-city children.
  Vision Statement: My vision is to become a nutritionist and teach parents how to provide better nutrition for their children, so they have more energy and mental alertness to learn effectively.

Do you see how one purpose statement can have a variety of corresponding vision statements? These are just three specific ways that a single purpose can be applied through an individual vision. Visions are specific and concrete.

Excerpt from Becoming a Leader, pp. 67–68. New Kensington, PA: Whitaker House, 2009.

My Purpose Statement:
"Provoking People to Pinpoint and Pursue Their Purpose."

My Vision:
To become a mentee of Dr. Myles Munroe and then a Certified Life Coach who teaches people to identify themselves, their value, and their personal purpose—empowering them to effectively impact their sphere of influence (society) with the right message, using the right methods, through their unique gifts.

CHAPTER 10

WHEN EDUCATION, PASSION, VISION AND PURPOSE COLLIDE

"It is a beautiful thing when a career and passion come together." - Unknown

EDUCATION AND VISION

You've probably heard the popular saying, "It's never too late for education."
Truth be told, sometimes—it's better late than early. I'll explain why in a moment.

Many people graduate from high school and immediately slip into college without a clear sense of what they truly want out of life. Even more concerning, most of us don't even know what we're meant to contribute to the world. But deep down, that's what we all long to do—give something back, leave an impact, and build a legacy. This drive is hardwired into our DNA.

Maslow's Hierarchy of Needs confirms this. At the top of the pyramid is self-actualization—the pursuit of personal growth, purpose, and fulfillment. And even beyond that is self-transcendence—the desire to leave a lasting mark, to make a difference beyond ourselves.

Yet the statistics show that something is deeply misaligned.
Only about 41% of U.S. college students graduate within four years, proving that the so-called "four-year degree" is more idealistic than realistic. Even more telling, 80% of students change their major at least once during their college journey.

Why? Because **uncertainty is the norm**.
Admissions advisors and counselors see it every day—students are torn between their personal interests and external expectations.

And this confusion exists because many young people haven't first identified their purpose.

Several factors contribute to the growing trend of delayed college graduation, but I want to highlight some of the main ones:

Changing or adding majors: Many students enter college without clarity. As they discover new interests or career paths, they switch majors—often adding years to their studies.

Retaking classes: Withdrawing from or failing courses forces students to retake them, further delaying progress.

Personal circumstances: Life happens—health issues, financial strain, and family obligations can easily derail academic timelines.

Course availability: Students often find themselves unable to register for required courses due to limited offerings, causing unwanted setbacks.

Part-time enrollment: Many students are balancing work or caregiving responsibilities, extending their academic journey over several years.

While only 41% of U.S. college students graduate within four years, that number increases to about 64% within six years. These statistics underscore the vital need for effective academic advising and student support systems to guide students through their educational paths.

Yet beyond these external challenges lies a deeper issue: **internal uncertainty**. Far too many young people embark on higher education without a clear sense of who they are, why they exist, or what they're meant to contribute to the world. They are visionless, and without vision, even their purpose gets lost in the shuffle.

CHAPTER 10

When we have a clear purpose and a vision for how to fulfill it, excuses lose their power. We move unapologetically, with focus and determination, overcoming every obstacle because our "why" is greater than any reason to stop. Purpose doesn't ask for permission—it compels action.

I emphasize that purpose is your why, and vision is your how. When students don't know why they're here or how they're meant to make an impact, they drift through life—and college—with little direction. This is why I believe discovering purpose and developing a personal vision should precede formal higher education. The sooner, the better.

The key challenge in life is simple yet profound: **knowing what to do.**
That's why one of my greatest passions is helping others—especially the next generation—find clarity, purpose, and vision. I am committed to championing global efforts toward self-discovery, purpose-driven living, and leadership development. We desperately need intentional spaces and programs where high school students are trained to understand themselves, align with their life's purpose, and develop a vision for their future—before they step into college or the workforce.

Because once you catch a vision, you stop wandering—and you start building.

> **"If you can't figure out your purpose, figure out your passion. For your passion will lead you right into your purpose."** - T. D. Jakes

TODAY'S UNIVERSITIES AND OUR CHILDREN'S UNCERTAINTIES

I love what **Howard Thurman** said, **"Don't ask yourself what the world needs; ask yourself what makes you come alive.**

And then go and do that. Because what the world needs is people who have come alive."

HELPING OUR CHILDREN DISCOVER PURPOSE

This is what our children need to be taught.

Maybe we can't help them pinpoint their exact purpose, but we can guide them toward it. It's vital to help them identify their interests, natural abilities, spiritual talents, and unique gifts—and then steer those toward their dreams and visions. Students always perform better in classes they enjoy. It's easier to study and stay motivated when the subject is aligned with their passion.

Remember, I've said this over and over again: Most people form their dream between the tender ages of 8 and 12, but they often get educated out of it—usually by unauthorized people.

PURPOSE PROVIDES DIRECTION

When you know your purpose, you have an advantage. You learn to conduct your affairs with clarity and intention. Purpose brings discipline and helps guide your educational path. The same applies to every goal in life—short-term or long-term.

When someone doesn't have a clear vision for their life, *anything goes*. That's why Proverbs 29:18 (NLT) warns:

> **"When people do not accept divine guidance, they run wild."**

Stay in your lane. It's uncomfortable to serve in areas where you aren't skilled, talented, or gifted.

CHAPTER 10

WHERE PURPOSE IS FOUND

We've already covered where purpose is found: in two places—**within you** and **in the mind of your Creator**. If you truly seek it, you will find it. Inquisitive people attract reasons—the *why*—for almost everything, including their own lives.

Psalm 84:11 (NIV) promises:

> **"For the LORD God is a sun and shield; the LORD bestows favor and honor; no good thing does He withhold from those whose walk is blameless." This reminds us that God does not withhold any good thing—whether it's your assignment, your purpose, or His perfect will for your life. Yet, part of discovering those "good things" lies within.**

Another place to search is within:

"The purposes of a person's heart are deep waters, but one who has insight draws them out." (Proverbs 20:5, NIV). God has already placed purpose within you, but it takes reflection, self-awareness, and divine insight to draw it out. The more you understand yourself, the more likely you are to position yourself in environments that cultivate your strengths and align you with His plan.

PASSION FUELS PURPOSE

What is passion? It's a strong, often barely controlled emotion—the juice of life. Passion is the **fuel** that drives purpose.

Dr. Myles Munroe once said:

> *"Leadership is the capacity to influence others through inspiration, motivated by passion, generated by a vision, produced by a conviction, ignited by a purpose."*

When you discover your purpose through your passion, you must then determine the specific knowledge required to fuel it. Ask yourself: *What purpose does my knowledge serve?*

Your major life goal should help you determine what knowledge you need. With this settled, the next step is to gather accurate information from dependable sources.

KNOWLEDGE IS POTENTIAL POWER

Educated people know where to find the knowledge they need—and how to organize it into **specific, actionable plans**.

Napoleon Hill wrote in *Think and Grow Rich*:

> "The word 'educate' is derived from the Latin word 'educo,' meaning to educe, to draw out, or to DEVELOP FROM WITHIN."

He also said:

> "KNOWLEDGE will not attract money unless it is organized, and intelligently directed, through practical PLANS OF ACTION, to the DEFINITE END of accumulation of money... Knowledge is only potential power."

Francis Bacon coined the phrase "Knowledge is power," but that was before we had instant access to nearly unlimited information. Today, we understand that **information is only useful when it's understood, directed, and applied**.

CHAPTER 10

Knowledge becomes powerful when it is applied toward a specific goal. Ultimately, **applied knowledge becomes wisdom**, and wisdom is the highest form of power.

This is why college degrees often fall short—they can represent general or miscellaneous knowledge, without a clear application. As we'll explore further in the next chapter, the people who change the world are usually known for **one specific thing**. They dominate in that area. I call this a **micro-niche**.

MY JOURNEY OF DISCOVERY

I was blessed to live and travel to other countries in my younger years. That experience, in many ways, was more formative to my calling than general education.

I did complete an associate degree in a field I didn't plan to pursue long-term. I still gave it my best for two years and enjoyed the experience. My professors even told me that my calling was elsewhere. I graduated and repaired computers for a short time, but deep down I knew it wasn't my purpose. I tried aligning my majors with my calling, but it didn't click right away.

Eventually, I pursued theological studies in various institutions. During my missionary work in Trinidad and Tobago (three and a half years), I studied Theology and Leadership. I also read many books on relationships and leadership development — topics that naturally drew me in.

When I returned, I got into **management training** and later worked in the **car rental industry**, where I immediately excelled. That job was a turning point. I was the company's top salesperson. During that time, I also pursued studies in **Christian Leadership** during evenings in Philadelphia.

BEYOND THE HUSTLE

Later, I entered the **fitness industry**. One of the employees I managed in the car rental business prior helped me achieve fitness goals. I slimmed down in just three months, and because I was advising others on nutrition, I ended up becoming a **sales general manager** for seven years at one of America's Largest Fitness Clubs Corperate Business. It was here I realized: **Sales was definitely part of my lane.**

Initially, I wrestled with the idea that transitioning from missionary work to corporate America felt like a demotion. But I received a divine revelation—this shift wasn't a **regression**; it was a **progression. A promotion** into my **purpose**. I wasn't just earning a paycheck—I was making an impact everywhere I turned. It was so fulfilling, I often forgot I was even employed by a company.

My previous experience as a missionary had prepared me for this. I started seeing my workplace as a **mission field**. Promotions followed naturally. Why? Because I treated my platform as a **tool for transformation**. That's when everything shifted.

Jesus said, **"Go into all the world"** (Mark 16:15). And guess what? Business is one of the most strategic platforms to spread Kingdom culture and help people discover purpose. It's a world—a major sphere of influence.

I didn't start in business to one day go into missions. I started in overseas missions so I could step into the business world equipped to influence it. I brought Kingdom values into the system from the beginning.

Some of you reading this book may take the reverse path—you'll begin in business and eventually find yourself on missions based on your purpose. Both approaches are effective.

Remember: **The twelve men Jesus called were all working men—fishermen, tax collectors, tradesmen.** He met them in the middle of their jobs and said, *"Follow Me, and I will make*

CHAPTER 10

you fishers of men" (Matthew 4:19). **He called them out of what they were doing, into who they were becoming.**

Purpose begins where you are—but it doesn't end there. Purpose often meets us in the middle of our work.

PURPOSE-DRIVEN EDUCATION

A few years later, I moved to SWFL and enrolled at a university that accepted all my prior credits—from colleges and life experience as a missionary. They condensed my degree into just one year. It was perfect. I majored in **Interdisciplinary Studies**. Every class captivated me.

They had me study Bob Proctor—whose conferences I had already attended in Miami, FL. I was amazed at how God orchestrated everything. Not that I really needed an education, but it was important for me - as personal goal because of the lifestyle I lived prior. I owned it to myself.

Ecclesiastes 3:11 (NIV) says:

> **"He has made everything beautiful in its time. He has also set eternity in the human heart; yet no one can fathom what God has done from beginning to end."**

This verse reminds us to trust God's timing. Every season and experience in life has meaning and beauty within the larger picture of God's purpose.

IF YOU'RE UNSURE, START BROAD—BUT NOT RANDOM

If you must attend college but haven't yet discovered your purpose, consider beginning with a field that keeps your options open while helping you explore your strengths, values, and natural interests. Choose a major that teaches you how to think, lead, and communicate effectively—skills that will serve you in any calling.

Some great starting points include:

- **Business Administration & Management** – Develops leadership, strategy, and decision-making skills essential for both entrepreneurship and organizational influence.

- **Communications** – Strengthens your ability to express ideas, connect with people, and articulate your vision clearly.

- **Leadership** – Focuses on personal development, emotional intelligence, and the principles of guiding others effectively.

- **Psychology** – Deepens your understanding of human behavior and motivation—insightful for any purpose-driven career.

- **Liberal Arts & Sciences / General Studies** – Provides broad exposure to multiple disciplines while you discern your path.

- **Philosophy, Ethics, and Humanities** – Sharpens your moral compass and critical thinking skills as you explore life's deeper questions.

CHAPTER 10

- **Undeclared / Exploratory Studies** – Gives you time to discover your strengths before committing to a specific track.

- **Entrepreneurship** – Equips you to identify opportunities, solve problems creatively, and build ventures aligned with your vision.

Remember, the goal is not simply to get a degree—it's to discover you. Education is most effective when it becomes a tool for purpose, not just a path to employment.

Choose something that aligns with your current interests.

But ask yourself: *Why commit to a long, expensive program if you haven't even detected your passion yet?* Why become a **depressed dentist** when you could be a **passionate musician**?

And if you're thinking, *"I need something to fall back on in case I fail,"* remember: **Being successful at the wrong thing is a form of failure**.

Seek not outwardly—but inwardly. Study your:

- **Desires**
- **Design**
- **Distinction**

SOCIETY DOESN'T ALWAYS GET IT RIGHT

Our educational system is often designed to produce employees—not assist in **self-discovery**.

Look at Bill Gates, Steve Jobs, and others. They left traditional systems to discover their authentic path. This proves that true wealth doesn't come from a job title—it comes from **your gift**.

As Proverbs 18:16 reminds us:

> **"A person's gift makes room for them and brings them before the great."**

This verse emphasizes that your unique gifts—not your degree, job, or title—are what open doors and lead to influence.

CHAPTER 11

THE TRUE DEFINITION OF LEADERSHIP: WHAT QUALIFIES YOU TO LEAD

> *"Leadership is the capacity to influence others through inspiration motivated by a passion, generated by a vision, produced by a conviction, ignited by a purpose."* — Dr. Myles Munroe

In the prior chapters, we discussed key points to help us discover our purpose. Once our purpose is discovered—what then? I've said numerous times throughout this book that we cannot retire from our purpose. It is something we carry with us throughout our entire lives. So what comes next after discovering and pursuing our purpose?

Leadership in that purpose.

TAKING THE LEAD:

Here's an inspirational acronym for **LEAD**:

- **L – Learn** – Stay teachable and always pursue growth.

- **E – Empower** – Help others rise by equipping and encouraging them.

- **A – Act** – Take initiative and lead by example.

- **D – Develop** – Invest in yourself and others to reach full potential.

Robert Schuller believed that resilience isn't about passivity—it's about actively steering your life through challenges. While phrases like "take it easy" or "take care" offer comfort, Schuller encourages us to "take control" and lead ourselves forward with purpose and determination.
He emphasizes the importance of **proactive leadership** and **personal responsibility** in his best-selling book, *Tough Times Never Last, But Tough People Do*. Ultimately, leadership has no real value if we're not taking action and are not truly in control.

In the realm of leadership, various definitions exist, each offering insight into the essence of effective leadership. One definition that resonates deeply with me comes from the renowned book *13 Fatal Errors Managers Make and How You Can Avoid Them* by W. Steven Brown. In this book, Brown articulates that **leadership is the art of achieving predetermined goals by leveraging the voluntary cooperation and efforts of others**. This perspective emphasizes the importance of collaboration and empowerment in leadership.

Moreover, Brown highlights the distinction between managing and leading by noting that **true leaders do not seek to control behavior, but rather aim to influence thinking**. It is a critical error to focus on controlling outcomes rather than shaping mindsets. Genuine leadership lies in **inspiring individuals to think independently** and embrace their roles as leaders within their unique areas of expertise.

CHAPTER 11

Effective leaders guide individuals toward aligning their passions and aspirations with organizational objectives, fostering a culture of growth and innovation. By encouraging individuals to develop their leadership potential, true leaders empower others to drive positive change and make a meaningful impact.

On the other hand, some mistakenly equate leadership solely with **influence**, overlooking how that influence is exercised. Influence without character can lead to **manipulation, intimidation, or fear-based compliance**. This limited perspective fails to capture the true essence of leadership, which involves **inspiring and guiding others toward a common vision**through collaboration and mutual respect.

Authentic leadership goes beyond mere influence. It involves fostering a supportive environment where individuals are encouraged to **unleash their full potential** and contribute meaningfully to shared goals. By prioritizing collaboration, empowerment, and personal growth, true leaders cultivate a culture of excellence and transformation within their teams and organizations.

For example, if I were to point a gun at your head and demand that you kiss my foot or get on your knees, I might get you to do what I wanted—but not in the right way. That wouldn't be leadership. It wouldn't be **inspiration**.

You can only inspire someone genuinely when you are **passionate about your conviction**. That's why I wholeheartedly agree with the quote I shared at the beginning of this chapter:

> *"Leadership is the capacity to influence others through inspiration motivated by a passion, generated by a vision, produced by a conviction, ignited by a purpose."* — Dr. Myles Munroe

As you can see, all these principles I've been sharing are interconnected. A person must first embark on a journey of self-discovery to uncover their niche. Once it's found, they must practice their gift until it becomes an embedded skill in their life. At that point, they'll become an expert at solving problems with that skill—and be ready to lead others.

So how do you lead someone toward a noble end?

Through **inspiration**.

Let's take a closer look at Dr. Myles Munroe's definition of leadership and examine its depth in this chapter.

The **Greek philosophy of leadership** traditionally asserts that leadership is reserved for the elite—a select few who are either born into power or chosen to lead. In stark contrast, our philosophy is this: **everyone is a leader**. Leadership is not about position or pedigree. Leadership is discovered when a person identifies their gift and begins using it to serve others.

The true value of every human being is the **gift** they were born to deliver to humanity.

WHO HAS THE POWER?

To illustrate this point, I love the analogy Dr. Munroe shares in his leadership book *I'm In Charge*. He uses a simple yet profound example titled **"The Battery and the Wire."**

He begins with a question:

> "Which part of a car is more important—the battery or the terminal wire?"

Most people would immediately answer, "The battery. It has the power."

CHAPTER 11

A car has around **60,000 parts**, and the battery might proudly claim:

> "I'm in charge of all of them. Nothing starts without me. I'm the battery. I have the power. Power! Power! Power! I'm the one who starts everything. Nothing starts until I arrive."

Sound familiar? Do you know people like that?

But now let's remove that tiny **red terminal wire**—the one that connects the battery to the rest of the engine. The battery might cost $150, but that small wire? Just $10. Even with 59,999 working parts and a powerful battery, **without that wire, the car won't start.**

You could have a car worth $70,000, $80,000, even $150,000—and still, it could be rendered completely useless by the absence of a $10 wire. You want to go somewhere. You have something to accomplish. But the car says:

> "I'm ready... but that little wire is missing."
>
> The battery still shouts, "I've got the power!"
>
> The spark plug chimes in, "I've got the fire!"
>
> The engine says, "I run the car."

But the little wire remains silent. It doesn't need to speak up. Eventually, all the other parts realize the truth and say, "Go find the wire!"

That **terminal wire** was created to transmit electrical current from the battery to the generator, and then to the engine, to ignite the spark plugs that start the car. In the domain of

electrical transmission, **the wire is in charge**. That's its area of leadership.

It might be small, but it can shut down the whole engine. Without it, nothing moves.

EVERY PART HAS ITS DOMAIN

Each part of a car is a **leader**—but only in its specific domain.

- A spark plug can never be a battery.
- A battery can never be a manifold.
- A manifold can never be a generator.

In the domain of the battery, the battery leads. In the domain of the wire, the wire leads. Each part is essential, not because of its size, price, or appearance—but because of its **function**.

This perspective on leadership **directly contradicts** the outdated belief that leadership is for an elite, "chosen" few—an idea often rooted in colonial or hierarchical mindsets that suggest only a privileged class is worthy to lead.

YOU ARE IN CHARGE

My view of leadership is this: **every person has an inherent gift**, and we are all called to serve that gift to the world.

You are a leader. You have power. Your gift is your power.

You are in charge **in your area of gifting—your domain**. You have a specific function to carry out, a leadership spot that only you can fill. Just as the terminal wire's value is determined by

CHAPTER 11

function and not price or visibility, your value is defined by your purpose, not by your platform.

Someone needs your gift. And likewise, you need the gifts that others bear in order to thrive.

> So, who's in charge?
>
> **You are.**
>
> Who's got the power?
>
> **Every one of us.**
>
> — Excerpt adapted from *I'm In Charge*, Dr. Myles Munroe

Therefore, you too have a leadership spot to fill and a function to carry out. Your gift determines that spot and function in this world. You are in charge in your area of gifting, your domain. When you find it and operate in it, you'll never have to self-advertise or get stuck in the hustle and bustle of life.

Just like Dr. Munroe states, the wire does not have to say, *"You need me. You can't start without me."* All the other parts soon realize it and say, *"Go find the wire."* Your gift serves a need in this world, and once you let that gift shine, it will usher you toward your destiny. Once it's shining, people will call upon you—because it ultimately shines the light and knowledge of what the Creator put in you. It's the treasure you came to the world with, and your generation needs it.

Again, let's look closely at this powerful definition and dissect it:

> "Leadership is the capacity to influence others through inspiration motivated by a passion,

generated by a vision, produced by a conviction, ignited by a purpose." — Dr. Myles Munroe

You can never effectively inspire, let alone influence, anyone outside of your domain—your area of gifting. If you try to do so outside of your sweet spot, it requires extra effort that can quickly turn into mere hustling or forcing. This won't be sweet at all, nor will it be like the unforced rhythms of grace you should flow in.

YOUR SKILL IS YOUR EXPERTISE WITHIN YOUR NICHE

I believe this is what Solomon meant when he wrote,

> "If the ax is dull and its edge unsharpened, more strength is needed, but skill will bring success." (Ecclesiastes 10:10 NIV)

When your gift becomes sharpened—developed and refined—it turns into a skill. A skill is like the expression, *"I can do it in my sleep."* What we mean is that it has become a part of us. Your work is no longer just a place you go to, but a combination of who you are and what you do.

Skill is now expertise—an ability to do something well. This comes through consistency. Practice makes perfect. This is when you are called upon to use your leadership role.

A fish doesn't learn how to swim, but it does become better over time. Stay in your gift and be consistent so you don't lose your advantage edge.

According to our definition, a leader is **capacity**—the maximum amount something can contain. It is the ability to influence the character, development, or behavior of people or things.

CHAPTER 11

- **Influence** — The capacity to affect the character, development, or behavior of a group or individual.

- **Inspiration** — The process of being mentally stimulated to feel or do something, especially something creative. Inspiring others is usually not making them followers but enabling them to become creative themselves.

- **Passion** — A strong, barely controllable emotion. Passion is the fuel to our intent or purpose. If you aren't passionate about something, who can you ask to follow or cooperate with you? Why would others want to? Passion narrows down your purpose by what lights you up.

- **Vision** — The ability to look beyond what your eyes see; tapping into your heart, the core of your being. What you visualize in your heart is more important than what your eyes see. Vision is a picture of a preferred future—a mental blueprint of the life you desire, driving your actions and decisions toward becoming your best self. Without vision, a leader is illegitimate—because leadership is not about position, but about purpose and direction. Vision qualifies and authenticates a leader.

- **Conviction** — True leaders are driven by conviction, not convenience. It is an unshakable belief in a cause, truth, or purpose that shapes a leader's actions, decisions, and character—even in the face of opposition, risk, or personal loss.

    - Conviction gives leaders courage—they stand firm even when unpopular.

    - Conviction gives leaders clarity—they aren't swayed by trends or pressure.

- ○ Conviction comes from vision and purpose—when a leader knows why they exist, they can endure anything without flip-flopping.

  "Authentic leaders do not chase followers; they naturally draw others towards them through their unwavering convictions." (RAH)

- **Purpose** — The ultimate "why" behind your life—your reason for being, the divine assignment encoded in your very design. Purpose gives meaning to vision, fuels conviction, and anchors leadership. Without it, life becomes aimless; with it, everything gains direction.

THE POWER OF BEING ASTUTE

Versatility is a Powerful Skill All Leaders Need in This Decade

Versatility is the ability to adapt—or to be adapted—to many different functions or activities.

Paul was a master communicator whose purpose was to be a light to foreign people. He was a man called to be a

> "Chosen instrument to proclaim my name to the Gentiles and their kings and to the people of Israel." (Acts 9:15b NIV)

Paul spread knowledge (light) to different audiences and people from various walks of life—from foreign people to kings, both Gentiles and the people of Israel alike.

CHAPTER 11

PAUL WAS ALWAYS ADAPTING WITHOUT ADOPTING TO EFFECTIVELY INFLUENCE

He describes how he became one (a slave-servant) with his assignment, in order to win or influence as many as possible:

> "Though I am free and belong to no one, I have made myself a slave to everyone, to win as many as possible. To the Jews I became like a Jew, to win the Jews. To those under the law I became like one under the law (though I myself am not under the law), to win those under the law. To those not having the law I became like one not having the law (though I am not free from God's law but am under Christ's law), to win those not having the law. To the weak I became weak, to win the weak. I have become all things to all people so that by all possible means I might save some. I do all this for the sake of the gospel, that I may share in its blessings." (1 Corinthians 9:19-23 NIV)

Paul used his freedom by becoming a slave to serve his gift. He became versatile to win as many as possible and to save some. The word *save* means to salvage. When a person is won over, they are brought back to their original state—they are safe, saved, and salvaged. They are literally rescued from a world of perdition (darkness) to an unshakable kingdom called the kingdom of God where they will experience light—the knowledge of who they are.

> "For he has rescued us from the dominion of darkness and brought us into the kingdom of the Son he loves." (Colossians 1:13 NIV)

The kingdom is our inheritance—our rightful place where we ultimately flourish as lights or stars in the sky. It's where we are kept from man's greatest enemy: darkness, which is ignorance.

BEYOND THE HUSTLE

Knowing who you are and being brought into this place of your unshakable kingdom is the ultimate pursuit and place of rest, where you'll live your unique unforced rhythm of grace.

A legitimate leader will never lead you to them but back to **you**—to

> "take your inheritance, the kingdom prepared for you since the creation of the world." (Matthew 25:34 NIV)

> "…and giving joyful thanks to the Father, who has qualified you to share in the inheritance of his holy people in the kingdom of light. For he has rescued us from the dominion of darkness and brought us into the kingdom of the Son he loves, in whom we have redemption, the forgiveness of sins." (Colossians 1:12-14 NIV)

Ultimately, winning people means bringing them to a foundational faith and position of strength through self-discovery and proper inheritance.

> "Therefore, since we are receiving a kingdom that cannot be shaken, let us be thankful, and so worship God acceptably with reverence and awe, for our 'God is a consuming fire.'" (Hebrews 12:28-29 NIV)

When a person is self-sufficient and knows how to go directly to their own Source, the one who won them and connected them in that direction has done a job well done—that is, fulfilled their life assignment effectively.

Paul describes this as

> "the ministry of reconciliation…" (2 Corinthians 5:18)

CHAPTER 11

Reconciliation is the restoration of a friendly relationship—having access to your Source (Father), God.

He states that it started with Christ over 2,000 years ago, and that he and we carry the baton and life work of ultimately restoring others unto this privilege:

> "God was reconciling the world to himself in Christ, not counting people's sins against them. And he has committed to us the message of reconciliation." (verse 19)

> "We are therefore Christ's ambassadors, as though God were making his appeal through us. We implore you on Christ's behalf: Be reconciled to God." (verse 20)

> To do this effectively, one must have the ability to adapt and be versatile as a wise person out to win souls. (Proverbs 11:30)

POWER OF INFLUENCE

Paul was in the presence of deep thinkers and Stoic philosophers. They said to him,

> "You are bringing some strange ideas to our ears, and we would like to know what they mean." (Acts 17:20 NIV)

It says regarding them that

> "All the Athenians and the foreigners who lived there spent their time doing nothing but talking

about and listening to the latest ideas." (Acts 17:21 NIV)

He boldly stood up in the largest city of Greece, but not before first carefully assessing it:

> "While Paul was waiting for them in Athens, he was greatly distressed to see that the city was full of idols. So, he reasoned in the synagogue with both Jews and God-fearing Greeks, as well as in the marketplace day by day with those who happened to be there." (Acts 17:16-17 NIV)

Paul was burdened by the ignorance in this society. A good question to ask yourself is, *What burdens or distresses you about the issues of our world?* Remember one of the questions toward self-discovery is, *What do I want to do for humanity?* Another is, *What makes me angry?*

Paul then stood up in the meeting of the Areopagus and said:

> "People of Athens! I see that in every way you are very religious. For as I walked around and looked carefully at your objects of worship, I even found an altar with this inscription: TO AN UNKNOWN GOD. So, you are ignorant of the very thing you worship—and this is what I am going to proclaim to you." (Acts 17:22-23 NIV)

Then he quoted one of their familiar poets:

> "For in him we live and move and have our being.' As some of your own poets have said, 'We are his offspring.'" (Acts 17:28 NIV)

At the end, the listeners were stimulated and wanted more:

CHAPTER 11

> "We want to hear you again on this subject." (Acts 17:32 NLT)

> "Some of the people became followers of Paul and believed. Among them was Dionysius, a member of the Areopagus, also a woman named Damaris, and a number of others." (Acts 17:34 NIV)

As you can see, he influenced the influential, which aligned perfectly with his purpose and calling. He was fully equipped for his leadership role.

The key was when they said,

> "We want to hear you again on this subject."

True leaders always whet their audience's appetite to learn—not impose but influence. Questions and inquisitiveness show a desire to learn. Ultimately, we are called to make learners, students, or disciples—perpetual students.

> **"ALWAYS BE PREPARED TO GIVE AN ANSWER TO EVERYONE WHO ASKS YOU TO GIVE THE REASON FOR THE HOPE THAT YOU HAVE. BUT DO THIS WITH GENTLENESS AND RESPECT."**
>
> **(1 PETER 3:15 NIV)**

This is one of my favorite verses in the Bible.

We too are called to be astute in our leadership role of influencing and impacting our sphere in society. Where are you called to work your life assignment? "Go into all the world!" (Mark 16:15). We should not be educated out of the world and into the church, but rather educated **in** the church **to** the outer world where the real problems lie. "In this world you will have trouble. But take heart! I have overcome the world." (John 16:33 NIV)

What sphere in our society burdens you? What are you passionate about? Remember, it is a beautiful thing when **Passion and Education Collide**. Get educated, equipped, and empowered where you will have the biggest impact. Maintain versatility in your knowledge base in this decade to ensure relevance in your purpose and area of influence.

What's your call and gift? Where can you be used mightily? Is it Education? Business? Are you passionate about Media? Do you carry a burden or interest in Politics or Government? Can you see yourself impacting or changing the Entertainment World? Are you possessed with assisting Families? What about solving problems in Religion like Paul?

"Go into all the world" means to get into these spheres of influence for their betterment. The word *world* is from the Greek *Kosmos*, meaning **"powers of control"** and **"institutions of influence."** "The earth is the Lord's, and the fulness thereof; the world, and they that dwell therein." (Psalm 24:1 KJV) So, let's restore all of it back to its original Owner—especially the systems that have forgotten their core values passed down from their Owner, the Lord!

The world can seem like a very intimidating place. It's vast and full of troubles. However, it is our assignment and it is not for cowards.

> "Ask me, and I will make the nations your inheritance, the ends of the earth your possession." (Psalm 2:8 NIV)

> When we are encouraged to be of good cheer (or take heart) in the face of a vast, troublesome world, we are reminded to adopt the attitude of "a lion, mighty among beasts, who retreats before nothing." (Proverbs 30:30 NIV)

CHAPTER 11

Attitude is your viewpoint, perspective, outlook, stance, position, and conviction. It's a fresh feeling about something or someone that results from a settled new way of thinking. Hopefully, this book has inspired in you the boldness needed not to retreat from your responsibility, as you are a world changer for your generation. Hopefully, it will assist you in valiantly assessing, addressing, and ultimately altering your sphere of influence—one mind at a time.

You are in the world, but not from it.

> "As you sent me into the world, I have sent them into the world." (John 17:18 NIV)

> "I am sending you out like sheep among wolves. Therefore, be as shrewd as snakes and as innocent as doves." (Matthew 10:16 NIV)

To be shrewd means to be astute. Astute, according to Webster's Dictionary, means "having or showing an ability to accurately assess a situation or people and turn this to one's advantage." This is what Paul did in this situation. He was in their world, ready and equipped with their knowledge. He knew his purpose and made students (followers) out of deep thinkers and religious people who were in search of meaning.

Learn from the systems of this world and use that knowledge to your advantage to accurately impact the world. Remember, your gift—when refined, developed, and used—will eventually have a greater impact on your world.

> "A gift opens the way and ushers the giver into the presence of the great." (Proverbs 18:16 NIV)

We should not fear those who can only harm the body, but instead, we should have reverence for Him who has the power to destroy both body and soul. It is essential to remember that light has come into the world, symbolizing your role as a leader. However, some may prefer darkness over light because they wish to conceal their deeds. Let us be guided by the truth and stand firm in our purpose.

> "Do not be afraid of those who kill the body but cannot kill the soul. Rather, be afraid of the One who can destroy both soul and body in hell." (Matthew 10:28 NIV)

> "This is the verdict: Light has come into the world, but people loved darkness instead of light because their deeds were evil. Everyone who does evil hates the light and will not come into the light for fear that their deeds will be exposed." (John 3:19-20 NIV)

YOUR PROVISION IS A PLATFORM FOR YOUR PURPOSE

You can go to a job, not just to earn a paycheck, but to make disciples (students) and have an impact in different spheres of influence. An income is what we get out of this world, usually through a job. An impact is what we give back to our world, through our gift.

You have your success—what you get out of this world—and then you have your significance—what you share and give back to your world. Many of you reading this book have found your success. Good for you. But know that it is only a platform for an even greater impact through your purpose.

CHAPTER 11

THE PARABLE OF THE WEEDS

Even though you are not of the world, yet you are still sent into the world—you are to grow together with its systems.

> *"Jesus told them another parable: 'The kingdom of heaven is like a man who sowed good seed in his field. But while everyone was sleeping, his enemy came and sowed weeds among the wheat, and went away. When the wheat sprouted and formed heads, then the weeds also appeared.'"* **(Matthew 13:24–26 NIV)**

> *"The owner's servants came to him and said, 'Sir, didn't you sow good seed in your field? Where then did the weeds come from?'"* **(verse 27)**

> *"'An enemy did this,' he replied. The servants asked him, 'Do you want us to go and pull them up?' 'No,' he answered, 'because while you are pulling the weeds, you may uproot the wheat with them. Let both grow together until the harvest. At that time, I will tell the harvesters: First collect the weeds and tie them in bundles to be burned; then gather the wheat and bring it into my barn.'"* **(verses 28–30)**

This parable stirred the disciples so deeply that they asked Jesus to explain it privately.

> *"Then he left the crowd and went into the house. His disciples came to him and said, 'Explain to us the parable of the weeds in the field.'"* **(verse 36)**

The power of influence is in **integration**. You can never influence or impact what you avoid. That's why He said, *"Let both grow together"* (verse 30). You cannot remove yourself from the systems and expect them to change or be restored back to their rightful Owner (the Lord).

> *"He answered, 'The one who sowed the good seed is the Son of Man. The field is the world, and the good seed stands for the people of the kingdom. The weeds are the people of the evil one, and the enemy who sows them is the devil. The harvest is the end of the age, and the harvesters are angels.'"* **(verses 37–39)**

KEY PRINCIPLE #1

You are sown (placed) in your spot, and that spot is in the world.
That is where you will enjoy what you are doing—within your niche. The Son of Man is the One who gives gifts to mankind, and those gifts are for **world influence and service**. This is where "both grow together" (verse 29).

The field is the **world**, and Jesus clarified in another passage:

> *"My prayer is not that you take them out of the world but that you protect them from the evil one."* **(John 17:15)**

We are meant to grow together so that we may **reconcile that sphere back to its Lord (Owner)**.

Notice it says, *"Then the weeds also appeared"* (verse 26). This means that the right seeds—those who are the sons (or people) of the Kingdom—were sown first. That's because the world **rightfully belongs to God**, and His intent from the very beginning was for mankind to manage it as good stewards for Him.

CHAPTER 11

> "AND GOD SAID, LET US MAKE MAN IN OUR IMAGE, AFTER OUR LIKENESS: AND LET THEM HAVE DOMINION OVER THE FISH OF THE SEA, AND OVER THE FOWL OF THE AIR, AND OVER THE CATTLE, AND OVER ALL THE EARTH, AND OVER EVERY CREEPING THING THAT CREEPETH UPON THE EARTH."
>
> *(GENESIS 1:26 KJV)*

THE PARABLE OF PURPOSE AND PERSEVERANCE

The **parable of the weeds and the good seeds** (Matthew 13:24–30) illustrates the **coexistence of good and evil** in the world. It teaches us that as we carry out our kingdom assignments, we will encounter challenges, opposition, and spiritual resistance.

Just as the wheat and the weeds grow together in the same field, we too will have to persevere in the midst of adversity. The parable highlights the importance of **discernment, patience, and steadfastness** in fulfilling our God-given purpose.

> *"The kingdom of heaven is like a man who sowed good seed in his field. But while everyone was sleeping, his enemy came and sowed weeds among the wheat and went away. When the wheat sprouted and formed heads, then the weeds also appeared." (Matthew 13:24–26 NIV)*

In this story:

- **The field** represents the **world**.

- **The good seed** represents the **people of the Kingdom**.

- **The enemy's seed** represents **corruption and deception**—an attempt to pervert God's original intent.

But God's Kingdom people are called to **grow through it** and **transform culture** with influence. Because in Kingdom reality, **opposition creates opportunities.**

KEY PRINCIPLE #2: YOU ARE PEOPLE OF THE KINGDOM

Though we live in this world, we are **not of it**. We were **sent** from God's Kingdom to serve on earth. As Paul wrote:

> *"For He chose us in Him before the creation of the world to be holy and blameless in His sight. In love, He predestined us for adoption to sonship through Jesus Christ, in accordance with His pleasure and will." (Ephesians 1:4–5 NIV)*

We are **ambassadors**, not bystanders. Our role is to represent Heaven, not simply watch from the sidelines

> *"We are therefore Christ's ambassadors, as though God were making His appeal through us. We implore you on Christ's behalf: Be reconciled to God." (2 Corinthians 5:20 NIV)*

As **Dr. Myles Munroe** taught, a Kingdom is the **governing influence of a king** over a distant territory, impacting it with His will, intent, and purpose—creating a citizenry that reflects His culture, morals, and values. This is the **Kingdom of God**, and we are His official representatives here on earth.

CHAPTER 11

KEY PRINCIPLE #3: YOU HAVE A KINGDOM MANDATE

Because you are a person of the Kingdom, you have a **mandate**—a specific calling to influence your sphere of life with Kingdom principles.

> *"As you go, proclaim: 'The kingdom of heaven has come near.'" (Matthew 10:7 CSB)*

This is not limited to religious work. Your **gifting**, your **skill**, and your **passion**—what you're naturally equipped and drawn to—is the very vehicle God will use to bring His Kingdom to earth.

> *"Your kingdom come, your will be done, on earth as it is in heaven." (Matthew 6:10)*

When you find your **niche**—your uniquely suited place in the world—you begin to **transform society from the inside out**, not by striving, but by flowing in the grace God gave you.

POWER FOR PURPOSE

The **Amplified Bible** brings clarity to the power behind our purpose:

> *"I can do all things [which He has called me to do] through Him who strengthens and empowers me [to fulfill His purpose—I am self-sufficient in Christ's sufficiency; I am ready for anything and equal to anything through Him who infuses me with inner strength and confident peace]." (Philippians 4:13 AMP)*

WINNERS SHINE

The conclusion of the parable of the wheat and weeds shows us the reward for the righteous:

> *"Then the righteous will shine like the sun in the kingdom of their Father. Whoever has ears, let them hear." (Matthew 13:43 NIV)*

Winners shine—**not because they imposed, but because they influenced**. True leaders **lead others back** to right standing with God through love, wisdom, and truth.

> *"Those who are wise will shine like the brightness of the heavens, and those who lead many to righteousness, like the stars forever and ever." (Daniel 12:3 NIV)*

A MAN'S SUCCESSFUL LEADERSHIP ACCOMPLISHMENT

In *The Spirit of Leadership*, Dr. Myles Munroe wrote:

> *"Humanity has the natural circuitry to have dominion over its environment. The greatest evidence of what a product can do or is capable of is determined by the demands made on it by the one who made it. Therefore, God's requirement that we dominate is evidence that the ability to lead is inherent in every human spirit."*

Leadership is not optional—it is **embedded** in your design. And purpose is the **pathway** to activating it.

CHAPTER 11

> **"Rulership is in our genes; dominion is in our makeup. We were designed to rule the earth."**
> – *Dr. Myles Munroe*

The apostle **Paul** was highly educated, and he ultimately established his gathering place in a public setting—the lecture hall of **Tyrannus in Ephesus**. He had discovered his niche. Paul was called and purposed to be a **light and teacher to the Gentiles**, and he was perfectly equipped for that specific audience.

At one point, he had to separate himself from religious individuals who refused to believe and even publicly maligned his message. The Scripture says:

> *"So Paul left them. He took the disciples with him and had discussions daily in the lecture hall of Tyrannus."* (Acts 19:9, NIV)

> *"This went on for two years, so that all the Jews and Greeks who lived in the province of Asia heard the word of the Lord."* (Acts 19:10, NIV)

Once Paul found his **right audience**, **right environment**, and **right niche**, he no longer had to **strive, hustle**, or **force his message**. The entire city began coming to *him*—to his setting. That's what happens when you step into the place you were designed to dominate.

Leadership is not about reaching everyone.

You're not called to everyone—you're called to "**whosoever wills**." When you're operating in your God-given niche, you won't have to chase people down. The right ones will be drawn to your voice and gift. Your ax head becomes sharp. Wisdom begins to direct your actions.

As it was in **Thessalonica**, momentum in the right setting can shake an entire city:

> *"These men who have turned the world upside down have come here also... saying that there is another king, Jesus."* (Acts 17:6–7, ESV)

Turning the world upside down was not a figure of speech—it was **radical change**, evidenced by the reaction of the public. Conviction has that kind of power. But with influence came **persecution**, as it always does for those truly called to lead.

Someone once said, *"The higher the level, the bigger the devil."* True leaders often **welcome adversity** as validation of their mission. It's an honor to suffer for what you believe and stand for. Conviction enables you to **stand in adversity**.

Before the transformation of Ephesus, Paul had to **break mental barriers**:

> *"Paul entered the synagogue and spoke boldly there for three months, arguing persuasively about the kingdom of God."* (Acts 19:8, NIV)

In that synagogue, Paul communicated the **Kingdom of God**—God's system and influence on earth—but his audience wasn't ready. His message clashed with **religious traditions** and **preconceived notions**. The greatest enemy to **self-discovery** is a closed mind. If you're unwilling to unlearn, or you think you already know it all, you'll stay stuck.

Once Paul **left that environment** and took his disciples with him, things began to flow. The results were undeniable:

> *"God did extraordinary miracles through Paul, so that even handkerchiefs and aprons that had touched him were taken to the sick... and the evil spirits left them."* (Acts 19:11–12, NIV)

CHAPTER 11

Imagine operating with such **kingdom influence**, where what others call "supernatural" becomes your **new normal**.

To **live beyond the hustle**, we must discover our **niche**—that **unforced rhythm of grace** where things flow rather than strain. Like Paul, **you are equipped for your purpose**. Through practice, discipleship, and faithfulness, your gift becomes sharp and skillful.

And here's what I love most from this passage:

> *"This went on for two years, so that all the Jews and Greeks who lived in the province of Asia heard the word of the Lord."* (Acts 19:10, NIV)

In the right environment, **with the right message, and the right audience**, **God will multiply your influence** beyond anything you could force on your own.

A MAN TAPPING INTO HIS CORPORATE LEADERSHIP MAN

Knowing what to do—and actually doing it—is one of the greatest challenges in life. I know of a specific organization, a church in South Florida, that changed its name from Flamingo Road Baptist Church to the simple and powerful name **Potential Church**.

Why did they make this change? They realized that the only way to be truly effective and to align with the lead pastor's vision was to help their students—and especially their youth—discover and develop their individual potential. This shift sometimes meant going against long-standing traditions and even risking offending the very religious organization they were once part of.

I'm not sure how long it took Pastor Troy to overcome these religious and traditional obstacles during the transition, but the results were remarkable. The church grew rapidly and became one of the fastest-thriving churches in America at that time, expanding with multiple locations across various cities and countries.

Their leadership was focused on helping others become who they were meant to be—helping them tap into their God-given potential. They serve in the west sector of Fort Lauderdale, which has become their ideal environment and headquarters for world influence.

> **"Crisis is the cradle of leadership."**
> **- Myles Munroe**

As stated earlier, I had the privilege of studying under Dr. Myles Munroe for four years, and I was further mentored by Trista Sue Kragh, who was also raised under Dr. Munroe's leadership. He once said, "We exist because there is a problem we were born to solve."

This world is full of problems—crises of all kinds. From orphaned children, poverty, and political corruption, to broken education systems, dysfunctional families, sexual abuse, depression, disease, genocide—the list goes on.

One of the simplest yet most powerful ways to identify your purpose is to ask:
What bothers me? What burdens me? What angers me?
Your answers are often clues pointing toward your domain—your area of gifting—where you were created to bring the Kingdom's influence.

Ministry is not confined to what happens inside four walls.
It's what you do with your life, your service, and your influence to bring God's Kingdom culture to a specific area of need in the world.

CHAPTER 11

Some key questions in the self-discovery journey include:

What do I want to do for humanity?
What is the most important thing I could do with my life?
The issues that irritate, grieve, or even ignite righteous anger within you are often signposts guiding you to your purpose. Why? Because at our core, we are not just preachers—we are problem solvers. "Crisis is the cradle of leadership."
Every time a crisis emerges, a leader is born—if they are the right person for the task.
Mother Teresa emerged from the cradle of deep poverty.
Moses rose from the cradle of lost identity and misplaced purpose.
Jesus Christ came forth from the cradle of brokenness and divine separation.
Dr. Myles Munroe arose from the cradle of poor leadership and a lack of national direction.

Dr. Martin Luther King Jr. sprouted from the cradle of racial injustice and systemic oppression.

Nelson Mandela rose from the cradle of apartheid, imprisonment, and national division.
What world crisis burdens you?
What cradle did—or will—you rise from?

CHAPTER 12

"THE EDGE OF PURPOSE"

HOW ONE ROOFTOP ENCOUNTER CHANGED A VILLAGE—AND A LIFE.

"For I know the plans I have for you," declares the Lord… (Jeremiah 29:11, NIV)

MY EXPERIENCE AS A MISSIONARY

How I was at the Right Place at The Right Time

BEYOND THE HUSTLE

(Original Picture from Guardian Express, Trinidad & Tobago)

I always wanted to do missionary work before embarking on my own career. I had this privilege in 1995, when I served in Trinidad & Tobago for three and a half years. It was there I presented the gospel to a whole community, where I lived among Hindus. It was very challenging. I believe it was designed to be a learning experience for me—preparing me for other avenues of service.

I can recall an especially outstanding occurrence while I served in Trinidad. It was in 1995 at a Hindu village.

I wasn't the most popular person there since I was introducing a new way of life to one of the first developed Hindu towns in the region, El Dorado Village. At first, I did not want to remain there, since I had to try too hard to win the people's favor. I became accepted after saving a young man from committing suicide. He

CHAPTER 12

was about to jump off the tallest building at the time, the Salvatori Building in Port of Spain, the nation's capital.

While traveling there, I was already fulfilling my purpose. I had a small-sized congregation that I pastored. But because the village was predominantly Hindu, many people observed our meetings from afar. They showed some interest, but not enough to come in while I would preach or teach. One day I witnessed a young 9-year-old being beaten by his uncle with a leather belt. I felt handcuffed, as if I couldn't do anything because it would've started more trouble for me if I interfered. As I stood there and stared, I immediately got a thought: "Enroll this young boy into school." That's what I thought loudly. Twice. The thought spoke, "A young lad not in school becomes idle, and idleness gets every youngster into trouble." Proverbs 12:5 says, "The thoughts of the righteous are right..." I believe that if we are steady, aligned, and wanting to do God's purpose in every scenario, our thoughts will lead us. We must confide in them.

Therefore, the following day I asked the mother, my neighbor, to get dressed because we were going to get this young lad's birth certificate to start the process of enrolling him in school. We went and found favor with all the employees that we came into contact with during that short process. It was at the Red House, the Parliament Building. One supervisor told me that because the cause and purpose were noble, we would have everything set up the next morning. This time I came alone, and I had my reasons. I just needed to make sure the mother did everything she was supposed to do. I also came alone the following day to avoid setbacks.

The next morning, I got off the public transportation—called Maxi Taxi (The Trinidadian Bus Services). I was speaking to a local woman about her purpose and what I was doing in her country. As we came off the public bus at the public square, I noticed a young man on the corner of the building's ledge. There was one individual on the pavement yelling, "I'll give you $40.00 if you jump." I couldn't believe what I was hearing—lots of people, lots of commotion. I then received a prompting in my spirit to go up and get him down. It was pretty clear. I believe it was the voice of God. How was I sure? Well, I remember reading in Isaiah 55:11 (NLT) years ago where it says: **"It is the same with my word. It will always accomplish all that I want it to, and it will prosper everywhere I send it."**

The following verse gets even better: **"For you shall go out with joy and be led out with peace; The mountains and the hills shall break forth into singing before you, and all the trees of the field shall clap their hands"** (Isaiah 55:12 NKJV). I'm positive that when you are being led by God's Spirit and word, there is a joy and peace that is unspeakable—and it is also the byproduct accompanying those who follow its lead. The second thing that happens when you step out on faith is that astonishing things begin to move out of your way—hindrances. Thus, "the mountains and hills break forth into singing, and the trees clap their hands." This speaks to the truth that even nature submits to God's purpose—how much more should people?

That same woman I was conversing with also happened to be walking in this direction. She let me know what was taking place. She made it known that this was a common occurrence. A problem that didn't subside. Young people were taking their lives almost every week in this country. After a small discussion, she motioned that she had to leave. When I learned she worked in the building, I proceeded to follow her. I said to her, "I'm going with you." She was clueless about what I was experiencing internally and said to me, "Okay! Let's go!" The guards stopped me at the entrance, but I simply told them, "I'm with her." When they looked at her, she nodded her head, and they gave me permission to enter the building.

Again, not knowing my true mission for entering the building, she insisted that I stop and meet her coworkers. I went with her while trying to rush the process. She insisted that all of them visit

CHAPTER 12

my service meeting for that coming Sunday. I gave them all the church's information and then left. I then took the elevator all the way to the top and when the doors opened, I met another woman as the elevator doors opened. She seemed to be a secretary. When she asked how she could help me, I asked her how I could get to the roof. She urged me to follow her, then ran through the hallways and instructed me to go through a small window and climb a ladder that would eventually lead me to the roof. After that, she told me to walk on the edge, all the way to the south side of the building. "That's where you'll find all the commotion," she ended telling me.

In a small prayer, I asked God for a sign. "If this is really from you, I want to be alone with the young man."

When I arrived to where this individual was located, I motioned to get his attention. It was difficult due to the crowd. There were many folks up there trying to convince him not to jump, including family members on the ladder of a fire truck. Police officers and fire officials were verbally abused by him.

After a few more minutes, I yelled out his name. When I finally got his attention, I told him, "I know the answer to your problem."

He responded, "What can possibly be the answer, at this point in my life?"

"JESUS," I replied. That is all I knew to say at this point in his life. When I talk to people about God and their purpose, I usually try to find common ground with them first. I try to identify the problem as well but, this was a matter of life and death, and the problem required an immediate solution. So, I worked backwards. The Name did carry a lot of weight at this time!

He stared at me with a tear coming down from one eye, but the crowd continued to distract us.

After a few more minutes I motioned to him that I was about to leave. I wanted to make sure he received a church pamphlet with the church's address on it. "I have faith I'll see you there this Sunday," I said. In other words, I assumed by faith that he won't go through with this insanity. In sales we call this a "take away." I made a paper plane while he gazed at me. It was almost as if he were saying to himself in a little shock, "What is this guy doing?" Thats exactly what I wanted.

A police officer in plain clothes approached me and said, "I don't know who you are, but I'm going to clear the building and leave you alone with him. I believe you're getting through to him." In less than a minute, the entire roof of the building was clear. I remembered the prayer I made to be alone with him. It was as if the Lord said, "Here you go! You're alone. Now do what I called you to do."

When I finished making the plane, I threw it towards him. The wind was not helping me at all, so I had to walk a little closer to him to pick it up. As I did this, he got closer to the edge to jump. I yelled, "WAIT! I just want to make sure you get this."

He kept his gaze on me as I took a quarter from my pocket and put it into the folded pamphlet. I had to fold it a little more to tighten it up. I wanted to make it heavier because of the wind. I had to get creative, in order to keep his gaze on me. While I was doing this, I had casual conversation with him about still seeing him on Sunday. I was reminded of Peter healing a crippled man in **Acts, Chapter 3**. He also needed the recipient of his message to keep his gaze on him. It was a crippled man. He said in **Verses 4–6 NIV, "Then Peter said, 'Look at us!' So, the man gave them his attention, expecting to get something from them. Then Peter said, 'Silver or gold I do not have, but what I do have I give you. In the name of Jesus Christ of Nazareth, walk.'"**

CHAPTER 12

I flipped the pamphlet to him, and he picked it up and opened it, as if he were ready to read it. By this time, he was already sitting on the ledge. As he opened the pamphlet, the quarter I placed in it fell from the ledge all the way down. I told him he owed me 25¢, because I needed it to make a phone call (it was my phone booth money. We didn't have cell phones in 1995). He laughed a little. That was the point. I remember thinking that his laughter was healthy and that it was preparing him for his encounter. I use a lot of humor when connecting with people.

I remember reading The Little Red Book of Selling by Jeffrey Gitomer, in it he states, "**If you can make them laugh, you can make them buy.**"

It speaks to the power of connection, authenticity, and emotional resonance in sales; people buy from those they like, trust, and enjoy. Humor lowers resistance and builds rapport instantly.

"IF YOU CAN MAKE 'EM LAUGH, YOU CAN MAKE 'EM BUY."

He looked in the tract, ready to read. Not knowing what the tract (pamphlet) was going to say, I yelled, "Let's read together!" I began to read: "DO YOU NOT KNOW THAT THE GATES OF HEAVEN ARE CLOSED FOR YOU UNLESS YOU ARE BORN AGAIN?" What a perfect introduction! "You think this is the end of your problem, but it's the beginning of an eternal problem," I explained.

After persistent conversation, he eventually felt comfortable enough to come closer. As we spoke, I was able to help him identify the root of his problem. He kept repeating, "How do you know all this about me? Who sent you?"

There was a moment when I called him a coward. Talk about a "take away." I said, "This is the coward's way out of life's problems." He was clearly shocked. I looked him straight in the eyes and repeated it, this time even more directly: "You punk! How could you just walk away—or jump, in your case—and think it's all over? I'm shocked. You seem intelligent and stable. You definitely have what it takes to confront this situation—and the others that will come your way. You're not mentally off; you're just emotionally affected. We've all been there. What are you, 17 years old?"

He stared at me, stunned. "How did you know my age?" he asked. "And how did you know I'm up here because of a woman?" Then again, with wide eyes, he repeated, "Who sent you?"

I shared a brief story with him. A year before heading to Trinidad and Tobago for this mission, I went through a painful heartbreak. I related it to his situation and made myself vulnerable—and it really hit home with him. By this time, he was in tears. In that moment, I caught a glimpse of something deeper: I was meant to go through that heartbreak and walk through the healing process, so I could one day comfort others—starting with him. My pain had become part of my purpose.

From his age to the very reason he was up there, it all became clear—he was emotionally overwhelmed by a broken relationship. In that moment, I sensed the spiritual gifts of knowledge and wisdom at work. Paul spoke about these in his letter to his students, the church at Corinth:

> **"There are different kinds of spiritual gifts, but the same Spirit is the source of them all. There are different kinds of service, but we serve the same Lord. God works in different ways, but it is the same God who does the work in all of us"** (1 Corinthians 12:4–6, NLT).

These gifts are like divine equipment that God gives us to fulfill His service and accomplish our purpose.

CHAPTER 12

It goes on to say, "To one there is given through the Spirit a **message of wisdom**, to another a **message of knowledge** by means of the same Spirit, [9] to another **faith** by the same Spirit, to another **gifts of healing** by that one Spirit, [10] to another **miraculous powers**, to another **prophecy**, to another **distinguishing between spirits (discernment)**, to another **speaking in different tongues**, and still to another the **interpretation of tongues (the ability to connect with the recipient in their language)**. <u>**All these are the work of one and the same Spirit, and he distributes them to each one, just as he determines.**</u> (1 Cor 12: 8-10 NIV)

Trust me, these gifts operate in the marketplace and in everyday situations in ways you wouldn't believe. I plan to write a book soon on how to practice this art—how the Lord works through all of us, ordinary people, to accomplish His extraordinary purposes. It truly is outstanding.

When he got close to me, he asked what I had in my hand. I responded, "A Bible." I unzipped it from its leather binder and opened it, and it landed on a passage in Luke: **"Blessed are the eyes which see the things that ye see: for I tell you, that many prophets and kings have desired to see those things which ye see, and have not seen them; and to hear those things which ye hear, and have not heard them"** (Luke 10:23b–24, KJV). I declared him blessed! In that moment, there was a deep sense of peace. It felt as if God was in full control—I couldn't even explain it.

It was amazing to think that just minutes prior to all of this, he was yelling, "The demons are tormenting me!" as he held his head with both hands. He was still in shock that I knew specific things about him. At that very moment, a few birds were flying overhead, as if they were anticipating a death. The newspapers later referred to them as "death birds," capable of sensing death—they were vultures.

But then the Author of Life stepped into the scenario! As Jesus said, **"I am the resurrection and the life. The one who believes in me will live, even though they die"** (John 11:25, NIV).

He also boldly declared, **"I am the way and the truth and the life. No one comes to the Father except through me"** (John 14:6, NIV). And just like when He said to the lifeless son of a widow, **"Young man, I say to you, get up!"** (Luke 7:14), Jesus showed up again—to speak life into someone ready to die.

Wherever you go on His assignment, you also carry the aroma of this same life. So don't underestimate the life-giving power you collaborate with to resurrect lifeless scenarios. As Scripture reminds us,

> **"For we are to God the pleasing aroma of Christ among those who are being saved and those who are perishing" (2 Corinthians 2:15, NIV).**

He then asked if she was coming, referring to the young lady who had pushed him to the edge. I felt it was okay to be honest and said, "She's not coming! The people who were here before me made you feel that way to keep you from jumping. I'm not here to lie to you. You don't want that kind of relationship anyway—that's a pity courtship, and they don't last. You're a good-looking young man with a future ahead of you, and there are plenty more fish in the sea," I added. "Why are you wasting your time on a shark? She's probably taken!"

"How did you know she was married?" he replied with shock one more time.

Again, it was as if the Lord was speaking through me. I didn't know how—I was just flowing. I seemed to know the details that had driven him to the edge of suicide. Gifts, not me. Remember, the equipment comes with the assignment, and all the praise and recognition belong to God, not us.

CHAPTER 12

We continued to converse and eventually became comfortable with each other. Then I told him I was hungry and asked if he was too. He replied, "Yes," so I said, "I'll buy the burgers, and you get the sodas. Let's go to the burger place downstairs." When he said he had no money, I agreed to treat him this time and said he could treat me next time. I was still working, if you know what I mean.

Seconds later, I explained that we weren't actually going to a restaurant, but to a mental institution—because he had kept these people's attention for so many hours. I knew what the real issue was, but they didn't. They were going to evaluate him. I told him, "Let's be responsible and go through the entire process. I'll be with you all the way."

Even though he had become comfortable with me, he was concerned that I worked for the police and was afraid of getting hurt. I assured him that I worked for the Lord and that no one was going to touch him. I assumed the mission was accomplished and signaled to the police that we were coming down. I yelled, "WE'RE COMING DOWN. NO ONE TOUCH US!" They put their hands up as if to say, "You have our word!" I then told the young man to follow me. He voluntarily took his bag and followed me.

With the help of police officers, I was advised and then escorted to go through the elevator. The crowd stared in amazement, and some were scattered all over the stairway and hallways. When we reached the lobby, the doors opened to reveal about seven very enthusiastic women waiting for us. They immediately surrounded us and embraced him. Some even kissed him and said, "We love you, son, and the devil was not going to have you. No more of this nonsense with our young ones taking their lives—it stops now. We were praying for you down here."

I thought this was quite remarkable. While I was preaching and problem-solving up there, they were praying and interceding down here. I believe these must all go hand in hand. It was no wonder I had such success in this situation—I was not alone. I was immediately reminded of the promise:

> **"Again, truly I tell you that if two of you on earth agree about anything they ask for, it will be done for them by my Father in heaven. For where two or three gather in my name, there am I with them."** — Matthew 18:19–20 (NIV)

From there on, I accompanied him as I promised.

The following morning, as I walked to the local grocery store to get my bread and coffee, I was greeted continually by everyone from the neighborhood on the way there. Prior to this, I never even got a "good morning", good afternoon", or good evening". They were watching closely to make sure I wasn't a fraud. That morning the woman who owned the grocery store told me the bread and coffee were on the house. She pushed them toward me, as she was already expecting me to walk into her shop at that time, and she smiled.

CHAPTER 12

She got a copy of all the newspaper articles placed them on top of the counter and said, "I told everyone that came into my store today that the pastor is a hero, and that's why everyone will respect you from now on. Thank you for saving that kid! One of our own."

As I walked back home, everyone kept on greeting me, right up to my stairway.

BEYOND THE HUSTLE

Five minutes later I get a knock at my door, "Pastor Robert, would you like some breakfast with curry in it?"

I said, "Yes!" and ran downstairs.

Ten minutes later, another woman offered a nice hot breakfast. I ran downstairs and said, "Yes!" This continued for the whole three and a half years I spent there, to the point where there were actual debates as to whose turn it was to cook for me. I had to break up arguments and manage my new cooking staff. This occurred for breakfast, lunch, and dinner and especially on Sundays. What good food the West Indians cook too! ***"Thou preparest a table before me." … "Surely goodness and mercy shall follow me all the days of my life" (Psalm 23:5a, 6a KJV).*** Things turn completely around for me from this moment on.

Through God's amazing work, they let all their young ones join our congregation. Some of the Hindus even attended. The ones that didn't would hear from afar but would always have my back for whatever I needed. Verse 10, from Acts 3, the same passage I shared about keeping the recipients gaze, stated, ***"When the people recognized him as the same man who used to sit begging at the temple gate called Beautiful, they were filled with wonder and amazement at what had happened to him" (Acts 3:10 NIV).*** From this moment on, everything was different. Everything God is involved in is always to get the people's attention on Him, not us. Lastly, do you know that when I looked at the news on television, my name wasn't even mentioned. Even the Guardian Newspaper stated, "Unidentified man, who fire officials thought to be a preacher, coaxes Joel Haynes from jumping off the Salvatore Building."

I said to myself, "God has a sense of humor."

He's entitled to all the attention, recognition, and glory. After all it's his work and way. We are just collaborating with him.

CHAPTER 12

I've learned that what God did—and still desires to do—is use the spiritual setting we call church to educate, equip, and empower us for effective marketplace influence, not the other way around. Many of us have been taught to use our gifts, callings, and lives for church development. By that, I mean packing out a building—the four walls—with people. That's okay, and it may even be part of the assignment for some leaders, as long as the objective remains the same.

Our call remains:

> **"Go into all the world and preach the gospel to all creation."** —Mark 16:15 (NIV)

INVADING CULTURE WITH KINGDOM INFLUENCE

I believe the most unforgettable experiences aren't acquired by sitting in pews and warming benches, but by stepping out in faith—after being educated, empowered, and equipped—and making ourselves available to serve a dying world at all costs, through the gifts God has given each of us.

We can't change a world we're afraid to enter. Too often, we've stayed comfortable in our sanctuaries, preaching to the choir while the people who need truth the most are still wandering—lost behind enemy lines.

TRUE INFLUENCE REQUIRES PRESENCE.

Jesus didn't avoid dark places—He walked right into them. He entered Samaria, a place avoided by the religious. He ate with tax collectors and sinners. He stood in places the self-righteous rejected. If we are going to bring light, we must be willing to walk into darkness. That means confronting fear, pushing past resistance, and even knocking on the gates of hell itself to reclaim what belongs to the Kingdom.

But here's the key: the gatekeeper must let us in. That's why we must be bold, strategic, and unshakable—not just loud.

THAT'S WHY WE SET OUR FACE LIKE FLINT.

> **"Because the Sovereign Lord helps me, I will not be disgraced. Therefore have I set my face like flint, and I know I will not be put to shame."**
> — Isaiah 50:7 (NIV)

Setting your face like flint means stepping into hostile territory without flinching. It means walking into systems, industries, and institutions the Church retreated from—and reclaiming them not with pride, but with purpose.

We must take this Kingdom message and invade every sphere of influence:

In Government — to restore integrity, justice, and truth in leadership.

In Business — to model ethical enterprise, generosity, and wealth as a tool for good.

In Education — to raise up future leaders grounded in purpose, identity, and truth.

In Media — to rewrite narratives and spread messages that bring light instead of fear.

In Arts & Entertainment — to inspire culture with stories that reflect God's creativity and glory.

CHAPTER 12

In Family — to restore values, heal generational wounds, and raise sons and daughters in purpose.

In Religion (the Church) — to equip, not contain; to send, not just gather.

This is where the real people live—not just in church buildings, but in cities, on stages, in boardrooms, classrooms, newsrooms, courtrooms, and creative spaces.

We are not called to hide behind stained glass—we are called to occupy until He comes.

> "Do business till I come." — Luke 19:13 (NKJV)
>
> "Go into all the world and preach the gospel to all creation." — Mark 16:15 (NIV)
>
> "Do not be afraid, little flock, for your Father has been pleased to give you the kingdom." — Luke 12:32 (NIV)

So wherever you go on His assignment, know this: you carry the aroma of life. Don't underestimate the life-giving power you partner with to resurrect what looks dead in every sphere.

> **"For we are to God the pleasing aroma of Christ among those who are being saved and those who are perishing."** — 2 Corinthians 2:15 (NIV)

It's time to walk boldly. To enter the gates. To speak with authority. The Kingdom is in you—for every space God sends you into.

www.ingramcontent.com/pod-product-compliance
Lightning Source LLC
Chambersburg PA
CBHW071951070526
44583CB00015B/1146